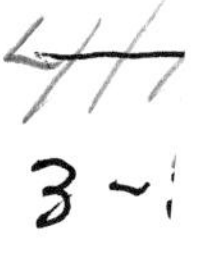

# Liberating Greatness

*The Whole Brain Guide to*
*an Extraordinary Life*

# Liberating Greatness

*The Whole Brain Guide to an Extraordinary Life*

Hal Williamson

with Sharon Eakes

Cover and graphics by

Barbara Curry

Grateful acknowledgment is made to the following for permission to reprint previously published material: From *Emotional Intelligence* by Daniel Goleman, copyright ©1995 by Daniel Goleman. Used by permission of Bantam Books, a division of Random House, Inc. Information on the HBDI™ and copyrighted graphics on Whole Brain Technology, reprinted by permission of Herrmann International, the Ned Herrmann Group, 2006. The list of virtues in Chapter 19 is reprinted with permission from the Virtues Project. Excerpts from *The On-Purpose Person,* Making Your Life Make Sense, by Kevin McCarthy, copyright ©1992. Used by permission of Kevin McCarthy.



Printed in the United States of America.

ISBN: 1-59571-122-8

Library of Congress Control Number: 2006922119

Word Association Publishers

205 Fifth Avenue
Tarentum, Pennsylvania 15084
www.wordassociation.com

Dedicated to Trudy, my late wife, the
mother of our children Sue, Hal, Patty
and Amy, and the love of my life for 43 years.

# Contents

# *Introduction*

*Regard man as a mine full of gems*
*of inestimable value.*
Bahá'u'lláh[1]

This book is about greatness in ordinary people. It is not about becoming famous, powerful or rich. It is about discovering the gems of your own natural greatness and polishing them into jewels. It is about acknowledging difficulties and moving past them. It is about finding your purpose in life, being your best self and having a positive impact beyond yourself. It is about the discipline of personal mastery.

Public-opinion pollsters have reported that those held in highest esteem by most people interviewed are neither the great artists nor the great scientists, the great statesmen or the great sports figures, but those who master a hard lot with their heads held high.

Life is wonderful! Life is difficult. Which is it? Or, can it be both?

Victor Frankl showed us that we can and do choose our state of mind. Through the remarkable story of his Holocaust survival[2] we learn that, regardless of the external circumstance of our life, we have choices. He was an inspiring model. How can we do what he did?

This book, conceptual and practical, is about understanding and unlocking the capacity in each of us. The pathways to that inner greatness are through the brain's vast neural circuit systems. When we see how amazing these pathways are, understand how they work and learn how to use them, we have discovered a tool of enormous power.

Over the past twenty years I have given a seminar series I called "Pathways to Greatness," to more than ten thousand participants—from the corporate setting to the factory floor, from churches to penitentiaries, from treatment centers to the community-at-large. Many have asked that a book be made available so they could continue the process of deepening their understanding of the principles put forth and to share with others what they learned. I present this book to fulfill those requests, to provide some of the recent findings about the mechanisms of our brains and to offer some simple mental tools to rewire your brain so you can become all you can be!

> *Greatness is...discovered in goodness, humility, service and character.*
> William Arthur Ward

Often at the close of the eight-hour program (usually presented over a span of four days), participants approached me and commented, "Hal, this is fascinating stuff you have shared with us. But how do we know that it works?" The principles, ideas and explanations find their origin in years of research, experimentation and, most importantly, in my own life experiences. Stories from my own life are woven throughout the book and serve as the most profound source of my knowing that this material works. I also share stories about how people have put these tools into practice and liberated their own greatness.

> *Don't ask yourself what the world needs. Ask yourself what makes you come alive, and go do that. Because what the world needs is people who come alive.*
> Gil Bailie

I am a seeker and a synthesizer. For years I have read articles and books on the brain, creativity, cognitive science, and self-help. While each contributed to my understanding of life, the work of Peter Senge is especially noteworthy in the unfolding of this book. In 1990, Peter Senge's book, *The Fifth Discipline,* arrived as if a gift from God.

> *Difficulty is the nurse of greatness*
> William Cullen Bryant

The discipline of systems thinking helped me recognize that the Newtonian approach to understanding cause and effect and stimulus-response did not accurately explain many of my own experiences. Systems thinking acknowledges the interconnectedness of influences upon a being. It further recognizes that the cause often leads to more than one effect and can also produce some unintended consequences. Time delays separating a cause from its effect can obscure one's analysis. I began to comprehend that the reason some self-help attempts worked and others did not had to do with the systems nature of things...and people. It also helped me to understand how we live in a world of systems embedded in systems.

The coming together of all of these influences culminated in the curriculum with its corresponding techniques. My ability to express the concepts in this book in a cogent way has been significantly enhanced by my marrying Sharon Eakes (See Chapter 1, Life Begins Anew), whose background in psychology enriched the material. Her voice throughout this book lends feeling and expression to my ideas.

## *How to Get the Most from This Book*

You will find this book most useful if you write down some things you would like to have, to do, or to be, in the future that seem difficult at present. I invite you to pause now and choose several goals from different parts of your life. Write them down here so you can refer back to them.

Family tree on disc - update

Career work past 65

Physical weight ↓ 150#

Financial [illegible]

Social c̄ friends 1 x month - dinner/lunch

Spiritual Ken baptized-

Intellectual finalize book for groups

Keep these in mind as you move through the book, but especially as you read Chapters 16 - 20. The book will help rewire your brain for the accomplishment of your own desired future.

Robert Frost reminded us that we choose our path in life.[3]

> Two roads diverged in a wood, and I -
> I took the one less traveled by,
> and that has made all the difference.

I invite you to begin your own journey on these pathways to greatness — to master the tools to change what you want to change about yourself, and get what you want out of life.

# PART 1

## THE JOURNEY

### *Hal's Story*

# 1
# *Hal's Story*

It was while looking back on my life's experiences, searching for explanations of how and why I overcame many difficulties that I came to believe my story might benefit others. This autobiographical sketch outlines a series of defining moments from which I learned lessons that have profoundly affected my life.

## *The Stage Is Set*

I was born in my parents' bed in a farmhouse in Cranbury, New Jersey, in 1934, but I'll begin with a memory of sitting at the dinner table when I was seven years old. It left a question indelibly etched in my mind that has taken a lifetime to answer.

My father appeared to be unusually upset by a phone call reporting some mischief on the part of my two older brothers. Now, what had they done? I never found out. All I know is that it was something bad and it brought shame to the family name.

At the evening meal my father didn't say anything. The meal ended, the table got eerily quiet, and my father pointed at my older brothers, Malcolm and Garfield. His face was red and his voice shook as he said, "Young men, I want you to remember, no matter where you go in this world, you are a Williamson. Don't you ever forget it!" My two brothers nodded their heads and apparently knew what he meant.

I didn't have the faintest idea what he was talking about."Remember, you are a Williamson." How could I forget that? Do you know what I believed him to say? You must behave and perform better than others. He never said that, but that's what I thought he meant.

A terrible feeling came over me when I heard my father's words, because I already knew I was "less than" other kids. How can a child in the first grade know that he is somehow less worthy than other kids? I knew. We had reading groups in my class. We had the blue birds and the red birds. The red birds were the slow reading group and the blue birds were the fast reading group. I was a red bird. Even in the first grade I wasn't performing as a Williamson should, was I?

Fig. 1-1 Hal at age seven

I began to listen intently at evening meals, as my father told the history of our family, hoping to learn more about what it meant to be a Williamson. Our first ancestors came to America in 1640 and settled in what is now New Jersey, across the river from New Amsterdam, now New York. I learned that my grandfather fought in the Civil War, was wounded and became a decorated veteran of that war. Following the Civil War my grandfather led a wagon train heading west, which was overtaken by Indians. He was one of the few survivors.

In the late 1930s, the height of the Depression, I had the sense that we were very poor. I gradually understood that my father had been a successful nurseryman and landscape architect in the 1920s. When the Depression hit, flowers and landscapes were the last thing on people's minds. I was learning what it meant to be a Williamson.

The next few years of my life had more tragedy in them than I could ever wish on anybody. In August, when I was eight, there was a gas explosion in our home. I was on the porch at the time and I was blown more than thirty feet in the air and across the driveway. I remember tumbling over and pushing the screen door off of me, racing up on the porch of the house and looking into the smoke-filled kitchen. I ran to tell my father, who was in the barn. I watched a neighbor rush into the house and bring out the blackened body of my brother Malcolm. All I could do was hold my head and scream. It was terrible.

Life went on, but sadly. I missed Malcolm. My mother was distracted with grief. Seasons came and went until I was ten years old, about to turn eleven. I remember a day in May. My father was very sick. A neighbor came and brought me home from school and said that my father's sickness had a name and it was cancer. They brought me to his bedside. That day I spent seven hours watching my father die. It was indescribably awful. It was not like the movies. I remember my father's mouth hanging loosely open as he convulsively breathed his last breaths. He was buried on my eleventh birthday.

All that remained of my family was my mother, my brother Gar, my younger sister Norma, and me. My Puerto Rican mother was just under five feet tall and weighed ninety pounds. I now know she was smart and gutsy. Then I wondered how she was going to take care of us. The year was 1945, and the country was at war. My mother took over my father's business and ran it. I don't suppose we were quite as impoverished as I thought we were, but I thought of us as poor indeed.

## *School Is Scary*

In the spring of 1947, when I was in eighth grade, an unusual thing happened. The principal from our elementary school came to our house. Let me tell you, it's never good when the principal comes to your house. Now he had come to see my mother, the widow Williamson. I was not at the meeting. I did not learn what transpired until many years later. Apparently, the school had decided not to send me on to high school. I was not going to graduate; instead I would be held back to repeat the eighth grade. My mother apparently said, "How can this be? We are just learning about this now. Why didn't you tell us sooner?" Well, they had planned to hold me back in earlier years but the tragedies in the family made them feel so bad they did not have the heart to do it. A test administered to eighth graders had revealed beyond a shadow of a doubt that I was mentally defective. I was, in fact, retarded. Retarded. My mother said, "Oh that can't be my Harold. Harold is not retarded; he is not defective." My mother pleaded with him to let me graduate from eighth grade. He said, "I will not do it. The only way I will let your son leave this school is if you put him in a school for slow children, where he can learn a trade."

Soon after that encounter my mother sold the farm. She had discovered a private preparatory school in a small city nearby that would take any student if the family had enough money. They would take kids, no matter how defective they were, and mainstream them. That's the word we use today. And so I was put in this exclusive prep school with some of the money my mother received from the sale of the farm.

How exclusive was this school? Let me tell you. In many of my classes there were five kids and one teacher. Think about that. I had some classes where there were three of us and one teacher. Even with that kind of attention during my freshman year, I barely passed. My grades fell in the low C/high D range. With that kind of academic performance I would never graduate from high school. The school's teachers and the headmaster grew concerned about my poor performance so they tested me again. Extensive batteries of tests. And you know what the tests revealed? They validated the previous tests. I was retarded. Retarded.

Now the teachers could be sure of my mental condition. Soon every kid in the school seemed to know that Harold, the boy from the farm, the hick from the sticks, the dumbest kid in the school, was mentally defective. I became the butt of every joke. My classmates tortured me. In English class the teacher would put a sentence on the blackboard. I would be asked what part of speech a word was. I didn't know. I just didn't know. And what would my friends do? They would whisper, "It's a verb, Harold, a verb." And I would say, "A verb". The teacher would respond, "Mr. Williamson, the word is a noun." And then the rest of the class would laugh. They would do it again and again, sometimes with correct answers, most often not. These were my friends?

I hated school. Math class was the only bright spot in my day because the teacher, Mr. Blake, was a kind man who seemed to like me even though I did poorly in his class. But I didn't have the awareness I have now. Coincidentally, he was also one of our athletic coach. And guess what? I was good in track and wrestling. He wanted me out on the field and in the gym performing for him. You know, over my freshman year, Mr. Blake became the number one man in my life. He became the father I didn't have. The sun rose and set on Mr. Blake. In fact, every opportunity I had I would try to put myself in his company.

Then I learned the truth. It was in the fall of my sophomore year, when there was one of those gatherings where parents and faculty get together. I would always go to those events. I never missed them. But I always, always went alone. It pains me to share with you the reason. I never invited my mother, for I was ashamed of her. My mother, with her short stature and her heavy accent seemed so different from the white, Anglo-Saxon Protestant parents of the other kids. My mother was the only person on the planet who believed in me. And I was ashamed of her. What a sad commentary on my state of mind.

That night when I got to the school I saw Mr. Blake near the door. He shook my hand and we began to talk. Then some parents came by and he turned to talk to them. I stood there with a cup of cider in one hand and a doughnut in the other, back to back with him, waiting for his conversation with the parents to end so that he could resume talking with me.

Well, it didn't work out that way. He apparently completely forgot that I was behind him. I could hear that he was talking to them about me, saying, "You know that boy Harold, he doesn't have it, he just doesn't have it," and, "Too bad. He is a nice kid, but he will never amount to anything."

Nothing I had heard up to that point in my life hurt as deeply as Mr. Blake's comments that night. As I burst into tears, I fled the hall and began to walk the streets of that small city. I couldn't go home. I had told my mother I would be out for the evening. As I walked that night and wept, I came to know the truth about me. I had suspected it in the first grade. And now I knew it. I didn't have it. Clearly in my mind I was not measuring up to "being a Williamson," whatever that meant. The most important man in my life had told the truth about me. By the time that evening was over I was filled with an overwhelming sense of inadequacy, for I knew the truth about myself.

I washed my face in a service station so my mother would not see that I had been crying. I went home. It probably wouldn't surprise you at all to find that over the rest of the year I did not do well in school.

With about eight weeks left in that school year, my mother took me aside and said, "You know, my son, you are not doing well in school and it is so expensive to send you there, I just cannot bring myself to spend any more money on your private school education. You are not making much of this opportunity. If you can't turn things around academically in the next few months, you must go to public school next year."

I hadn't realized that it was a significant financial burden on the family to send me to private school. If you looked at the way my mother dressed me to go to school, you would never say, "There goes a kid from a financially stressed family." I know now that for her it was not a sacrifice. She did it because she wanted to. She loved me.

But now I was terrified. There had been twelve kids in my class in my farming community. Now I was in a school with as few as five kids in my class. And my mother was talking about sending me to a public school with thousands of kids! I was absolutely scared to death. That was on a Thursday.

## *A Revelation and a Catalyst*

That Sunday morning I found myself in church. Oh, please don't think I was spiritually inclined. I wasn't. In our household, what happened on Sunday? On Sunday, we went to church. We weren't asked if we wanted to go to church. We went to church and that is why I was there, putting in my hour. Not paying attention, I couldn't wait until the benediction came down. I remember sitting there, feeling quite tortured by what I had learned on the Thursday before. As I sat rethinking the conversation with my mother, an unfamiliar voice filtered into my consciousness. It came from the pulpit and turned out to be the voice of a visiting pastor. I opened the bulletin and looked at the sermon title. It was a single word: Excellence. I do not know why, but that morning I sat up and listened. (My RAS, which you will learn about later, was working.) As the pastor spoke, he made one point again and again. The point was simply this: the gap between average performance and excellent performance is very small. And there really isn't anything you can't do or be if you want it badly enough and are willing to work hard enough for it. And then he enumerated countless average men and women down through the ages who, through determination and hard work, had stepped across that gap and snatched a measure of excellence. The talk by that visiting pastor was a catalyst.

Let me tell you, when I left church that morning my spirits soared. You see, I felt I had found a philosophy I could put to work in my life. I knew what I was. Below average. With a big effort, why couldn't I be average? And, with an extraordinary effort why couldn't I step across that gap and snatch a measure of excellence? Why not?

The following day I threw myself into my studies. A couple of positive experiences stand out from this time. The first happened following an essay exam in history class, my junior year. Mr. Holly, the teacher, called me to his desk after reading my exam. "Did you write this?" he asked. I trembled as I answered, "Yes." Exam in hand, he marched me to the headmaster's office, threw it on his desk and said, "Read this." I was petrified. After reading the essay, the headmaster said, "This is the best piece of writing I've seen in years." I was amazed.

The second experience was in my senior English class where I had given a speech on "Getting a Good Night's Sleep." When I finished, the whole class applauded. This had never happened before. I walked over to Mr. Coyle, the teacher, and as he handed me the paper with my grade on it (an "A") he said, "You have a gift."

Two years later, I graduated at the top of my class. You may be thinking, "Isn't that wonderful? Now he certainly must have felt adequate." Oh, no, no. For you see, no one knew the truth. What was the truth? I'll tell you about the truth.

Two years earlier, the Monday morning following that catalytic Sunday service, I rose at 3:00 am to study, retiring on Monday night at 8:00 pm and getting up on Tuesday at 3:00 am to study, repeating this, frequently seven days a week as well as a number of days in the summer months, for the next two years. If you ever discovered the truth about me, what would you know? He is one dumb kid. All he ever does is study.

## *Higher Education and Working — The Disconnect Continues*

Amazingly, I got into engineering school and graduated from the University of Wisconsin in Madison, using the same study methods. I married Trudy, a wonderful woman I met in prep school who also attended the same university, and we were raising a family. I had decided to become a patent attorney and went to Washington D.C. to work in the U.S. Patent Office determining whether or not people's ideas were patentable. I went to George Washington University School of Law at night.

Then it happened. It was near the end of the third year of a four-year program of work and study. One day I needed a case file I had worked on the previous week. I figured it would be helpful in preparing the file on a current, similar case. I went into the file room and I could not find the file. It was missing. I got the card that was used to check files out and instead of the person's name who had taken it, there was a code number. I went to the clerk and said, "Who has my file?" She said, "I can't tell you." I said, "Come on now, I am responsible for that file." I demanded that she produce the file. Finally she said, "Mr. Williamson, I am not supposed to tell you who has that file, but since you insist, I'll tell you. That file is in the hands of the Commissioner of Patents." Well, if you do not know anything about the Patent Office, the Commissioner of Patents is the head guy like the Chief Executive Officer, who runs the whole place. I said, "What does he want with it?" She said, "I thought that would get your attention. Let me tell you something else. For the past three months, every week someone from the Commissioner's office comes down here and goes to the file room and takes four or five cases. And do you know whose they are? They are always yours. Nobody else's."

You have no idea how scared that news made me feel. What were they doing? My experience so far led me to believe the worst. They were building a case to fire me. I was heartsick. I could not bring myself to tell my wife that I was in the process of being canned. I could not sleep; I began to lose weight.

Weeks passed, maybe a month or more. I remember the day it happened. It was a Tuesday at 11 o'clock in the morning when the call came to report to the Commissioner's office immediately. The dreaded day had come. I did not even know where his office was. It turned out that it was on the top floor in the Commerce Building. There was a big corridor parallel to 14th Street in downtown Washington, D.C. and many corridors teed on it. One of them teed right on his office. As I walked down the corridor, I could see that his office door was open. I could even see him inside. Let me tell you, it felt like I was walking the last mile before my execution.

As I neared his office, I could see him standing inside, behind his desk, talking to someone on his right. I hunkered against the wall to my right and looked in and, my gosh, it was my boss he was talking to. My boss didn't look very happy. I thought, *I am not going in there.* I got near the door and my boss saw me and gave me one of those head motions, you know, *get your backside in here.* I stepped into the

Commissioner's office and as I did I literally froze dead in my tracks. When I looked to my right, there were two men with flash cameras. Flash cameras. Oh my goodness, they are going to take pictures of it. What was about to happen? I could already see, in my mind's eye, my picture on the front page of the Washington Post. You know, with a convict's number on it and a caption that read, "Young Examiner exposed as a fraud, drummed out of the Patent Examiner's Corp." But there was something wrong with the picture. The Commissioner was smiling. He had his hand extended, so I came over rather tentatively, and took his hand and he pumped my hand as he said, "Mr. Williamson, let me be the first to advise you that you have been selected the Outstanding Patent Examiner of the Year. I want you to know that you are the youngest in the history of the Patent Office to receive this award."

Knowing my prior experiences, you might well think, "Wasn't that wonderful? He certainly must have felt adequate after that." Quite the contrary. I was scared to death. For, you see, they didn't know the truth. What was the truth? For the three years preceding the award, I had worked almost every Saturday. My boss didn't know. I had a big docket. I had great responsibilities. I was never paid for those Saturdays. It was assumed we took Saturdays off. What had they done? They had counted six days of work as if it had been done in five. At the end of three years I had broken the productivity record in the U.S. Patent Office. I wouldn't be surprised if I hold it now, nearly 40 years later. No one is going to ever break the productivity record unless what? Unless they are willing to work six days and get paid for five. Now what did I believe? I believed that they would soon discover that this was part of a plot of mine. I had cheated in getting this award by sneaking in on the weekends to work. I lived in fear that I would be discovered.

## *Moving Up and Falling Down*

I left that job when I graduated from law school and worked for several years as a patent attorney in New Hampshire. Then I got a job at the Westinghouse Airbrake Company in Pittsburgh, Pennsylvania. After several years as a division patent counsel there, I was invited to join the executive offices of the company, where I worked for the next six years. At age 37, I was the youngest executive. I remember the day the top executives invited me to lunch. They met me in the lobby and said, "Hal, we are going out for lunch and while we are out the rest of the company is going to learn that you have just moved into the executive offices of this company. You will be one of us. A small handful of men who run this business." That afternoon they brought me up to the executive suite, in a prestigious building that stood on the point where the Allegheny and Monongahela Rivers come together in downtown Pittsburgh. They showed me into my new corner office and the door closed behind me. I stood there by a corner window looking down on the Monongahela River on the left and the Allegheny River on the right. The confluence of these rivers forms the Ohio River, which stretch as far as the eye can see. As I stood there that day I experienced a moment of truth. I suddenly saw a pattern of my behavior that had begun many years earlier. In my late teens and twenties, every day was the same for me; I experienced overwhelming feelings of inadequacy. Every day I would strive to do what? To do my best. To "be a Williamson," whatever that was. And here I was, 37 years old and living the same pattern. The new job, which was quite a promotion, made me feel bad because the belief wired in my brain told me the truth. The truth was that I was a below-average person.

To compensate, I put in unreasonable hours and worked very hard. Then what happened? People gave me plaques, commendations, promotions. This recognition made me feel worse. Cognitive dissonance! (See Chapter 9.) I was a phony and a fraud. Everyday I expected to have the truth uncovered. It was a vicious cycle.

I had a remedy. In my late teens and early twenties, I had discovered something remarkable. I discovered a way to make those terrible feelings disappear. For you see, that was when I discovered alcohol. When I drank, oh, when I drank, those feelings went away. I would feel inside of my head like normal people look: all together.

By the time I reached the executive office, I knew that alcohol had become my best friend and that this was a problem. I would no more dream of facing a day without a drink than without food or air. There I was, standing in that grand office having made it to the top. And I had a moment of truth. I knew if I kept drinking I would lose that job.

On June 16, 1971, I joined a fellowship (hereafter referred to as The Fellowship) of men and women who had banded together to solve their common problem: drinking. It was not nearly as easy as it sounds. In fact it included unbelievable physical and mental anguish. Suffice it to say, I haven't had a drink since. No week of my life passes now that I don't spend a few hours in the company of men and women who find themselves today as I did then, searching for an answer....a better answer than we found in the bottle.

The next five years of my life were remarkably good. Why were they good? Westinghouse Airbrake sent me on to graduate business school. They knew I was in The Fellowship. I was sort of the company's resident drunk-made-good. I mean it was known and accepted. "Hal is in recovery." It was not a big deal; I didn't have anything to hide. And it was grand. At the end of five years with promotions and pay raises I headed a team that successfully fought a hostile takeover of the company. Lots of pats on the back. Then the company was about to be attacked by another company in a hostile takeover. And so the company fled to what is called a White Knight. That's what they call a friendly merger. The bigger company was

American Standard Company in New York. Now, what happens with a merger? There were two people for every job and at the age of 42, I was suddenly unemployed.

## *Surviving Unemployment*

I thought I would quickly find work somewhere else, but I didn't. I tried to launch a franchise business, but things didn't work out well. At the end of six months I was out of money. I had used up my 26 weeks of unemployment benefits. I had used up my severance pay. I had two kids in college and was unable to find work. I was desperate. I would search for work all day and find myself unable to sleep at night. Soon I was as anxious as I'd been during the last days of my drinking. I couldn't sleep and if I did fall asleep, I would wake up in the middle of the night with my mind racing.

Then I remembered something said by a wise, long-time member of my recovery program, a man who actively supported my recovery. This older gentleman said, "You know, Hal, at some point in your recovery it may seem that the world is going to come down on you. When that happens, I urge you to look in the basic text of The Fellowship, because somewhere in the pages of that book will be an answer to every problem that you will ever face in recovery."

I remember a particular night, six months without a job, unaware that I would spend three more years without work. I carried the recommended book to bed with me that night, sat up, turned to page one and began to read. I would read that book from front to back, if need be, to see if there was an answer for me. Early in the book I came upon a passage where the author seemed to be speaking to me. He said that if you were disturbed, no matter what the cause, the first thing you must do is quiet that disturbance. He said to do it was simple. Begin to repeat something you have committed to memory: a prayer, a poem, a song. Over and over again. If no prayer or poem comes to mind, find a passage in a book that is meaningful to you and read it again and again and again. That night no prayer or poem came to mind, so I turned to a passage in this book that was especially meaningful to me. I propped myself up in bed and began to read. I remember the page that it began on, the bottom of page 83. (I changed "we" to "I".)

> If I am painstaking about this phase in my development, I'll be amazed before I am half way through. I am going to know a new freedom and a new happiness. I will not regret the past nor wish to shut the door on it. I will comprehend the word serenity and I will know peace. No matter how far down the scale I have gone I will see how my experience can benefit others. That feeling of uselessness and self-pity will disappear. I will lose interest in selfish things and gain interest in my fellows. Self-seeking will slip away. My whole attitude and outlook upon life will change. Fear of people and of economic insecurity will leave me. I will know how to handle situations which used to baffle me. I will suddenly realize intuitively that God is doing for me what I could not do for myself.

The passage went on in a way that was important to me and hearkened back to the words of the pastor in my youth.

> Are these extravagant promises? We think not. They are being fulfilled among us — sometimes quickly, sometimes slowly. They will always materialize if we work for them.

I do not know how many times I read the passage that night. But I can tell you this. When I woke in the morning, I found the book on my chest. And I had had my first peaceful night's sleep in six months. This was a practice I repeated every night for the next three years.

And what did I discover that night? I discovered something that you will discover in Chapter 6, namely that you can think only one single thought at a time. Who chooses the thoughts that you have? You do. It's the thoughts that you have that produce the feelings that you experience. And the person who controls the thoughts is you.

That was the second great lesson in my life. The first one, you can guess, happened when I was sixteen. Although I did not understand it back then, I discovered that I was a right-brained kid in a left-brained world (See Chapter 11). But I discovered that I also had a left side of my brain. And do you know what? If I used it, it worked exceedingly well. I never was retarded. I discovered that in my sixteenth year, but did not fully understand why for another 36 years, until I reached my early 50's.

The next three years of being unemployed were bad beyond description. Most of my work was at minimum wage. I borrowed heavily against the house to put my kids through college. My brother Gar, bless his heart, helped cover many of my oldest daughter's college expenses.

The last job that I had during this painful time was delivering phone books. Phone books. I don't think I will ever forget that Saturday morning when I dropped a stack of phone books on the stoop of a fine home in a suburb of the city. I was unaware the owner of the home was a senior executive who had been at the same level I was in another company there in the town. He did not know that I had lost my job. When I dropped the books on the stoop, apparently the sound carried through the screen door. As I was walking away, he came to the door and recognized me. I remember him shouting, "Hal? Hal is that you?" I remember thinking, *oh, good heavens, he saw me. Don't look back. Don't look back. Don't let him know what has happened to you.* And then I could hear his footsteps. He was running after me. I stopped at the gate and I looked back and I said, "Yes, John, it's Hal. I brought you your phone books." We stopped and talked a minute. I felt humbled and embarrassed. From the executive offices to delivering phone books was an enormous step down.

## *Making the Best of It*

Finally, I was offered a job in Rockford, Illinois, by the Sundstrand Corporation, a large aerospace company. It was a wonderful offer, with a terrific salary. However, something seemed to be wrong. I was being offered a position as a Junior Patent Attorney. That did not seem right. But I accepted the job and showed up to start my work there. When I arrived, I learned that the title in the job offer was not a mistake. I was to be a Junior Patent Attorney. Junior Patent Attorney is a title you give a person when they leave law school. First job out. I had twenty-two years of experience.

The boss would come to my desk in the morning and give me work to do that day. He would come back at five o'clock, pick up the completed work and take it home, critique it with red ink, then bring it back in the morning for me to do over again. I mean, after all, I was a Junior Patent Attorney.

I arrived in Rockford $100,000 in debt. Now, the question was, should we declare bankruptcy? We made the very personal decision that we would not do that. We decided to pay off what we owed. It took eight years. (More details in Chapter 17)

My aging Cadillac, which creditors did not even want, was a gas guzzler. Because I couldn't afford to drive it, I went to work most days on a 50cc Honda Moped. I had the only moped in the executive parking lot. Brooks Brothers suits and a moped. Strange as it may seem, that was not a humbling experience. That was all I could afford. I will admit that many who saw me riding my scooter thought I was quite eccentric. And let me tell you this, when it got down near 0° it hurt to drive that thing.

## *Working on Myself*

The difficulty of these times was made easier because I began to work on myself. Since 1971 when I got sober, I'd been doing what I was told to do to stay sober. It worked to stay sober, but somehow I felt fake. I knew how to "act as if", but it wasn't authentic. *Who am I really?* I wondered. I tried every self-help technique I could find. All of them promised change and accomplishment. They filled me with hope. Some seemed to help. None lasted.

Then, in 1985, while at a conference of Couples in Recovery at Lake Geneva, Wisconsin, I had what was to be a defining moment! Dr. Robert Henry, the CEO of a big city hospital, gave the keynote address. It was about brain dominance and its impact on our behavior.

The morning after Dr. Henry's talk I woke up excited and hopeful. We had completed a survey called the Herrmann Brain Dominance Instrument™, which determines how a person likes to think. When I saw my own thinking style profile, I was riveted! It didn't match the picture of myself I presented to the world. Maybe the brain held clues for both understanding myself and changing my behavior! Dr. Henry also advocated practicing affirmations, which I totally dismissed for the moment.

But I began to study the brain. I read every book I could find on the brain. I attended a training called Investment in Excellence®. I became certified to administer and interpret the Herrmann Brain Dominance Instrument™.

As I learned, I began sharing some of what I learned with friends and acquaintances on weekends in my home.

## *Birth of "Pathways to Greatness"*

It had taken me ten years to go from Junior Patent Attorney to Director of Patents for the Aerospace group at Sundstrand, at that time a billion-dollar-in-sales operation. I had made it to the top again.

In the fall of 1991, a decision was made at the highest levels to terminate research and development as a major function in the company. Two hundred scientists would be let go; only 25-30 would remain. The day they made that decision they also made a profound decision about patents and invention. If you don't need research and development, do you need patent attorneys? No, you don't. That very day they made the decision to terminate the General Patent Counsel. They came to my office and told me, "Hal, we just terminated the General Patent Counsel."

What were they telling me? It was all over, wasn't it? Where do you go when you are 58? Do you find a place in industry? No. In private practice? No. What did I know? I knew I was in the budget for the rest of the year. So I arrived at work every day to sit and think. It felt like those years of unemployment in the seventies, when every day ended the same way for me. But, in the seventies I knew nothing of the lessons I had been describing in what I came to call the "Pathways to Greatness" program, referring to the neural pathways in the brain. I knew nothing about affirmations and visualization and how to rewire your brain. I also had no idea of the significance of thinking style preferences, much less of finding my purpose in life. In the seventies I'd repeated to myself again and again the promises from the basic text of The Fellowship, until I fell asleep, not realizing they were affirmations.

One painful day in the office I reflected on those affirmations I had committed to memory, and I found myself speaking them out loud:

> If I am painstaking about this phase of my development I'll be amazed before I am half way through. I'm going to know a new freedom and a new happiness. I will not regret the past nor wish to shut the door on it. I will comprehend the word serenity and I will know peace. No matter how far down the scale I have gone I will see how my experience will benefit others.

That was it! Did you hear that? "No matter how far down the scale I have gone, I will see how my experience can benefit others." You know what I would do? I would put together a curriculum that explained the lessons I had learned in my life, and the results of my brain research, somewhat as I had been doing informally at home. I would ask Harry Stonecipher, the CEO of my company, for eight hours of his time so that I could share this program with him.

Luckily, a neighbor of Harry's had attended one of the informal programs in my home and raved about it to him. That got me in the door. God bless Harry. After experiencing it, Harry asked me what I wanted to do with the "Pathways to Greatness" program. I said that I wanted to bring it to all the employees of the company. Harry responded, "Okay. Do it. You'll have to attract people to come voluntarily. We'll see how it goes. If it's not working at the end of the year, you will be out of a job." I accepted the offer on the spot.

In the first few months, attendance at the programs was low. Usually a manager and a few key staff members would show up, checking it out. Weeks, or sometimes months later, their entire departments would attend the program. Before a year was up, the scheduled classes were filled to capacity, requests for the program began to fill my schedule to the limit, and I had a waiting list. News of the personal and professional usefulness of the training spread by word of mouth. I was asked to offer the program on weekends at my home for employees' family members, which I did.

In three years, nearly six thousand employees, from all over the country, participated in the program. I learned later that literally hundreds of employees wrote notes to the company's CEO expressing their appreciation for making the program available for all employees.

## *An Abrupt Transition*

It has been said that every story has a beginning, a middle and an end. Some stories have no ends; they are the ongoing chapters of life. I like to think my life is like that. Some chapters cover decades while others cover only a single day.

I would like to share one of those single day chapters in the story of my life. My wife, Trudy, had joined me out on the lecture circuit, touring the country, assisting me as I was delivering the curriculum that you will experience by reading this book. Our plan was to spend the balance of our life together, 24 hours a day, traveling and delivering the "Pathways" material.

Etched in the neural circuits of my memory are the events of that day, Oct. 19, 1994. We were in Miami. It was a special day weather-wise, because the first bubble of crisp, dry Canadian air had pushed its way into Miami Lakes. The humidity was gone. We left Shula's Resort Hotel together and began our morning walk, heading west. As we got near a toll road, an interstate that crossed the road we were on, we paused and then headed south across the divided highway. We got to the broad, palm-lined island in the middle and I held my hand back toward Trudy, who was walking slightly behind me to my left, to stop her until the traffic was clear. It cleared very quickly, because one hundred yards away to our right there was a traffic light and all the traffic had stopped. An exit ramp coming down from the south and off the toll road fed the traffic light from that direction. I saw a car heading down the ramp. I assumed the light was about to change. I reached back to grab Trudy's hand in mine as we started to cross the last leg of the highway. We were almost safely across. They tell me I had my foot on the curb we were heading for, when a car exiting the Interstate raced down that ramp, beat the yellow light and came east on Miami Lakes Drive. The driver was blinded by the rising morning sun. He never saw us. He hit us both.

I remember becoming conscious and frantically trying to sit up. I looked down and I could see my bones sticking through my pants. Then someone's hands were on my chest with more hands on my head. A man was saying "Don't move, don't move." He pushed me back down on the pavement and just before my eyes filled with blood, I looked for Trudy's right hand that I had been holding. And she was gone. I had lost her. I wept and my body shook. I wept tears of sorrow for myself. Forty-three years is a long time to have been together.

But along with the tears of sorrow were tears of relief and thanksgiving, for you see, my Trudy was at a place with the God of her understanding, where there would be no chemotherapy, no agonizing death from the cancer most people did not know she had.

To everything there is a season and a time for every purpose. A time to be born and a time to die. It was not my time to go. This strengthened my belief in the purpose of my life. I decided to leave Sundstrand and strike out on my own, taking the "Pathway to Greatness" program to a wider audience. I called my new company Hope Unlimited.

## *Life Begins Anew*

Following the accident I felt terribly alone. In forty-three years of being together, Trudy and I had developed quite a rhythm. Now it was as if the music had stopped.

In the months that followed, I returned to work. My neck was broken; my right leg had a compound fracture, but I did what it took to get moving again. Because I felt strongly that it had not been my time to go, I wanted to dedicate the rest of my life to living my life with purpose, a life of love, a life of service to God and my fellow man.

But, by the time eight months had gone by, gnawing loneliness dominated my feelings, even when I was engaged in my work. I often thought of the Frost poem. I had taken the spiritual path on the road less traveled. And it was my sense that there were not a lot of us on it. There seem to be a lot of us when we gather at conferences, because we are all in one room. But on the roads of daily life, I felt quite alone. So, I began to accept the invitations of friends to stop at a church where there would be other people like me, people who were widowed, divorced, and single. But somehow it was all wrong for me.

I remember going home after one such gathering and thinking to myself, *I can't do that. I can't do that anymore.* At that moment I was overwhelmed with the reality that the life I had known with Trudy was over — forty-three years, a remarkable life with a remarkable woman. As I lay in bed that night, I realized that I would most likely be alone for the rest of my life.

I decided to just throw myself into my work. I would live my life on purpose. I would devote every waking moment of my life to my work. I would dilute none of my energies with looking for somebody else. I was so overwhelmed by that thought that I got out of bed and knelt by the side of the bed in the darkness and I literally wept for myself. I was going to be alone forever. I prayed, "Oh God, oh God, if there is to be someone in my life won't you please put that soul on the road that I am traveling now."

On October 19, 1995, the one year anniversary date of Trudy's death, I had arranged to deliver the "Pathways" program to the therapists and patients at Gateway Rehabilitation Center, in western Pennsylvania, one of the largest drug and alcohol treatment centers in the state. I wanted their evaluation of this material for purposes of treatment. When it was over, I told my life story and the story of Trudy's death.

The Vice President of Treatment Programs, Sharon Eakes, came up to talk with me when I finished. I had known Sharon twenty-five years earlier, when she was a new therapist there. Now she practically ran the place. She said "Hal, you know, we have something in common. Do you remember Gene Curley, a doctor?" I said "Yes." I did. She told me she had married him. Then she said, "Gene died of a heart attack four years ago. And during his autopsy they discovered that he had small tumors in both lungs. He would have developed cancer. He was spared the same terrible death that your Trudy was spared."

We fell into easy conversation, and before we parted, I promised to send her Danah Zohar's book *Quantum Self* and Sharon promised to send me a paper she'd written on Chaos Theory.

I headed back to the Midwest that night. A day or two later my daughter Sue came to my house. We were now working together, taking our message of hope around the world. I told Sue, "I had a dream last night," and I shared the dream with her. I usually don't remember the details of my dreams and it is not my nature to share my dreams with others. This one was vivid. The dream involved Sharon. Sue suggested that I write Sharon and share the dream with her. I said, "No way!" but later thought, *Why not?* Referring now to the letter, which Sharon still has, I can tell you what I wrote to her:

> What I am about to share may strike you as odd. In fact I can rarely recall having shared with another the type of experience I am about to share now. I have no idea of the meaning or significance, if any, of my experience. The experience involves a dream I had two nights ago. It was a vivid dream that began on the streets of a city. The city street bustled with activity. The dream opened with you and me meeting at a crosswalk in mid-street. We both appeared surprised to meet this way. Your characteristic and perpetual smile appeared spontaneously when first we recognized each other. You said nothing. I spoke and simply said, "Shall we dance?" And you nodded your assent. We both seemed to know that we were to waltz. You placed the fingertips of your right hand in my upraised palm. With my right arm lowered to receive your left arm, we began to dance. It was

> most awkward at first as I tried to lead and you tentatively began to follow. Within moments our individual steps and movements fell into a smooth and flowing pattern that allowed us to glide effortlessly up through the middle of the street toward a rise that crested on what appeared to be the highest point in the city. As we arrived at the crest, the music that only you and I seemed to hear, softly ended. We stopped our dance and after but a fleeting moment we drifted apart as if guided by an unseen conductor. I slowly bowed at the waist and you simultaneously curtsied with a deep flourish. And this is the way the dream ended. I woke refreshed with the details of the dream foremost in my mind.

We began to correspond and meet. And on May 27, 1996, in Inverness-by-the-Sea in northern California at 12:00 noon, Sharon and I were married.

One life ended in the middle of a street. A second life began in the middle of a street, in a dream.

# PART 2

## THE THEORY

### *These Amazing Brains!*

# 2
# *Meeting the Brain Again For the First Time*

## *Why Learn How the Brain Works?*

It was the fall of 1985, at George Williams College, on the banks of Lake Geneva, Wisconsin. I awoke one morning filled with the feeling that something big had happened that would allow me to change. I jumped out of bed, put my jeans over my pajamas, pulled my shoes on untied and stepped outside of the cabin.

The night before, as I described in Chapter 1, I'd been in the company of about twenty other men and women, couples, who'd come together for a weekend to work on improving their relationships. The speaker, Dr. Robert Henry, had talked excitedly about brain dominance or thinking style preferences.

All I knew about the brain were some textbook definitions, which I found of no help at all in directing my life. After listening to Dr. Henry, it became clear to me that inside my brain there was an architectural structure that often dictated my behavior. I'd seen a graphic presentation showing the relationship between my most natural and comfortable ways of thinking and my brain structure. It was a puzzle to me, but seemed to hold promise. This could be the key to understanding myself and becoming more authentic and comfortable.

For 15 years, I'd been doing what I'd been instructed to do in The Fellowship: Pray in the morning, pray at night and if I couldn't believe, make believe. I was told to keep it simple. I was told to "act as if," and that behaving well would eventually come naturally. These things were working. It was helpful. I loved service work. But there was something about me that I knew was inauthentic. I knew how to act nice. I knew how to respond to challenges. But, truthfully, acting in a way that was completely acceptable was uncomfortable. It didn't feel natural. And apparently it didn't convince others either. Sharon remembers me during that time as a pompous man.

I had tried and been disappointed by every self-help technique I could find to improve my state of mind. On that crisp fall morning of 1985, as I told you in Chapter 1, I was filled with new hope that a study of the brain might help me both understand myself and become the person I wanted to be.

When I returned home, I began to read everything I could find about the human brain. In the chapter that follows, I attempt to describe what I discovered: the development of the brain, the architectural structure of the brain and the role and function of many of the components that make up the brain. It has been a fascinating journey.

> This may all seem like more than you need to know about neural circuit development. The purpose of describing it in such detail is to enable you to understand the basics of brain circuitry, which will help when you want to rewire your own!

I am using the word architecture as a metaphor. Think of it like the architecture of a home. A home includes many rooms, a dining room, a kitchen, a family room, a bathroom. All of these are laid out in a way to give you access to and from the different rooms. Specific activities take place in each room, but the overall collection of rooms makes the building a home. In the description that follows, I encourage you to pay attention to the various elements and functions of the brain, thinking of them as the rooms and furniture of a home. In a dining room we eat meals, but we cannot eat meals unless they're prepared in the kitchen or brought in from outside. We can talk about what's needed in a dining room: a table, chairs, adequate lighting. We can come away with some appreciation of the need for this particular room in the house and how it relates to the other rooms. I hope that when you leave this chapter in the book, you will come away with a sense of how the sections of the brain operate together. This understanding will help you with the rest of the book, which is about how you can take charge of your life and experience a fresh sense of hope, rooted in the faith that, with the tools presented, you, too, can begin to live an authentic, purposeful life, a joyful life, with an ebullient state of mind that you may never have realized was within your grasp.

If it seems too much like biology class, I urge you to skim or skip the paragraphs laden with technical language, read the call-out boxes in each chapter and go to Part 3 for the tools. Understanding how the brain works will be meaningful to many people, but using the tools does not require that you understand the inner workings of the brain's structure. In the last chapter you'll read how I created the "Pathways to Greatness" program to share the lessons I'd learned in my life so other people could benefit from them. These life lessons didn't make clear sense to me until I was exposed to the concept of thinking style preferences. The next few chapters will tell you what I learned when I began to study the brain and why it fascinates me.

## *The Birth of a Brain*

The mind has been called a lot of things: a treasure, a curse, a phenomenon complex enough to blow your mind! The mind could be defined as the sum total of neural processes that take place in the brain. Your mind is what your brain does. If the mind resides in the brain and the brain is connected to all regions of the body by a nervous system, then understanding how the brain and nervous system come into being will help us understand how the mind works.

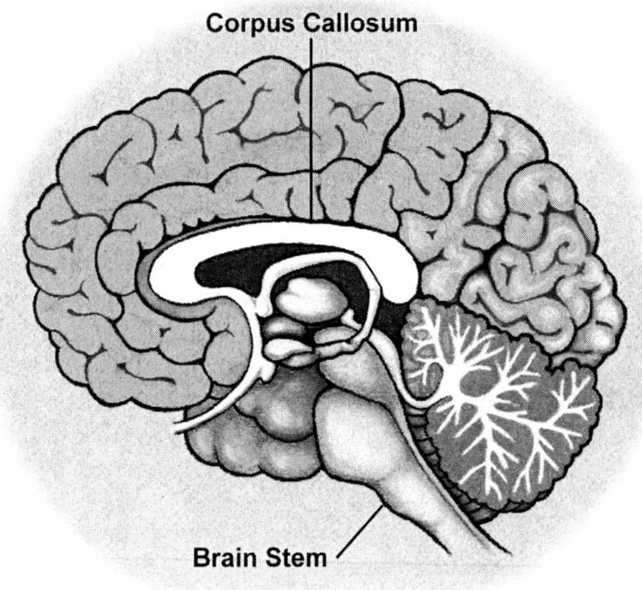


Fig 2-1 Cross Section of the Human Brain

In the beginning, the brain is just a group of cells in an upper layer of an embryo. Within three weeks of its appearance, this group of cells is distinctly different from other cells in the embryo. Imagine that these brain cells are located at the top of a tube which will eventually contain the spinal cord. Brain cells such as neurons and glial cells, that nourish and mechanically support the neurons, continue to split and migrate in a symmetrical manner, gradually building up the right and left hemispheres of the brain, filling the top of the tube.

When we say that the neurons migrate, we mean that the cells move from one place in the developing brain to another place in the embryo, where they set themselves down and go to work. Each neuron appears to know exactly when and where it is supposed to go. When it arrives where it was headed, each cell begins to perform the role and function written in its genetic instructions. Should the neuron arrive ahead of schedule, it waits until other neurons arrive that, by their design, are intended to be laid down first. This process is so complex that those studying it often wonder in amazement how the neurons know so clearly when and where to go. Science now has an answer: "God only knows!"

## *Making Electricity via Neural Circuits*

It gets even more complicated. Each of the neuron cell bodies (left side of Fig. 2-2) that migrates and arrives at its destination sprouts a structure called an axon, or nerve fiber.

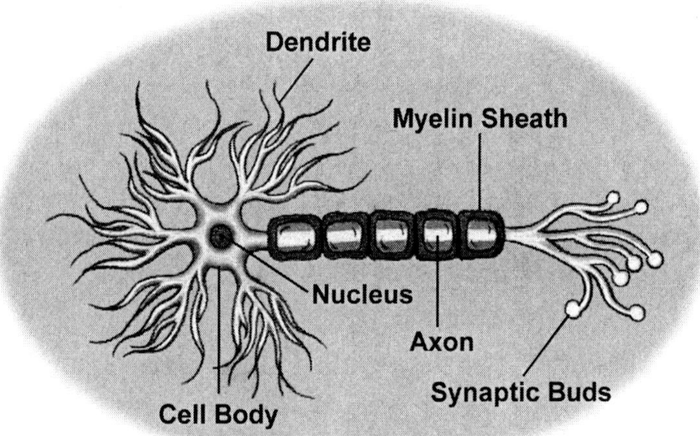


Fig. 2-2 Neuron

This nerve fiber grows to a predetermined length and then branches, much like a seed placed in the ground that sprouts and sends a shoot up which then branches out. At the end of each nerve fiber branch is a synaptic bud (right side of Fig. 2-2).

The nerve fiber is covered by a myelin sheath that serves as electrical insulation (segmented center section of Fig. 2-2). As the cell body is sprouting, it is also generating structures called dendrites. These dendrites take on the appearance of roots that extend from a sprouted seed (left side of Fig. 2-2).

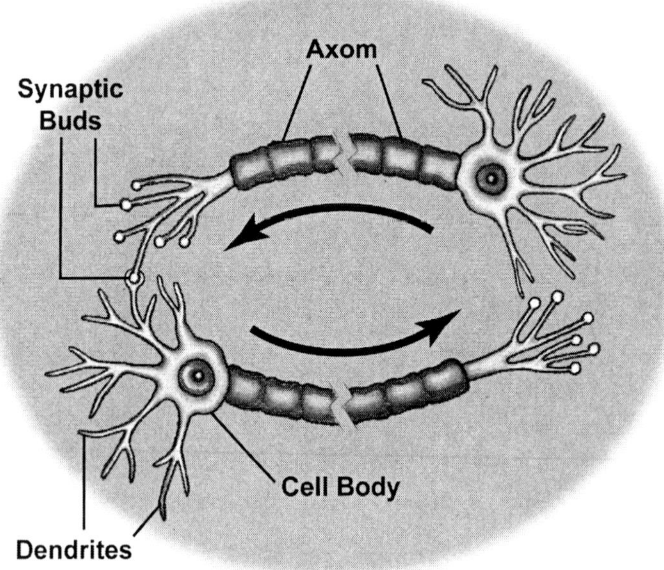


Fig. 2-3 Simplified Neural Circuit

A synaptic gap is the space between the synaptic button of a branch of one neuron and the dendrites of a neighboring neuron, best seen on the left side of Fig. 2-3. Electrical potential from one cell body travels by way of the insulated axon across the synaptic gap and into the dendrites of another neuron, where an electrochemical signal is triggered in the cell body of that neuron. This signal is delivered via the nerve fiber to thousands of adjacent neurons and, presto, we have neural circuits.

A neuron with its dendrites, cell body, axon, branches and synapses connected to another neuron is an electrical circuit. It is not *like* an electrical circuit; it *is* an electrical circuit. These elementary neural electrical circuits form the basic building blocks of the brain and the nervous system.

## *Speed and Size*

As awe inspiring as this brain-building process is, an additional factor makes the phenomenon even more astonishing. Speed! The neurons are dividing and migrating at a rate of a quarter of a million per minute! This activity continues unabated for the balance of the nine months of gestation.

It is presently believed that the resultant cell division produces 200 billion neurons. Of these 200 billion neurons, about half die or are pruned away during brain development. Scientists tell us that the dead cells are absorbed by the body and then eliminated as waste. In other words, half our brain is flushed down the drain. No one appears certain as to when cell death and pruning stops. Some believe the process is complete prior to birth; others believe the pruning process continues during the first few years of life and again in the teen years.

For a long time it was believed that 100 billion neurons were all we ever got. However, evidence of neurogenesis (new cell growth) has recently been detected in the brain's hippocampus, a structure near the base of the brain believed to be involved in long term memory storage.

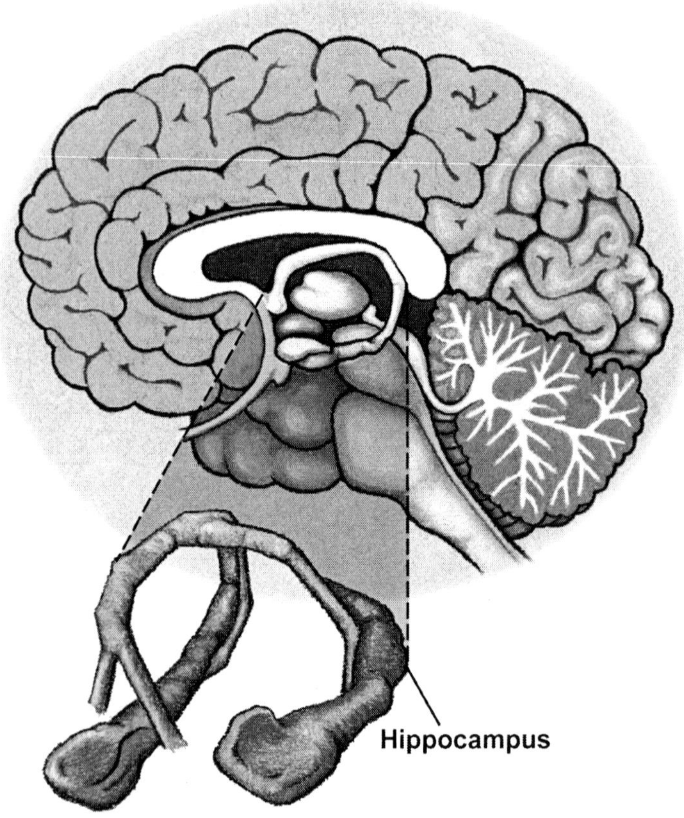


Fig. 2-4 The Hippocampus

It also appears that people who have experienced a stroke grow new neurons that push to the site where neurons have died from lack of oxygen.

How complex is this system of 100 billion neurons? Can you picture it? It is hard to get a handle on a number that large — or connections that small. Let's try to get an understanding of this complexity by comparing it with something humans have created — the entire phone system for the planet. If we take all the phones in the world and all the cell phones (there are over six billion people on the planet), the number of connections and the trillions of messages per day do not equal the complexity or activity of a single human brain.

## *The Wrinkling of Our Grey Matter*

In the days following birth there is a veritable explosion of neural circuit growth. Circuits develop massively and arrays of neural circuits increase in physical size as neurons continue to branch and interconnect with the dendrites of adjacent neurons.

Eighty percent of the brain system's storage capacity is in the cerebral cortex, an eighth-inch thick, highly-wrinkled surface layer of the brain where, it is believed, 80% of the 100 billion brain neurons reside (Fig. 2-5).

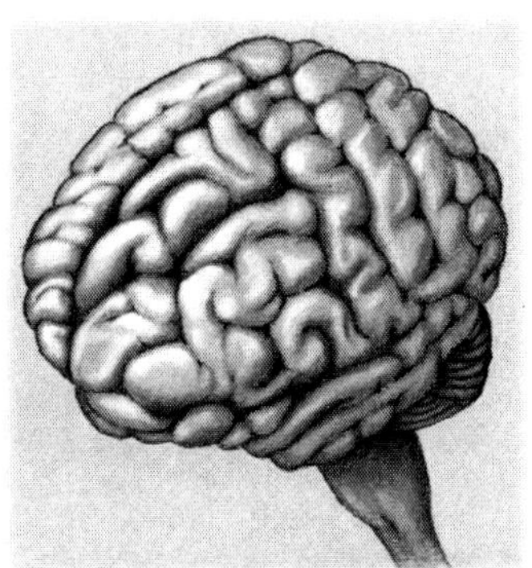

Fig. 2-5 The Cerebral Cortex

When the cortex begins to grow in size as a result of neural circuit development, it is interesting to note that the cortex does not get thicker, its surface area simply gets larger. While the brain grows rapidly, the heavy bone structure in the temple region of the skull grows very slowly, causing the cerebral cortex to buckle, much as a carpet that is too large for a room develops folds and ridges. The growing cortex folds up upon itself and results in its wrinkled appearance.

## *Electrical Connections for Movement and Sensing*

Different regions of the brain include neural circuits that perform specialized functions. Among the first special-purpose neural circuits to form are the circuits that generate electrical power. These circuits apparently combine glucose and oxygen from the blood stream of the mother that passes through the placenta for use in the developing brain. Electrical energy is needed in the operation of the brain and nervous system that extends from the brain into the body. It is currently estimated that the total electrical power generated by these circuits can reach 25 watts, more than enough to power a night light.

It is these electrical signals transmitted from the brain through nerve fibers to muscles in the body that bring about muscle contraction and relaxation. So you want to crawl, walk, throw a ball, type? It is by way of these orchestrated contractions and relaxations of muscles that any and all physical actions take place.

What about circuits that process electrical signals from sensory organs? Neurons migrate to all organs and regions of the anatomy and therefore to the eye, inner ear and all over the skin surface of our body. Neurons that have migrated to our finger tips set themselves down and sprout nerve fibers that extend back through hands, arms, our spinal cord and into the brain. The muscles in our arms, hands and fingers are controlled by neurons in the brain by way of the nerve fibers that extend from the brain to the muscles of the arms, hands and fingers.

In other words, we have neural circuits that go from the brain to all regions of the body. And we have neural circuits from all regions of the body feeding information back to the brain, all in the form of electrical signals.

## *Circuitry for Thinking, Learning and Remembering*

Scientists currently estimate that at birth the human brain has only 24% of the 100 billion neurons wired to generate power and process data from our senses. The remaining 76% of the neurons are apparently destined to serve as an onboard biological camcorder/data storage bank to record processed and sensed data and provide a vast array of memory storage circuits.

Our brain processes and records sensed data. Our mind combines these storage bytes into electrical signal patterns, or memory traces. Broadly speaking, the results are what we know as our own personal thoughts about the world.

> The more times the same or a similar sound or image is delivered by an electrical message to the same region of the brain, the stronger that circuit becomes and the easier it is to retrieve the stored information.

A number of theories have been proposed to explain how the 76% of the memory storage neurons cooperate to store processed information. The theory I find most convincing holds that neurons and neural circuits convert sensory information into electrical signals. Each signal has unique characteristics specific to its source. So, the electrical signals from sounds are different in character from electrical signals carrying visual images. In this model, the nature of the electrical signal causes ends of the nerve fiber branches to migrate toward nearby dendrites. At the point of contact, a little button called a synaptic bud instantly develops and establishes an electrochemical connection. The nature of the electrical signal being sent controls the nature of the electrical signal generated in the receiving neuron. A unique series of branching and connecting dendrite circuit paths form creating the memory storage circuit. Subsequently, each time this specific image or sound is experienced, it is delivered into this specific neural circuit. The circuit paths may become massive.

In this model virtually all sensed information becomes physically recorded in the neural circuits that form in the brain. Retrieval becomes the issue. This book will assist you in appreciating how and why a variety of conscious mental techniques will cause special-purpose neural circuits to form that ease the retrieval of stored information.

## *Hearing Circuits*

People often ask, "Does the brain sense and record information prior to birth?" The answer is "yes." We now know that the inner ear of a developing infant is fully formed by the eighth month of gestation. What does the unborn infant hear and record in its brain? Primarily the sounds of its mother's breathing, heartbeat and voice. Also there are studies indicating that newborns respond to other voices heard frequently during pregnancy and to music the mother may have listened to repeatedly while pregnant.

It should not be surprising to learn that, especially in the first few weeks of life outside the mother's womb, when a fussy infant's head rests on the mother's chest, it is comforted by the sound of its mother's breathing and heart beat. These sounds are familiar and match the heartbeat and breathing sounds recorded in the womb. It is this familiarity that dominates the infant's senses and produces a state of peace.

When fathers of newborns try to comfort them by holding and rocking them, the peaceful state is not so quickly established. In time, if the father plays a role in physically nurturing the infant, his heartbeat and breathing will be recorded in the infant's brain.

Now, think of children learning to talk. They hear the sounds used in their native language over and over. They attempt to talk. At first these attempts are only approximate, having the tone and inflection of language. But gradually, as the language neural circuits are reinforced through what they hear repeatedly, they begin to put together understandable words and sentences.

## *Seeing Circuits*

We know now that fetuses record sounds in their neural circuits. Do they see anything before birth? No, because light cannot enter the womb of the mother. The next logical question is, when a newborn infant is exposed to light at the moment of birth, does the infant see anything? Well, not until the brain's ability to make sense of what the eye "sees" is developed. (The next two paragraphs are for those like me, who are fascinated by the details).

The retina, an internal surface in the back of the eyeball, is like the film or digital recording surface in the back of a camera. It is comprised of about 130 million photoreceptor cells. These cells are like neurons in that each has a nerve fiber that connects with other cells which combine signals from the photoreceptor cells into a smaller number of nerve fibers. The nerve fibers exit at a single location behind the eyeball to form what we call the optic nerve. The optic nerve is a bundle of nerve fibers connected to the occipital lobe region of the cerebral cortex, referred to as the visual cortex (Fig. 2-6), at the back of the brain near its base.

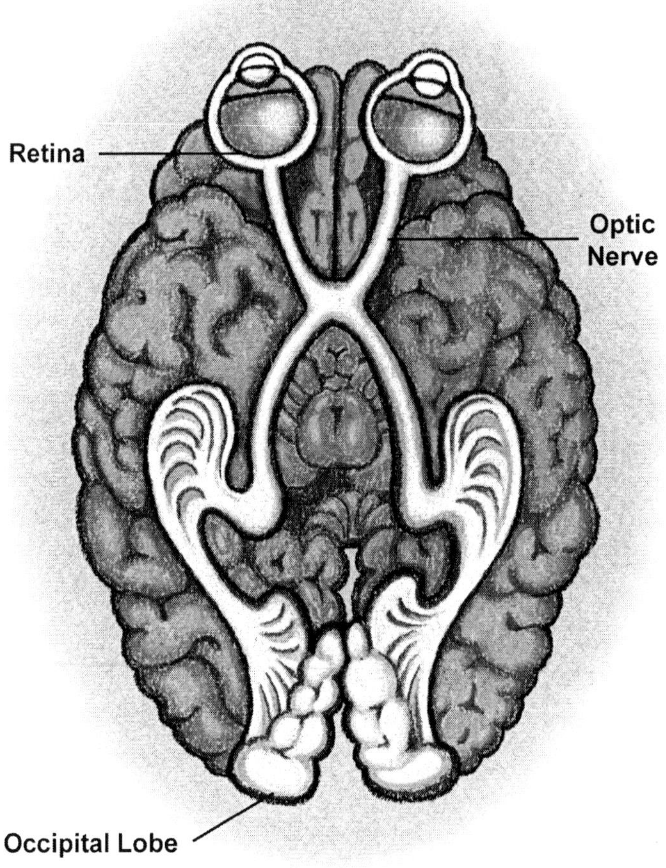


Fig. 2-6 Visual Cortex

Each of the photoreceptor cells generates an electrical signal when a beam of light strikes it. The electrical signal passes back through an associated nerve fiber, which delivers it to neurons in the occipital lobes. A bright light generates a strong signal in the photoreceptor cell, whereas a faint light beam generates a small one.

So, now the question is, how does the infant learn to see? The visual cortex translates visual images received from the retina into images that are recorded in neural circuits. Immediately after birth and upon exposure to light, the electrical signals from the photoreceptors of the retina begin traveling to the visual cortex via the nerve fibers of the optic nerve. The arrival of these signals drives neural circuit development, which records the images in the visual cortex.

## *Flexibility (AKA Plasticity)*

Imagine that the process just described is much like a camcorder that is always on, recording everything that falls within its field of view. While the camcorder metaphor is useful, it falls short due to the complexity of the nervous system. To fully function as a metaphor, we would need a camcorder beyond the scope of today's technology, one that simultaneously recorded not only sound and sight but also taste, touch and smell.

As late as the 1980's, it was believed that the human brain was completely wired prior to birth, and all that was necessary was to program the existing, pre-wired brain, much as you would a computer. In this model, the brain was thought of as a "blank slate" (tabula rasa) at birth that was programmed by life's experiences. This blank slate metaphor led proponents to conclude that the environment or culture in which a human developed controlled the programming of the pre-existing neural circuits in the brain.

This computer analogy of the brain was useful in explaining much of human learning and behavior. The computer model included neural circuits for processing in all of the five senses and assumed there were separate neural circuit configurations to store the information received from each of the five senses. The assumption was that neurons such as hearing neurons or seeing neurons were permanently distinct from the beginning.

The computer model was found to be inaccurate in the late 1980's, when it was discovered that neural storage circuits have more flexibility than previously thought. While there are separate fields of neural circuits in the cerebral cortex that do by and large store sight, sound, taste, smell and touch information separately, they are not necessarily limited to one special purpose. Under certain circumstances, neurons originally assigned one role can be recruited for another purpose.

Evidence of this was discovered when an experimenter placed a patch over one eye of a newborn kitten for 48 hours. The remaining eye was left open to receive light and process images. What surprised the researchers was that when the patched eye was uncovered, it had lost its capacity to cooperate with the neural processing circuits in the visual cortex. When only one eye was allowed to process light and images the optic nerve of the uncovered eye delivered signals to the entire visual cortex and had apparently commanded nearly all the visual field neurons for its own use. There were few, if any, visual cortex neural circuits available for the use of the other eye once it was uncovered. The remarkable result was that the cat was blind in one eye for the balance of its life. In a similar fashion, an infant born with a cataract (an opaque lens that blocks light from entering the eye) will be blind in that eye for life unless the cataract is removed immediately.

We now appreciate that while neural circuit storage fields in the brain may appear to be special purpose, they are not. We have all known blind people with exceptional hearing. The explanation lies here. When an infant enters the world with a birth defect that prevents the optic nerves from sending electrical signals from the eyes back to the visual cortex, the visual neural circuit storage fields become available for use by other signal-processing centers in the brain. Therefore, the blind develop exceptional hearing, and their tactile sense becomes much more sensitive than that of sighted people.

One of the most remarkable examples of this was observed in a child who had the entire left hemisphere of her brain removed, which should have rendered her unable to speak, understand words and move the limbs on the right side of her body. To everyone's amazement the little girl learned to read, write, handle math, move about and eventually live a full life, including a higher education!

Brain plasticity — when a portion of the cerebral cortex is being used for a purpose different from the genetically instructed function — seems to be a characteristic of neural circuits when the brain is in development prior to puberty. At puberty, plasticity decreases when there is an influx of hormones into the brain which appear to fix the neural circuits already formed, hard-wiring them, as it were.

## *Not One Brain, but Three*

Up until now we've talked about the brain as a single entity. Some scientists say that the body has three brains — the familiar one encased in the skull or cranium, and two lesser known, but vitally important ones, found in the heart and gut. The three brains are interconnected and when one gets upset, so do the other two. Some scientists feel talking about three separate brains is just a different way to talk about the exquisite complexity of the central nervous system. For the sake of understanding the power of the brain, we'll describe the three brain theory in this section.

## *The Brain in the Gut*

The brain in the gut consists of a complex network of neurons located in the esophagus, stomach, small intestine and colon. These neurons are like those found in the brain in the head. Much like the cranial brain's activity, the brain in the gut learns, remembers, acts independently, and produces, as they say, "gut feelings."

Until recently scientists believed that the gut's complex neural network was wired directly to the cranial brain. Command signals from the brain delivered via the vagus nerve were believed to affect primarily the overall activity of the neural circuit networks in the gut, with the vagus nerve that connects the cranial brain to the gut having only a few thousand nerve fibers. It is now known that the gut has at least 100 million neurons. Much has yet to be learned about the brain in the gut and its role in human behavior. While this book does not explore the role and function of the brain in the gut, it should be understood that not all human behaviors can be traced exclusively to the brain in the skull.[4]

## *The Brain in the Heart*

In 1991 Dr. J. Andrew Armour's research5 revealed that the heart has a complex, intrinsic nervous system that is sufficiently sophisticated to qualify as a "little brain" in its own right. The heart's brain is an intricate network of several types of neurons, neurotransmitter proteins and support cells like those found in the cranial brain proper. Its elaborate circuitry enables it to act independently of the cranial brain — to learn, to remember, and even feel and sense. The heart's nervous system contains around 40,000 neurons that detect circulating hormones and neurotransmitters and sense heart rate and blood pressure information. A fascinating book detailing this small brain in the heart is The HeartMath Solution by Childre and Martin.

## *The Three Brains Working Together*

The heart's nervous system translates information into neurological impulses and sends them to the brain through several neural pathways. These nerve pathways enter the brain in the brainstem at the base of the brain. The process triggers the brain to send out signals which have a regulatory role over many of the body's organs, such as the heart and the stomach. This part of the nervous system is called the autonomic nervous system, controlling involuntary actions in the body. These signals, which influence the heart, blood vessels and other glands and organs, also cascade into the higher centers of the brain where they may influence perception, decision making and other cognitive processes.

Fig. 2-7 is a causal loop diagram which depicts the brain in the head shown with arrows to and from the brains in the heart and gut.

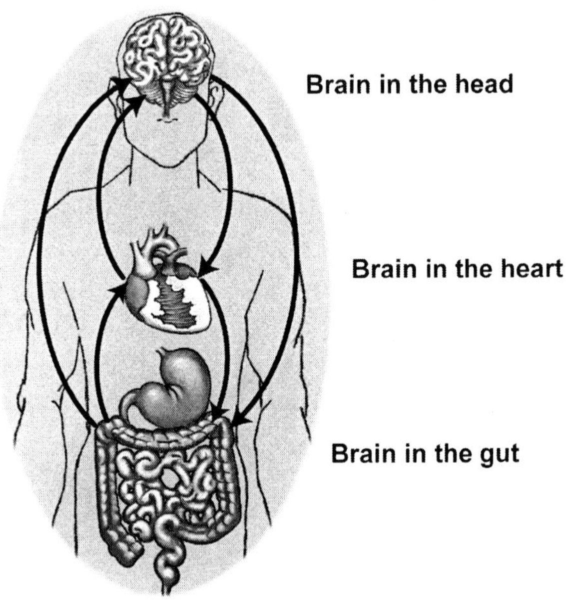


Fig. 2-7 The Three Brains – a Causal Loop Diagram

For those readers not familiar with causal loop diagrams, which feature prominently in systems thinking literature (see Chapter 13), a causal loop diagram tells a story of a system. The arrows help create the narrative by showing the direction of influence or interdependence. A systems thinker would say the diagram above tells the following story: "Neural activities in the brain in the head influence neural activities in the brain of the heart and the brain in the gut. Similarly, neural activities in either the brain in the heart or gut influence the brain in the head, and the brain in the gut influences the brain in the heart." Talk about interdependence!

Examples of these connected circuits are found in the "butterflies" we feel in our abdomen when we are about to give a speech, and the visceral dread we may experience as we sit down to take an exam. Another example is the way we may choke up and spontaneously bring our hand to our heart on seeing the picture of an orphaned child.

The role and function of these three brains in the human body have been fully defined by each person's genetic instructions. In this view, sensory data are processed not only by the cranial brain but also by gut and heart neural circuits and stored in neural circuits spread throughout the intestines and heart.

# 3
# *Learning*

## *We Know What We Know*

At this point we need to examine a basic principle about how the mind/brain/body learns that is critical for understanding the balance of this book. The principle is as follows: If you haven't experienced something before, you won't know what it is. In the language of the brain, if there are no previously sensed and stored experiences, the mind will not be able to compare incoming information and match it with stored information. People know what they are experiencing only if there is a match between what has been stored in the past and what is being experienced by their senses in the present. In other words you don't know what you don't know.

> If you haven't experienced something before, you won't know what it is.

An example of this is the story of Australian aborigines who, when seeing a white man on a horse for the first time, assumed the man and the horse were one. At a later time when a man on a horse passed by with sheep, the aborigines assumed the sheep were the wives of the horse-man. They matched information based on their stored knowledge. Whether accurate or inaccurate, it was based on their reality.

You can see from this principle of "knowing" that everything we experience via our five senses (that is, sight from our eyes, hearing from our ears, smell from our nose, taste from our tongue and touch from our skin) is processed and stored in the neural circuits and memory storage neurons of our brain.

## *I Am a Slow Learner*

Back in elementary school, tests determined I was a "slow learner" or "retarded." Intelligence was measured by how quickly I could think and not whether my thought processes produced sound reasoning and effective outcomes. If I were a child today, I would undoubtedly be categorized as having a "learning disability." In any case, in the face of my childhood performance, it would have been unrealistic to believe that I could do what I have done, namely, complete engineering school, law school, obtain a graduate degree in business and become a successful patent attorney. Perhaps the desire to understand this discrepancy sparked my intense interest in the brain!

As you will soon see, what transformed me from "retarded" to "highly competent" was nothing more than....drum roll...exercise!

## *Exercising Muscles*

Let us now pause and dwell upon some well known attributes of muscle development in humans. Imagine, if you will, that you are given a 30 pound barbell designed to be held in one of your hands. Next assume that you are instructed to hold the barbell in your left hand and flex your left arm at the elbow raising the weight to your shoulder, and do this twenty times a day for the next two years. The instruction is that you NOT do the same activity with your right arm. Play along with me and assume that you actually followed these instructions. What will we observe at the end of the two years? The biceps in your left arm will be perceptibly larger than those in your right.

Assume next that you are instructed to cease weight lifting with the left arm and report back 20 years later. What do you think your left arm will look like after normal use for 20 years? More than likely its size and shape will closely approximate the size and shape of the right arm. In other words, the left arm muscles will have wasted away through lack of use. Lack of exercise results in the wasting away of muscle and connective tissue and the reduction in overall muscle size and strength.

## *Off to School We Go*

Let us now return to the developing brain and explore what is happening there during the twelve years a child is in school, involved on a daily basis with a variety of mental tasks that involve reading, writing, and arithmetic. If he is lucky, he will also be exposed to art and music.

In later chapters we will explore in detail the right and left hemispheres of the brain. For now, you may already know that the left hemisphere of the brain handles reading, writing and arithmetic, whereas the right side processes art, music, and interpersonal relationships, among other things. For purposes of this exploration, pretend that you are able to remove and examine the brain of a student after twelve years of schooling. Compare the size of the left hemisphere with that of the right. Is there a difference as a result of twelve years of mental activity? Of course. The size of the left hemisphere is larger than the right. If we examined this same brain forty years later, we should not be surprised to find, absent further schooling or an occupation that required extensive mental activity, the left hemisphere is not larger than the right. As in the example of exercising the left arm — the brain is like a muscle.

So when do portions of our brains begin to shrink from lack of use? The answer for most people is: the day you leave a formal learning environment. Not only is there a change in physical size, but also in memory circuit function and efficiency. An example is Gina, a woman whose first language was English. She spoke only English until age twelve. Then her family moved to Mexico and she learned Spanish. She spoke Spanish from then until middle age. By then she was speaking, thinking and dreaming in Spanish. Later in life Gina found that although she could still speak English, she had lost much of her English vocabulary.

## *Good News*

The good news is that any time, up until the moment of death, you can generate neural circuits and continue to enhance the performance of existing ones. Good nutrition and mental exercise are basic elements in retaining and restoring mental capabilities. Lifelong learning has been shown to delay the onset of some disorders found in elderly people, such as Alzheimer's disease.

The other good news is that the human brain has a virtually infinite storage capacity. This claim is supported by the fact that each neuron and its branches can form interconnections to dendrites in up to 15,000 adjacent neurons. In theory each nerve fiber branch-to-dendrite connection provides for a single storage bit and combinations of bits form storage bytes. Assume, if you will, that you could count all the connections at the rate of one per second. Gerald Edelman, the 1972 Nobel Prize winner in medicine, tells us that it would take you 32 million years to finish counting. If this is true, then isn't it fair to say human brains have unlimited storage capacity?

# 4

# *The Limbic System – Understanding Some Mysteries about Behavior*

When you see the small size of the limbic system compared to the massive right and left hemispheres of the brain, you might assume that it has a smaller role in mental processing and human behavior. Nothing could be further from the truth. The limbic system might be likened to an automobile's accelerator pedal, which is small in size relative to the vehicle's engine and power train, but oh, so important if you want to go anywhere! An understanding of the limbic system's role and some specialized functions in the mind/brain/body system is helpful, especially if you want to make changes in your life.

The limbic system is a group of brain structures that is involved in both emotional response and memory management. Several subsystems contribute to the overall functioning of the limbic system. In the sections that follow, we will explore two of them, the hippocampus and the amygdala, in detail.

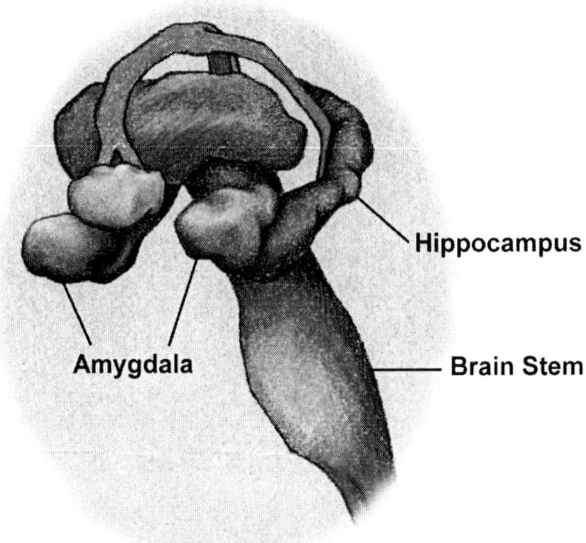


Fig. 4-1 The Limbic System

## *Site of Memory*

The limbic system serves as a sort of switchboard to route incoming sensory information to its storage location, and to retrieve data from storage. It is thus essential to learning. It is believed that all information derived from our senses — touch, taste, smell, hearing and sight — passes through the limbic system. There, the incoming data may be tagged or coded on the way to the cerebral cortex for storage. It is this tagging or coding that allows the data to be retrieved from the cerebral cortex in the future.

Information not tagged or coded in some way is delivered directly to the cerebral cortex where it is all recorded. This untagged information creates a contextual memory or background for embedding tagged and coded data. Untagged information, including everything you have experienced over the course of your life, every book you have ever read, everything you have seen, is stored in the trillions of neural circuits in your brain. Later in this chapter and in Chapters 8 and 18 you will learn how you can search for, find and consciously retrieve untagged information that will aid in dealing with problems or concerns that arise in your daily life.

## *Center of Emotional Processing*

The limbic system is the chemical factory of the brain. The chemicals produced there affect our emotional states. The limbic system is often referred to in evolutionary terms as the mammalian brain that developed in time after the reptilian brain known as the brain stem. In his book Descartes' Error6, Dr. Antonio Damasio, a neuroscientist at the University of Iowa, makes the point convincingly that these chemicals in some way affect all thought processes that take place in the brain. Thus, there is no such thing as a completely rational, analytical, logical thought that is free of emotional involvement brought about by the chemicals released by the limbic system.

In her 1997 book, *Molecules of Emotion*[7], Candice Pert demonstrates that molecules of the chemicals that are involved in emotional states circulate all through the body. These chemicals influence all the feelings we experience.

## *The Brain as a Sensory Camcorder*

As described earlier, our sensory systems are connected to the brain in a manner suggestive of a video camcorder that records everything we experience. What I am suggesting by this metaphor is that virtually everything we experience and all of our thoughts about our experiences are stored in our neural circuits. However, if the information is not tagged on its way to the cerebral cortex, it is generally not retrievable. Books on developing a highly efficient memory describe a host of mental techniques that aid in tagging information in the neural circuits of the cerebral cortex. For many individuals these memorization techniques are effective, but they can also miss by just a hair. I knew a Mrs. Eligator who, while traveling in Europe, ran into a man she had previously met. This man had probably used a memorization technique, because he approached my friend warmly, saying, "How nice to run into you so far from home, Mrs. Crocodile."

There are some situations that we tag and remember without consciously trying to do so. The physiological conditions attendant to tagging information, as well as retrieving untagged information, are of particular interest to me. In many "Pathways to Greatness" workshops I asked participants if they could remember in vivid detail what they were doing during any random ten minute interval eight months earlier. No one could. They said it was impossible. They could not recall where they were, who they were with, exactly what they were doing or what was happening around them during the ten minute interval.

In order to demonstrate the inherent ability we have to perform this type of vivid recall, please look at the dates below and then reflect on where you were on these dates (assuming you were born) and what you were doing at any given ten minute interval that immediately comes to mind.

- November 22, 1963
- January 28, 1986
- September 11, 2001
- February 1, 2003

In the matter of the November date in 1963, do you have any specific recall as to where you were at the moment you learned of the Kennedy assassination?

My wife Sharon remembers November 22, 1963. She was in the middle of a class called New Mathematics, which she didn't especially like, at the University of California, Davis, where she was an undergraduate student. A man came in and whispered to the professor. The professor turned white, then told the class he'd received a report that President Kennedy had been shot, and he wanted to find out more, so the class was given a break. The class went outside and formed small, distraught groups, anxious for more information. Those were not the days of instant news, or portable radios or phones people carried with them. After what seemed an agonizing period, the class was called back into the auditorium and told the President was dead. Everyone sat in stunned silence without moving for a very long time. Sharon remembers tears streaming down her face and passing crying people as she rode her bicycle home.

In a similar manner, reflect upon where you were and what you were doing in January, 1986, when you learned of the Challenger accident, September 11, 2001, the terrorist attack on the United States, and most recently the Columbia tragedy on February 1, 2003.

Why do we remember some sensory experiences in vivid detail but not others?

## *Chemical Tagging of Information*

Bad, threatening, awful, frightening or tragic input typically causes the limbic system to flood the brain with neurotransmitter chemicals similar to those associated fight or flight reactions. When chemical flooding occurs, neural circuits-in-formation absorb these emotionally-generated neurotransmitters, causing automatic tagging of the incoming information. This chemical tagging of memory circuits allows the vivid recall of events such as those remembered above.

An obvious downside of chemically tagged memories that are

highly charged with negative emotions is that they can be recalled so vividly and be painfully relived years later. This is one reason people who experienced childhood trauma or abuse often require therapy in order to move forward.

There is, however, a profoundly significant upside to this chemical tagging of memory circuits. When we have highly charged, positive experiences, we flood the brain with neurotransmitters of the type associated with joy, happiness and excitement. Reflect back over your life's experiences and vividly recall some powerfully positive experiences you have had. Although you may not realize it when you recall these positive experiences, the brain is re-flooded with the neurotransmitters that tagged neural circuits forming at the time of the original experience. We will use this fact in Chapters 16-18.

### *Other Useful Tidbits about the Limbic System*

The limbic region of the brain also controls your emotions regarding sex and hunger. You don't want anything to happen to this part of your brain! Scientists tell us that this is a very primitive part of the brain. Because it operates below the level of conscious awareness there's no way you really know what the limbic region is asking for. This part of the brain is so dumb that if it is asking for sex, you may be able to turn it off by having a chocolate sundae. And if you want something sweet to eat, you might turn that off by having sex.

Given my history, it stands to reason that when I learned it is the part of the brain involved in hunger and addiction, I developed a keen interest in the limbic system. When a person ingests alcohol, cocaine, tobacco, or any of the other mind and mood-altering drugs, this is the part of the brain that is affected. This part of the brain also is involved in overeating, another of my past challenges. (See Chapter 15 for that story.)

Alcoholics have an abnormal craving for alcohol. What is often recommended when they experience such a craving for alcohol? "Have a dish of ice cream. Eat a candy bar." The limbic region of the brain is so undiscriminating it doesn't know the difference between a drink and a candy bar. Although a high protein food would give longer relief from hunger (or a craving), it makes perfect sense that Alcoholics Anonymous groups often serve donuts. Sweets give quick relief.

## *Brain Waves in our Daily Lives*

We've all heard of brain waves, but they are not widely understood. Brain waves are electrical impulses given off by brain tissue. The interesting thing is that there are different types of brain waves, each type classified by a range of frequencies that correlate with different mental activity levels (Fig. 4-2). Even though the brain wave signals look different, with the exception of delta, each one may have identical thoughts, ideas, knowledge and information embedded in it.

The *beta wave* signal has a frequency between 12 and 27 cycles per second (CPS) and is predominant when we are fully awake and consciously engaged in the world around us. Using the vehicle/limbic system metaphor with which we began this chapter, we might think of the beta wave's 12-27 CPS as revving up the engine or accelerating from idle to cruising speed.

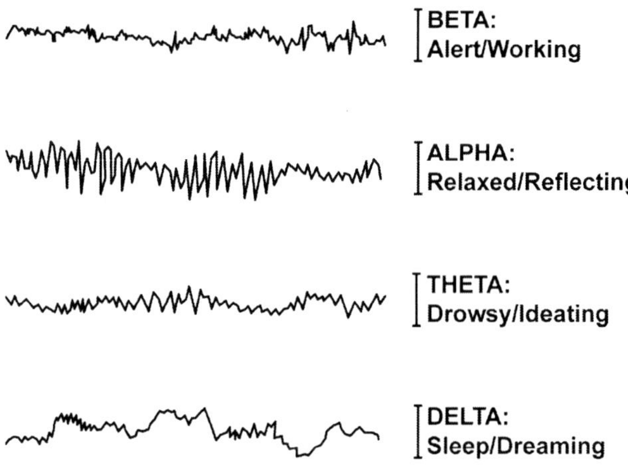


Fig. 4-2 Brain wave chart

The *alpha wave signal* varies between 7-12 CPS. This may be likened to a range of gentle engine idling speeds. We typically experience the alpha wave state when we are relaxed both physically and mentally. Meditation practices often elicit alpha brain wave activity. Alpha brain waves are also linked to daydreaming, fantasizing and a general sense of detachment. When we close our eyes to listen to music or relaxation tapes, alpha waves are in operation. Alpha wave signals disappear in some individuals when they open their eyes after relaxing. With practice, however, many people are able to stay in an alpha wave state with their eyes open.

The *theta brain wave* state is a very deep state of mental relaxation, a state believed to be experienced during hypnosis. The theta brain waves range between 4 and 7 CPS. Theta brain waves can be thought of as the mental signals that transport our mind into our subconscious where we have access to all our tagged and untagged memories stored in the neural circuits of our cerebral cortex. In the theta range, information flows easily between conscious and unconscious mental states.

*Delta brain waves* vary between 1 and 4 CPS. The delta state of mind predominates when you are asleep. Delta waves go from sleeping and dreaming to deep, dreamless sleep, allowing the brain to be in a nearly complete state of rest.

### Good News about Theta Waves

I first discovered the value of the morning shower early in my career as a patent attorney when I had the task of uncovering the gist of an invention buried in a complex technical context. I will never forget one particular morning when an awareness of great clarity, the gist of the invention, came to my conscious mind as I showered. It literally felt as if someone had turned on a light in my head and I could now see clearly what I had been searching for.

To my utter dismay I was late for work that day and rushed through my dressing, skipped breakfast and arrived at work literally out of breath. I sat at my desk, pen in hand, and drew a total blank about the grand, illuminating thought that had come to me in the shower. I had lost it! But why? My cognitive error was my failure to consciously tag the thought before delivering it to the cerebral cortex for storage and retrieval.

Today I frequently cut short a shower to make sure I get to a pad and pencil to record my theta state solutions to problems. I also know people who use waterproof tape recorders in the shower so they always capture the brilliance of the theta state.

There is more good news involving the theta state and the subconscious. Take any problem — personal or work related, practical or abstract. Ask your subconscious to work on the problem while you sleep. You have probably had this experience before, and the insights of many famous thinkers have come in this way. Give the problem to the subconscious just as you fall asleep and wake up from the theta to the alpha and beta states in the morning with the solution in hand. Some people keep paper and pen beside the bed to record great solutions that surface at 3 a.m.

In our sleep-deprived culture this powerful problem solving technique becomes short circuited when total restful sleep time is always interrupted by an alarm clock. The alarm clock does exactly what it is intended to do — quickly drive your mental state from delta deep sleep, through theta, then alpha to a fully alert beta state. When this occurs, any solution to the problem carried into the subconscious and solved during sleep is likely to be lost by the rapid movement through the theta state to higher states.

However, sometimes these inspirations can be retrieved if you step into the shower as soon as your alarm clock wakes you. The steady flow of water onto the head, shoulders and back induces a theta state in many people, freeing solutions to problems which then bubble up into the conscious mind.

The theta state also apparently occurs in occasional moments of the day when we appear, by our outward behavior, to be fully conscious and alert. Do you recall times when you have finished a day at work, gotten into your car to drive home and upon nearing your home become consciously aware that you had absolutely no recollection of having driven through rush hour traffic? Many who have had such experiences worry that they could have killed a pedestrian or run a stop sign or red light if they were so out of it.

Don't worry. During your drive home a significant portion of the brain's muscle motor control circuits were under the control of theta brain wave activity. The theta waves access subconscious neural circuits for conscious use. These include all required physical activity essential to driving your car safely. These activities had been performed countless times in the past and can be performed almost automatically. (See more about solving problems in Chapter 18.)

### *Brain Waves and Efficient Sleeping*

Imagine that your day is ending and just prior to getting ready for sleep your mind is active with thoughts that trouble you. These thoughts may involve personal concerns or simply searching for a solution to a problem you are living with. Assume that these thoughts dominate your mental state as you lie down and close your eyes. Most people are unaware that the moment the eyes close and stay closed, the brain interprets this as the intention to go to sleep. It triggers the release of the hormone melatonin, which induces a slowdown of brain wave activity from beta through to alpha, to theta into delta and deep sleep. Any troubling thought or problem embedded in your last conscious beta brain waves is first converted into an alpha wave form and then into a theta wave form, which allows the troubling thought or the problem to be delivered into the subconscious mind that never completely shuts down. The last conscious thoughts you transport into your subconscious circulate there while you sleep. Unless you have posed a challenge for your subconscious to work on in the night, the troubling thoughts you took into sleep with you will be there in the morning, waiting to resurface as the brain moves from deep sleep back through the theta state toward alertness.

Sleep/wake cycles range between 90 and 110 minutes. As we come out of deep sleep to a lighter sleep state, the troubling thoughts carried into the subconscious rise back into our lighter, more conscious sleep state, where they bring about full wakefulness and a troubled conscious state of mind. Once you are aware of this theta wave transport of your last conscious thoughts into sleep, you have the knowledge necessary to prevent disturbed sleep patterns that find their origin in real or imagined distressing circumstances present in your daily life.

Here is the secret: a key element of peaceful, restful sleep is to ritualistically quiet your thoughts and focus your last conscious thoughts on positive, peaceful subject matter. It is not surprising that all the world's great religions urge their followers to end each day with a prayer that they take with them into their subconscious while they sleep.

For the past thirty plus years my last conscious thoughts each day have been the following:

> Dear Lord, thank you for another sober day. I humbly pray for knowledge of your will for me and the power to carry it out. I am divinely guided. I take the high road, the road less traveled. God reveals a way when I have lost my way.

As a small child I can remember my mother each night at my bedside reading an uplifting story and reciting a simple prayer with me. This set a peaceful tone as I drifted off to sleep, often before the story and prayer were over. However, bedtime rituals of story and prayer ended when my mother was left with overwhelming grief and responsibilities following the death of my brother and then my father. For the next thirty years I turned to prayer only fleetingly, and then only when I was in trouble and sought rescue from circumstances of my own making.

After joining The Fellowship in my late thirties I began to follow their suggestions to thank my Higher Power for another sober day before drifting off to sleep. To this prayer I add the affirming thoughts noted above. I sleep like a baby.

### *How Do We Remember? Gratitude for the Hippocampus!*

The hippocampus is a part of the limbic system that sorts information. We remember what we understand; we understand only what we pay attention to; we pay attention to what interests us, what suits our fancy at the moment.

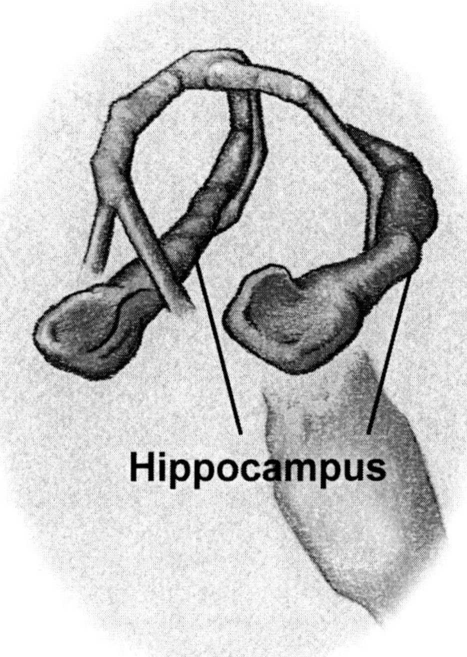


Fig. 4-3 The Hippocampus

In his book *The Owners Manual for the Brain*[8], Pierce J. Howard, Ph.D. notes that

> Long-term memory appears to be located in the cerebral cortex. Apparently, hippocampal short-term memory communicates with the cortex through what we call simple human will or effort; over time, it establishes chunks in long-term storage.

There are some experts in the study of memory who suggest "short-term memory" is a misnomer. The hippocampus provides for what is called "immediate memory." The hippocampus functions as a buffer region that can hold thousands of pieces of data for two seconds or less as the stream of data is headed toward the cerebral cortex where it is recorded as background information. For example, when you look up a phone number that you have never seen before, you will forget it a few seconds later unless you keep repeating it. The incoming flow of information is continuous. This flow will carry the new phone number with it and store it as context, unless the mind pays special attention to it.

What must happen before a long-term memory circuit will be formed in the brain's cerebral cortex? Clearly something read or thought one day, and revisited some days later, would not have received enough attention to be remembered. Multiple repetitions every day for a number of weeks will almost always ensure that the information is stored in long-term memory. Retrieval of the data is another matter. It is always helpful to consciously tag the information to be stored in long-term memory.

Since metaphors often give life to a concept, think of the hippocampus as a large room with three doors. One of the doors is an entrance and two are exits. Next imagine that in this room there is a balcony that goes around the room. The balcony serves as a site from which to observe what is happening in the room below. The entrance is that region in the base of the brain where all sensory information flows into the brain for processing. This sensed information is mostly untagged. It is simply raw, unprocessed data. The first exit door leads to the long term memory regions in the neural circuits of the cerebral cortex. The second exit door also leads to the cerebral cortex and vast arrays of neural circuits which store information that the mind does not consider worth paying attention to.

Imagine that part of your mind is always perched somewhere in the balcony, watching the inrush of all sensed information, serving as the traffic director. As a practical matter, there is so much information rushing in that the mind is challenged to detect and direct information that is worthy of attention.

The hippocampus has the capacity to hold information in storage for days or weeks at a time. The mind is always looking for information that is received multiple times. Accordingly, information that repeats many times is considered by the watching mind to be important and therefore worthy of storage in long term memory. In the hippocampus big room metaphor we may think of the mind reaching down from the balcony and directing these repeated groups of information toward and through the exit door that leads to long term memory storage and easy retrieval for future use as required by the mind/body system,

The room is almost constantly overflowing with data coming in from the senses. The storage capacity of the hippocampus is vast, but still limited. Neuroscientists suggest that during the hours when we sleep, the mind sorts through the day's sensed inputs, organizes them and sends them out the second door to be stored as context for all experiences.

We are not sure how the mind determines what is worth paying attention to. We are sure that information repeatedly entering the hippocampus deserves attention and a place in long term memory.
A recent discovery found that the hippocampus is the only structure in the brain that generates new brain cells, that is, new neurons. The significance of this is not fully understood, but it certainly leads one to speculate that our mind/brain has increased capacity to store and learn throughout our lives.

TIP: Have you ever found yourself in a room of your house and you can't remember why you went there? Where is the thought that took you to the room? It's still in the hippocampus "big room." To remember it, return to the exact place where you had the thought which you've now lost. The image your brain was receiving at the time of the thought will come again and your mind will remember effortlessly – it's embedded in that context.

## *Emotion, Memory and the Amygdala Hijack*

These days it is common to read reports of "road rage" in the press. In a recent incident, a male driver in rush hour traffic was cut off by a car driven by a woman. The male driver leaped from his car which was then stalled in traffic, sprinted to the woman's car, reached through an open window, seized a small pet dog from the front seat and threw the dog beneath the wheels of passing traffic. The dog was killed instantly. The man walked back to his car without a word and drove off.

In his groundbreaking book *Emotional Intelligence*[9], Daniel Goleman comments on road rage of this nature.

> Such emotional explosions are neural hijackings. At those moments, evidence suggests, a center in the limbic brain proclaims an emergency, recruiting the rest of the brain to its urgent agenda. The hijacking occurs in an instant triggering this reaction crucial moments before the neocortex, the thinking brain, has had a chance to glimpse fully what is happening, let alone decide if it is a good idea. The hallmark of such a hijack is that once the moment passes, those so possessed have the sense of not knowing what came over them.

You are fortunate if you have not had the experience of blowing up or simply losing it. Goleman indicates that such neural hijackings originate in the amygdala, a pair of almond shaped structures on the right and left sides of the brain stem in the limbic area of the brain, below the hippocampus.

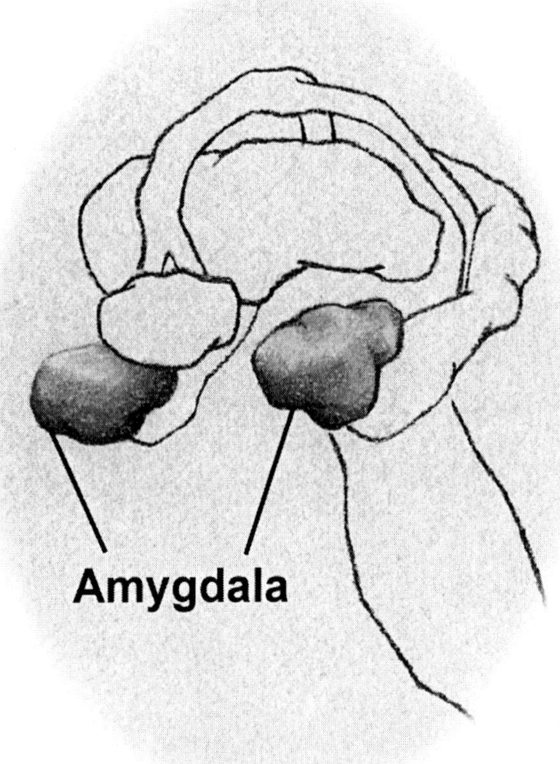


Fig. 4-4 The Amygdala

Goleman says that while the hippocampus and amygdala of the limbic system "do much or most of the brain's learning and remembering, the amygdala is the specialist for emotional matters." When impulse overrides rational thought, the amygdala is taking control. Goleman goes on to say:

> It is in moments such as these — when impulsive feeling overrides the rational — that the newly discovered role for the amygdala is pivotal. Incoming signals from the senses let the amygdala scan

> every experience for trouble. This puts the amygdala in a powerful post in mental life, something like a psychological sentinel, challenging every situation, every perception, with but one kind of question in mind, the most primitive: 'Is this something I hate? That hurts me? Something I fear?'
>
> If so — if the moment at hand somehow draws a 'Yes' — the amygdala reacts instantaneously, like a neural tripwire telegraphing a message of crisis to all parts of the brain.

Goleman's metaphor is compelling.

> When it sounds an alarm of, say, fear, it sends urgent messages to every major part of the brain: it triggers the secretion of the body's fight-or-flight hormones, mobilizes the centers for movement, and activates the cardiovascular system, the muscles, and the gut. Other circuits from the amygdala signal the secretion of emergency dollops of the hormone nor-epinephrine to heighten the reactivity of key brain areas... and
>
> The amygdala's extensive web of neural connections allows it, declaring an emotional emergency, to capture and drive much of the rest of the brain — including the rational mind.

Daniel Goleman's book is must reading for anyone who wants a better understanding of the neural circuits involved in emotions.

To summarize, the body's sensory organs, the eyes, nose, ears, etc., all send electrical signals to and through the limbic region of the brain. As these data signals pass through the limbic portion of the brain, they are coded and recorded in the cerebral cortex. Once recorded, this stored information is available for comparison with subsequent experience and can then be processed rationally by the cerebral cortex to provide output signals to initiate appropriate behavior.

A history of all prior emotional experiences is recorded in the amygdala's neural circuits. Accordingly, when the cerebral cortex compares incoming data with prior recorded experiences and concludes that a strong emotional response is in order, an electrical signal triggers the amygdala to command a fight-or-flight response. For years scientists believed this was always the way the amygdala became involved.

It is now known, however, that the nerve fibers that deliver coded information to the cerebral cortex also include a very small number of fibers going directly to the amygdala. These nerve fibers are delivering the same information to the amygdala that is being delivered to the cerebral cortex for rational processing, but some of them arrive at the amygdala before getting to the home of rationality. Imagine the amygdala sitting there with its huge record of emotional experiences, recorded over a life time. This amygdala, with its slightly fuzzy pool of emotional memories, may feel there is a match with incoming data that is similar but not exactly like what's been stored. When this small, fast, incoming stream of information gets to the amygdala and hits an apparent, emotionally charged match before the rational cerebral cortex has had time to process it, the amygdala becomes highly sensitized and unstable. The amygdala is triggered to send command signals to all regions of the brain to take complete control of the mind/brain to initiate a full range of behaviors in response to the incoming data. There may be an inappropriate blow up. The behaviors can be as irrational as seizing a small pet from the front seat of a car and deliberately killing it, as described earlier.

### *My Amygdala Hijacks*

In my own life I can look back on a few instances when I experienced what I now know were amygdala hijacks. They all occurred when I had been drinking. When I stopped drinking I experienced few if any of these types of outbursts in my marriage or with my children.

In the last twenty years I can count on the fingers of one hand the times I experienced highly charged emotional outbursts. I recall that two of them were with my secretary, and my behavior brought her to tears. She was an excellent secretary in all respects. Given my long history of having a sober and emotionally balanced role in my personal and business life, I was completely at a loss to explain to myself why I reacted the way I did. Following these outbursts I was always embarrassed and would immediately act as if nothing untoward had happened. I don't believe I ever apologized. Today, I keenly regret my actions.

Soon after my marriage to Sharon, I was dismayed to realize that on occasion I would reply to a simple observation she made in a way that was nasty or hurtful. Sharon did not ignore these outbursts. Calmly but clearly, she advised me that my outburst was hurtful and that there was no rational basis she could think of that warranted such behavior. I will be eternally grateful to Sharon for bringing me up short when I had an outburst and for Daniel Goleman's book on emotional intelligence.

As I read Goleman's description of an amygdala hijack, it became apparent that while my outbursts seemed to happen instantaneously, they actually were preceded by a pattern of subtle emotions that I can best describe as a vague feeling of irritation with the other party. Upon reflection I now recall that every outburst was preceded by these vague feelings of irritation. I am pleased to report that many years have passed free of outbursts now that I am consciously aware of the presence of the precursor feelings of agitation. When I feel them arising, I simply acknowledge to myself (and sometimes out loud) that the event happening appears in some vague way to match some long-forgotten happening. This awareness allows time for my cerebral cortex to rationally process the incoming information.

### *Preventing Amygdala Hijacks*

Therapists working to help abusive parents stop abusing their children and those working with perpetrators of domestic violence have long appreciated the importance of interrupting the cycle of violence at the very beginning. They knew this from experience, even before the recent discoveries about the role and functioning of the amygdala. A major goal in such treatment is to recognize one's own early symptoms of an impending amygdala hijack. This may be the vague feeling of irritation I experienced, tightness in the chest or stomach, ringing in the ears, shallow breathing or some other clue. With practice, one can learn to prevent a crisis by recognizing this early sign of emotion and walking away, breathing deeply, doing whatever it takes to buy time. Buying time lets the information reach the cerebral cortex for rational processing, thus preventing the quick response of the amygdala to the early information.

> TIP: To control your own amygdala hijacks, learn to identify your personal early warning signals. Instead of interpreting these as triggers to blow up or come out fighting, use them as your internal alarm system to buy time, allowing your rational brain time to receive the information and react appropriately.

# 5

# *Neural Circuits and the Subconscious Mind*

Our ability to be aware of and understand what is happening in our environment depends directly on the recording of previous sensory experiences stored in the neural circuits of our brains. Our personal thoughts about these experiences are also stored in neural circuits. (See Chapter 4.) We use both types of memories to make sense of current experiences, but this comparison generally happens on a subconscious level, below awareness.

## *The Undiscriminating Subconscious*

In many ways a conventional tape recorder is a good metaphor for the subconscious mind. I can turn the recorder on, speak into its microphone and record the following, "My name is Hal Williamson and I am a billionaire. I own five homes on the west coast and three on the east coast." The truth is that I am not a billionaire and the only home I own is a small, inland cottage. When I play back the recording I will hear exactly what I said into the microphone. The tape recorder will never interrupt the playback to announce that what had been recorded is false.

There is, however, a critical distinction between our subconscious mind and a tape recorder. Our conscious mind is the gatekeeper that determines whether the incoming data should be accepted as true and recorded as such or be rejected as being false or inaccurate.

From time to time in workshops I will ask a participant if we have ever met before. An example was a participant named Andy, who responded that we had not. I asked what he did for a living. He told me he was an accountant. I then announced that I was completely unqualified to comment on his basic abilities to perform his daily tasks, but went on to say that I would comment anyway. I then told the other workshop participants that I know for a fact that Andy is grossly incompetent in his field and further that if I could find a way to have him removed from his current position, I would do so. In this situation both Andy and the other workshop participants knew that everything I was saying was totally unfounded, false. Andy's conscious mind could push away my comments, labeling them untrue. However, when I asked Andy to describe his emotional reaction to my negative public statement concerning him, he indicated that he experienced negative feelings. I then asked him if my comments that were now recorded in his memory could, in any way, affect his performance of what he does in his daily life. He responded, "Of course not." However, his subconscious stored an obviously false evaluation as a negative experience.

## *Once We Have It — We Have It — In Our Neural Circuits*

When we master a skill, then abandon it for many years, we will usually be able to return to it in short order. All we have to do is make a conscious mental effort to call upon the behaviors in the hardwired circuits where we stored the skill.

Learning to ride a bicycle is a mental and physical activity that drives the development of a huge number of neural circuits. These neural circuits allow your nervous system and muscles to keep a bike balanced and moving. If you have not ridden a bicycle in 20 years, mounting one, putting your feet on the pedals and gripping the handlebar feel awkward at first, but you quickly regain confidence and feel at ease again riding that bike. Once these neural circuits are in place, behaviors stored in them flow freely, with little conscious effort.

## *Free Flowing Thought and Behavior*

Not all mental activity produces physical behavior. Tagged information stored in memory circuits may be retrieved with little or no mental effort. Information stored in interconnected neural circuits is generally recalled as a whole thought.

For example, most people have recordings of the months of the year as a sequence of single words representative of each month. When I speak of "free flowing" behavior from your neural circuits, I want you to actually experience the feeling of this free flow. Start by reciting aloud the months of the year beginning with January. If you are in a place where you cannot say these out loud, then actually move your lips as you would if you were saying the months out loud. Easy, right?

There is no question that you know the months of the year. Now repeat the months of the year in reverse order and make a mental note of how much slower the process is when you try to pull data from neural circuits in reverse.

How did that feel from the standpoint of mental effort? Harder and slower going backwards? Okay, so you can say the months of the year forwards and backwards. Now I want you to experience the increased mental effort it takes to say the months of the year alphabetically.

Almost without exception people attempting the alphabetical

recitation of the months of the year begin by firing the neural circuits that contain the months of the year in a forward direction, (January, February, March, April), stopping mentally when they get to the first month that begins with the letter "A," which is April. The effort continues until August is reached and there is a momentary pause as they ask themselves, "Does the letter "P" which follows "A" in April come before "U" that follows "A" in the month of August?" The answer is "yes," and the forward recitation of the months continues until December is reached. Whew! Repeating this task again and again will ultimately result in an alphabetical list of the months. It will require a continuous, conscious mental effort. This is the opposite of free flowing!

I doubt if you are motivated to get really good at saying the months of the year alphabetically, but if you were, you could. Repeating them over and over would eventually result in strong neural circuits and they would flow freely.

This example of the ease of saying the months of the year forward and the difficulty of saying them backwards or alphabetically is intended to give you the experience of how easily things flow from strongly established neural circuits. In the same way, we want our desired behaviors to flow as freely as saying the months of the year from January to December. Techniques to make desired behaviors flow freely are given in Part 4 of this book.

# 6
# *An Orderly Universe*

## *A Long Time Ago — Man Was Pretty Smart: Order In the Midst of Chaos*

What can we learn about brain development from the historical evidence, of the people who were responsible for construction of Stonehenge, a semi-circular arrangement of stone monoliths in an open field in a southern region of England, during the thousand-year period 2000-1000 B.C.?

Research indicates that these stones weighed as much as fifty tons and had been quarried nearly 240 miles away. The task of transporting them over water and forested land is unimaginable, especially when it is noted that the wheel had not yet been invented. These huge stones were dragged!

The stones were arranged in the general form of a circle in an intriguing pattern. It is suggested that if one were to position himself at a point remote from Stonehenge and watch the night stars and planets appear to ascend from the horizon, there would be four nights of the year when the stones in the field and the stars in the heavens would be perfectly aligned. Astonishingly, these four nights herald the first day of summer, the first day of fall, the first day of winter and the first day of spring.

The designers of Stonehenge had to have understood something about the relationships among the moving earth, the sun, planets and stars in an expanding universe. We can see Stonehenge as man's first intergalactic computer, providing him with precise indications of changing seasons. No doubt this information was of great value to an emerging agrarian society, providing information about when to plant and when to expect a harvest.

There are many implications in the sheer fact of Stonehenge: the ability to imagine and implement what must have seemed impossible; the understanding of order in a complex universe without modern tools; the shared vision and patience to carry such a project to completion through what must have taken many generations. Part of what is suggested by Stonehenge is that from time immemorial, man has sought and discovered that the universe has a hidden order that expresses itself in a multitude of ways.

I hope that you will accept that there is much in the universe that is orderly. If you can accept this premise of order, then the material that follows may prove profoundly useful.

## *Born To Plan*

Whether you know it or not, when you do something as simple as plan your day, you are relying on the universe to be an orderly place. You are also doing something uniquely human. Teleology is a philosophical doctrine that holds that all of nature is goal directed, and that humans are the most goal directed of all.

It is always humbling to note the wisdom of someone like Aristotle, who was a philosopher in the third century B.C. He wrote that the world we live in and the universe as a whole appear to form an orderly continuum, from where we live on earth out through the heavens. Aristotle, as well as others of his time, believed that the presence of observable order in the universe allows man to plan. Aristotle said that man is a purposeful creature who can anticipate the future and behave in ways calculated to realize his intentions. Aristotle also put forward the idea that man is the only creature on the planet who can imagine a future and plan for it.

Planning involves setting forth a series of doable, implementable steps that take you from where you are to a goal. The steps involve a series of cause and effect events that lead to the goal's attainment.

What is the opposite of order? The usual response is "chaos," which means the absence of order. If the world were totally chaotic, planning would be impossible. In other words, an orderly universe is required for planning. This also helps to explain our response when the chaos level of the universe seems accelerated, such as today, when changes in every area of our lives can happen at the speed of light. Effective planning becomes more difficult and we humans are alternately excited and scared by the seeming unpredictability of things.

## *Who Created Order?*

Aristotle observed that the presence of order in the observable universe produced a profound philosophical effect on our minds. When we see and experience order in the natural world, whether it be the day followed by night, or the seasons of the year, we experience a deeply felt "knowing" that there must be something or someone that created the order. How could there be order without a creator of the order?

In the Judeo-Christian world the creator is called God. In other cultures, the creator is given different names. Aristotle concluded that nearly all religions and cultures in the world believe in some superior power and are drawn to that belief by the inherent nature of the human mind.

## *Can Animals Plan?*

Animals do not appear to have an awareness of any higher power operating in their lives. Then again, how do we know? Maybe we and Aristotle are just interested in distinguishing ourselves from the lower forms of animal life. We think of ourselves as being superior to lesser forms of animal life because we humans have free will and the power of choice.

The behavior of some animals would lead us to believe that animals can and do plan. For example, when the weather turns from cold to warm and you see a bird on the lawn with a twig in its mouth, you might say to yourself, *Ah, that bird is planning to build a nest.* You continue to watch the bird gather twigs, string and other nest-building materials. Soon you see a nest taking form in a nearby tree. Did the bird consciously plan to build a nest? Well, it sure looks like it. But the truth is that a bird doesn't build a nest as part of a conscious plan.

Earlier you read that at birth the human brain has only 24% of its 100 billion neurons hardwired in place to process sensed information. The remaining 76% of the neurons are available to store inputs from the outside world as well as our thoughts about those inputs. In the case of birds, they and most lower forms of life have between 86% and 98% of the neurons that control their behavior hardwired into neural circuits at birth. That leaves a skimpy 2-14% of the neurons available to plan or process new information.

Let's approach this from the extreme case. If a bird had 100% of the neurons in its brain hardwired in neural circuits prior to birth, would the bird be able to learn anything? No, for there would be no neurons available to store new information from the environment. Studies of birds that have been hatched in incubators and have never associated with adult birds show they build perfect nests without further instruction. We call these hardwired instructions "instincts." It is therefore apparent that planning is not an appropriate description of the steps involved in a bird's nest building activity.

Monkeys' brains are about two-thirds the size of humans, with only about 80% of their neurons hardwired at birth and they have some capacity to learn and develop simple strategies to obtain what they need. There are clever squirrels, pigs and other warm-blooded creatures that seem to be able to learn and use behaviors that obtain what they need or want. Many of us have known smart dogs or cats. In fact, our cat, Bonkers, is a near genius. He knows when I've opened a can of tuna even when he's upstairs and I'm downstairs, and he tries to block the door with his body when I'm leaving the house with a suitcase. Suzanne Delzio and Cindy Rebarich, D.V.M. have written a book called *Felinestein, Pampering the Genius in Your Cat,* which teaches you to cultivate smartness in your cat. Read carefully, the book is actually about consciously building and reinforcing the small percentage of available neurons to get the cat to perform amazing feats like fetching a ball.

Let us now explore the orderly manner in which neural circuits in the human brain affect our perceptions and beliefs.

## *Seeing What We See*

To experience the principle of neural circuit operation, take a look at the illustration of a woman's face which follows. Variations of this illustration are found in the course material of many training programs.

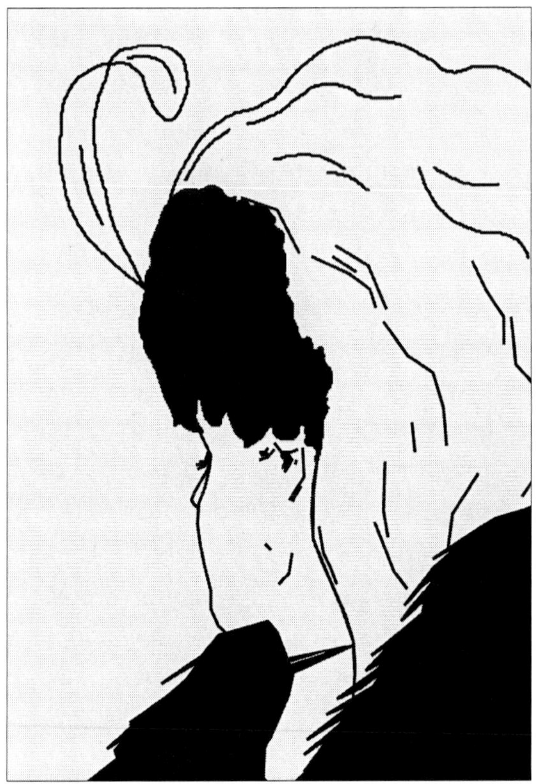

Fig. 6-1 Old Woman/Young Woman

Even if you have seen the picture before, please answer the following questions to yourself as if you were looking at the picture for the first time. Fig. 6-1 includes representations of both a young woman's face and an older woman's face. Do you see one or the other or do you see them both? All three responses are common.

Why do some see only one face, while others see only the other face? Why are some people able to see both faces? Before this question can be answered in terms of neural circuit operation, we will need to explore the operation of the human eye and its neural connections to the brain.

As noted in Chapter 2, the lens of the eye focuses light reflected from objects onto the retina. The retinal image is delivered by electrical signal through the optic nerve to the circuits that process image data. The processed information is then delivered into a vast web of neurons in the occipital lobes, where these waiting neurons cause neural circuit formation. This neural circuit formation records what has been captured by the lens of the eye.

Imagine for a moment that I have my eyes open and am looking at your face. Reflected light from your face enters my eyes and signals from the retina are sent back to the occipital lobes where neural circuits record the image of your face. I now close my eyes and the image of your face is no longer present on the retina of my eye. I open my eyes and there you are again and I send the same image information back to the vision fields in the occipital lobes, where it is recorded.

The first time I see you, I create a neural circuit representing your face. When I see you the next time, the image of your face is delivered to a previously created neural circuit that most nearly matches the incoming image. If the image is identical or nearly identical, the appearance of the second image strengthens the original imprint. If the image is slightly different, it is delivered in what might be thought of as a slightly overlapping image onto the earlier image. Current research indicates that the brain records the same image in only one place. We don't have multiple images of a single face stored in several places. You can think of it in terms of images stored in a continuum from young faces to old faces.

In summary, before we can understand or recognize what we are looking at, we must have seen and recorded an image previously that is the same or similar to the incoming image. If the incoming image is identical to a stored image, we will know what we are looking at. If the incoming image is similar to what has been previously recorded, we will be consciously aware of the similarity.

### *We Do Not Know What We Do Not Know*

In Chapter 2, I said that "we know what we know." The inverse is also true. "We do not know what we do not know." To "know" means that at some point in the past our physical senses have received information that has been recorded in our brain and our mind has processed the information and recorded our thoughts about it.

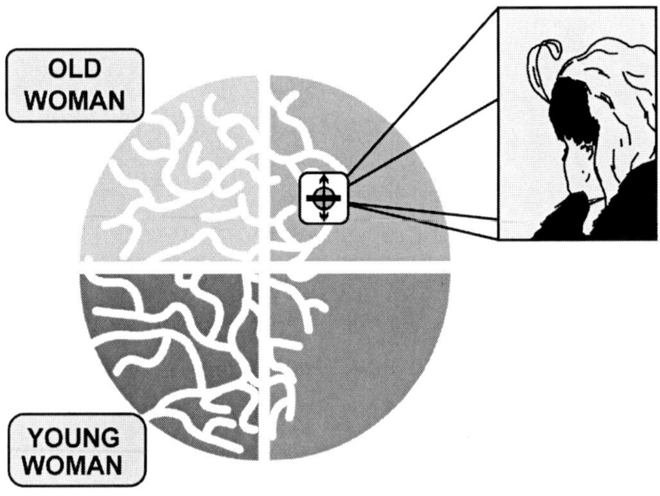


Fig. 6-2 Seeing the Old Woman/Young Woman

Let us turn now to what happens in the brain when we view the old woman/young woman image.

Fig. 6-2 is a picture of the brain with a black switch lever. The double headed arrow through the switch lever is intended to convey that the switch may move up or down to complete one of two circuits. Think of the mind as being in control of the switch. To the left you see a pair of blocks with the legend "Old Woman" and "Young Woman". The message here is that somewhere in the brain images of young female faces have been recorded and that in some other region of the brain images of old female faces are recorded.

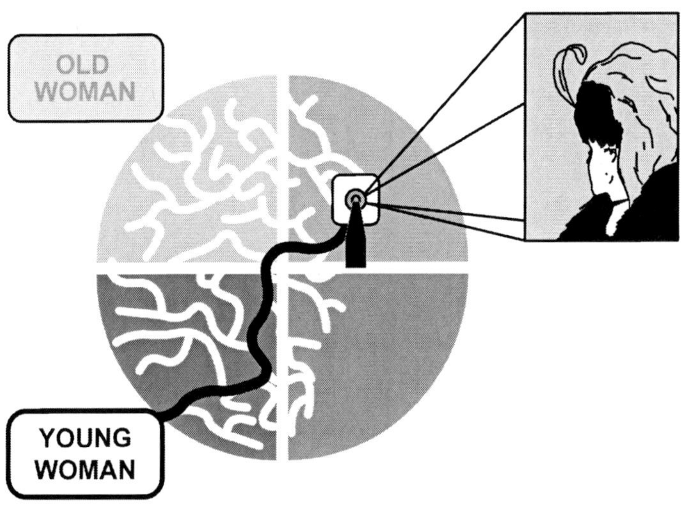


Fig. 6-3 Old Woman/Young Woman – Switch Down

In Fig. 6-2, the switch is in a neutral position. The image of a female face is shown, indicating that you have seen the image. In Fig. 6-3, the switch has been moved downward by the mind and a circuit (shown in full line) has been completed between the female image, the switch, and the "young woman" image stored in the brain. At the moment the circuit is complete the mind concludes that the image is that of a "young woman".

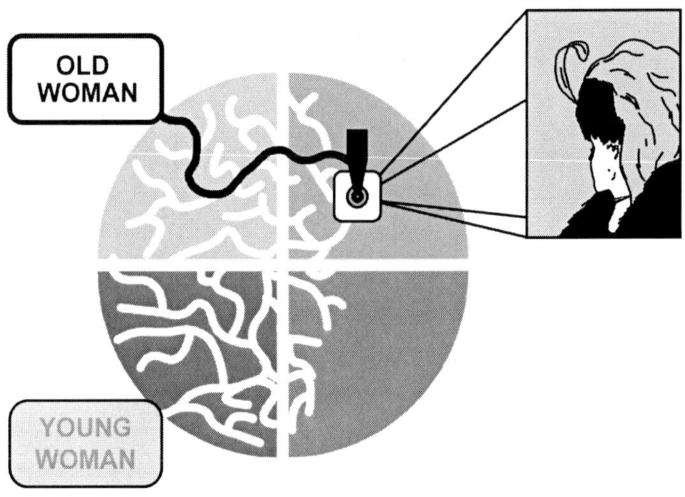


Fig. 6-4 Old Woman/Young Woman – Switch Up

Fig. 6-4 shows the switch in an upward position and depicts a completed circuit between the female image, the switch, and the old woman.

Frequently people identify only the young woman and not the old woman or vise versa. If you are one of those who can only see the young woman, focusing your attention on the necklace on the throat of the young woman may help you to see the old woman. This necklace becomes the mouth of the old woman; the ear of the young woman becomes an eye of the old woman, and the chin and cheekbone of the young woman become the hooked nose of the old woman. Do you see the old woman now?

On occasion when people are able to make the switch from young to old or vice versa, they become unable to throw the switch and return to their original perception of the image.

## *One Thought at a Time*

The sole purpose of this exercise is to demonstrate that the conscious mind can only process a single thought at a time. If, in fact, a person can only consciously process a single thought at a time, why do some people say they can perceive the young and the old images simultaneously? The answer is simple. The mind is able to switch circuits in about three thousandths of a second, which creates the illusion that two separate perceptions are happening simultaneously. A similar experience arises when we watch movies which are projected one frame at a time at great speed. The brain's neural circuitry can switch quickly, but not quickly enough to distinguish the separate frames. We perceive the separate frames as a continuous, uninterrupted image that appears to change in real time.

Return now to the image of the female faces and focus your perception on either the young or the old image. Notice that when you consciously look at one image you cannot perceive the other image concurrently.

## *We're Missing Things*

There is another profound lesson to be learned from this experience: As we observe the world and focus on a specific facet of our environment, we may well fail to discern other information in the same environment because we have not completed a circuit between what our senses are receiving and previously stored information.

> We may be missing more than we know.

Now focus your attention on the framed words which follows. Please read the statement once and only once.

> FINISHED FILES ARE THE RESULT OF
> YEARS OF SCIENTIFIC STUDY
> COMBINED WITH THE EXPERIENCE
> OF MANY YEARS OF EXPERTS.

Now read it again. This time as you read, please count the number of letter Fs as you come upon them.

How many did you discover? Most people readily report finding between three and six Fs. If you discovered seven Fs then you have identified all of the Fs.

Now that you know that there are seven Fs, read the framed statement once and only once again, while counting the letter Fs. Did you find them all? Some find them all on the second try. Others find the same number as originally discovered or a few more, but not all seven. If you found them all on the first try, ask an acquaintance to read the framed statement once and then again in the counting mode. More than likely he will miss some.

Why does this happen? Psychologists offer this explanation: humans become conditioned by past experience to overlook certain information. If this is true, then simply unconditioning the individual will allow the missing Fs to appear.

If you did not find them all, you can be unconditioned by looking at the sentence yet again. This time focus your attention on the second line and the second full word, which is "OF". Now count the number of "OFs" in the remaining lines and voila, you will find all seven of the Fs. Missing the Fs has to do with the fact that we see with our brain, not our eyes. Our eyes merely focus images on the retina which sends the information via the optic nerve into the brain where the incoming information is compared with what we have stored. When there is a match, we become consciously aware of what we are looking at.

Then why don't we all see all of the Fs when we try to count them? When we read, we read entire words as units. In the United States, most children are taught to read phonetically, by creating the sound of the letters that form a word. As the words are sounded out, they are audibly perceived by the brain and the reader has an awareness of the word as it has been heard and recorded before. Accordingly, most individuals will pronounce the letters "OF" phonetically, which sounds like "OV". Thus they will not perceive the F in "OF" when they are counting Fs.

This simple experiment effectively illustrates how we miss information. When many people are initially asked to read the words to themselves, they pull into play the neural circuit that interprets "OF" as "OV." When they are then asked to read it again, the "OV" neural circuit, having just been employed, responds again and the F of the "OFs" is missed.

Many workshop participants have suggested that when we learn to read we mentally skip unimportant words and that is why we miss the Fs in the "OFs". In an extensive set of experiments with statements that included multiple uses of the word "Be" as well as words with the letter B in them, virtually all participants identified the correct total number of Bs.

The most tangible evidence supporting the explanation of the neural circuit block arising because of the phonetic pronunciation of "OF" as "OV" came in a workshop I led at an industrial worksite in Rochester, New York. Participants in a large group of employees included a dozen hearing impaired workers. I was provided with an assistant who signed my lecture and instructions for the hearing impaired employees, most of whom had been deaf since birth. When these employees were asked to count the letter Fs, without exception they counted all seven of the Fs. For the hearing impaired there are no neural circuits that represent the phonetic pronunciation of "OF" as "OV".

### *Even Bigwigs Miss Things*

It is important to note that education and natural intelligence have nothing to do with the appearance of neural circuit blocks of the nature just described. In the 1990's I had presented the "Pathways to Greatness" program one-on-one to Harry Stonecipher, then CEO of Sundstrand (later CEO of McDonald Douglas then The Boeing Company from which he retired. See Chapter 1).

Like many others, including myself, Harry found only three Fs on his first try. I told him that there were, in fact, seven Fs and suggested that he was not trying hard enough. In order to motivate him to try harder, I suggested we make a wager as to whether there really were seven Fs, as I claimed, or only the three he had found.

At the time I was presenting this material to him, I was an employee of the company. I proposed that if I was wrong and there were only three Fs, then I would resign from the company and forfeit any pension benefits I had due me. Harry responded, "What do you want from me if you are right about there being seven Fs?" I responded that I would expect him to assign his pension to me. Harry was silent for a moment and asked if he could study the statement again before betting. I said, "Sure". He examined the statement for a long time. Then he said, "You're on, boy". After the unconditioning, which produced a strong expletive from Harry, we laughed over the certainty he had felt when he made the wager. After all, he had two eyes and obviously if the information was there he would see it! (By the way, I'm still waiting for Harry's pension.)

> The amazing truth is that we may not see what is there, if there is something in the brain's neural circuits that blocks our perception.

In summary, three factors may contribute to our missing what is right in front of us.

1. We can only consciously think one thought at a time.
2. We may not have seen it before so there's no match in our stored database.
3. We may have neural circuits in place that block our perception.

# 7

# *Truth — Belief — Behavior*

It is our perception of the truth that controls our behavior. This is true even when our perception conflicts with what appears to be incontrovertible evidence. An example of this principle is the recently described behavior of Harry when he was told that there were seven Fs in the phrase he had studied. He knew that there were only three, because he had two eyes and he trusted his ability to count. If there were more Fs, he would have seen them. Hence his willingness to enter an outrageous wager that would put his future pension at risk.

As we move forward, it is important to be aware of neural circuits that may block our perception of the truth. I have delivered the Pathways workshop over many years to thousands of participants. During that time a number of people have come back to experience the curriculum a second, even a third time. A number of these repeat participants still find fewer than seven Fs when asked to read and count the Fs in the previous exercise. This time, however, they know that there are more Fs than they count and will refuse to make a wager as to the accuracy of their F count. They have a memory that there are seven Fs in the phrase, so they know their counting of the number of Fs is somehow in error.

## *Breakthrough Behavior*

What happens to behavior when we don't know commonly accepted truths? History is filled with examples of people who have accomplished remarkable results simply because they did not know what could not be done. This may explain why most physicists and mathematicians come upon their greatest discoveries in their early 20's and 30's.

My favorite story in this regard, though, involves a sporting event that takes place annually in Australia. The event is a foot race between the cities of Sydney and Melbourne, a distance of about 600 kilometers (372.6 miles). A large cash prize is paid to the winner. Runners from around the world enter the race. The race and the activities that precede the race are media events. On the day prior to the race, when runners arrive to sign up and get a starting spot in the running, reporters are always looking for human interest stories.

In this setting in 1983, some reporters observed a man standing in line who appeared to be out of place because of his clothing and apparent age. Dressed in bib overalls and rubber overshoes, with an abundance of white hair peeking out from his straw hat, the man looked more like a homeless person than a marathon runner. Maybe he thought the lines of people were standing there for some sort of handout. When asked his name, he said he was Cliff Young. When asked if he knew why he was standing in line, he told them he was waiting to sign up for the race. Asked if he knew how long the race was, he said that he did and that he had read about it in the newspaper. He volunteered that he was 61 years old.

Needless to say, the reporters, sensing they had a newsworthy story in the making, asked if he had ever run in a race of this nature before. He answered that he had never run in any race of any kind since he was a child. He told them that he was a potato farmer and thought his working life on the farm kept him fit and qualified him to enter the race. Cliff Young seemed oblivious to the fact that most of the other racers had run in marathon races all over the world.

Given the length of the race, it is not surprising that, at the time, it was considered to be the only race in which a person could actually die completing it. Sports medicine experts had studied the physical demands of the race and concluded that in running 600 kilometers, the human body would fail if the runner ran more than 18 hours in any 24 hour period. It was widely accepted common knowledge that at least six hours of rest/sleep are required to avoid the risk of over-exertion and death.

It should not surprise you that Cliff Young received a starting position at the very end of a huge number of runners.

By this time you probably suspect that despite all the odds, Cliff Young won the race. What cannot be imagined is the margin by which he beat his nearest competitor. He finished with a lead of a day and one half! How on earth could he have accomplished this remarkable feat? The answer is in what he did not know. He did not know that he was supposed to sleep! Think about it for a moment. If you lived your entire life on a remote potato farm in the back country of the Australian bush, would you ever have heard of a foot race of any kind where runners stopped to sleep? At the end of about 18 hours, all of the racers stopped to sleep. Cliff Young caught up while they were sleeping and by the time the sleeping runners woke up, he was in the lead, a lead which he never gave up.

Now the Australian public knew the truth and people expected that Cliff Young would drop dead before crossing the finish line. It is reported that the interest in Cliff Young's running effort was so noteworthy that a vehicle with a TV camera and a satellite up-link provided a television image of Cliff running twenty four hours a day.

Of special interest was a clock in a corner of the video picture. Why do you suppose there was a clock? As you may be aware, Australians are sporting people and unofficial betting pools had materialized all over the country with promised payoffs to the bettor who most closely predicted Cliff's moment of death. Needless to say, there was no payoff.

Public interest mounted and radio and TV talk shows began interviews with doctors and physical fitness experts, trying to determine what it was about Cliff Young's racing strategy that allowed him, at his age, to defy death. While it was true that Cliff did not sleep, he did stop from time to time, to eat and use the bathroom. When he stopped, reporters would crowd around him, peppering him with questions. Among other matters they determined that Cliff's diet consisted primarily of potatoes, pumpkin and beans, washed down with large quantities of water. This amazingly simple diet became the subject of talk shows that featured dietitians, who generally concluded that it was probably the pumpkin in his diet that produced his incredible stamina. Once the public began to believe that it was the pumpkin in Cliff's diet that was miraculously keeping him alive, it was reported that during the week of the race there was the greatest run on pumpkin in the history of the Australian continent.

The lesson here is that people act in accordance with the truth as they perceive or believe it to be, even when conscious logic contradicts such a belief. The Cliff Young story is a fine example of a situation where an individual did not know what was commonly believed to be the truth and, being ignorant of what he could not do, did what was believed to be impossible. In Cliff's case, his absence of a belief allowed him to defy death. (Cliff Young died in November, 2003, at the age of 83. He continued running almost until his death. The Cliff Young Australian Six Day Race is named in his honor.)

## *The Power of Belief*

Let us now look at another set of events involving the power of beliefs. This one centers on the speed with which a person can run a mile. In the early 1950's when I was a teenager living in New Jersey, it was popularly reported that no person could run a mile in less than four minutes. Runners came exceedingly close, but never finished in less than four minutes. It was conjectured that if the four-minute mile were to be broken, it would probably occur in Atlantic City, New Jersey, where a measured straight mile race was scheduled on the wooden boardwalk every year. There were no curves to slow the runners and the resilient wood surface of the boardwalk provided an advantage to the runners. No one ever broke the four minute barrier in Atlantic City.

Anyone living at that time will remember the front page newspaper headline on May 7, 1954. The previous day Roger Bannister, a 25-year-old British medical student, had run a mile in 3 minutes, 59.4 seconds on the Iffley Road Track in Oxford, England. He had broken the four-minute mile!

More amazing than Bannister's accomplishment was the fact that in the months and years that followed it was not uncommon to have two or more runners break the four-minute mile in the same race. It appears that once the old belief was dropped, new possibilities for all running athletes opened up. How powerful is belief?

# PART 3

## MOVING FROM THEORY TO APPLICATION

*Getting Ready To Act*

# 8
# *Never Again Miss What's Important!*

## *The Role and Function of the Reticular Alerting System*

As explained in Chapter 4, all sensory information passes through the limbic system of the brain on the way to the cerebral cortex, the wrinkled surface of the brain, where we process all conscious thought. The brain stem extends down to the spinal cord, linking the spinal cord to the limbic system and the cerebral cortex. Within the brain stem is a mass of neural circuits called the reticular alerting system or the reticular activating system (RAS). The RAS is completely wired and fully formed at birth.

Presumably the mind allows only information it considers important to get through the RAS to the cerebral cortex for conscious processing. In a metaphorical sense, the RAS acts like a filter that grabs and holds onto information of value at any given moment for conscious processing. All other information is allowed to pass through to the cerebral cortex to be recorded and treated as long-term memory or background information, which provides the context for embedding significant information.

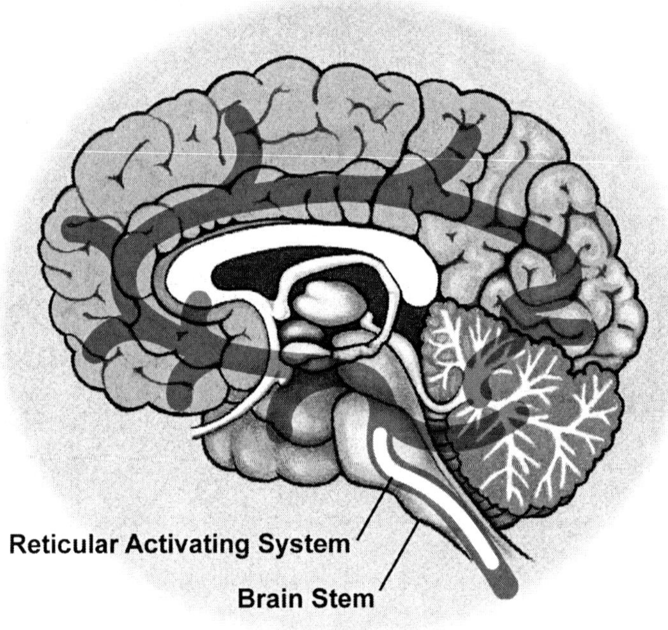


Fig. 8-1 The Reticular Activating System

The brain stem contains neural circuitry responsible for maintaining wakefulness and selective attention. In a state of general consciousness, your mind may drift and incoming information may pass unnoticed. In the state of selective attention, you filter sensory input and focus on that which is relevant and important to you.

The RAS in the brain stem is about the size of an adult's little finger, and it is essentially hardwired to the cerebral cortex. The right cerebral cortex, the part of the brain that processes images, has far more neural connections to the RAS than the left cerebral cortex, which processes analytical and logical thoughts. The DNA of a person (or any other critter) pre-wires the RAS to respond to life-threatening visual and auditory stimuli, for example, the shadow of a hawk falling upon a rabbit's visual field. Only hawk shadows result in the rabbit either freezing or fleeing. Likewise for a cat, loud noises trigger instant flight away from the source of the sound. If you have a cat, check this out by dropping a book on the floor. The cat will be gone in a flash!

## *The RAS at Work — a Miracle!*

When I began to read about and study the role and function of the RAS, I found myself reflecting upon a series of events that transpired some 30 years earlier that now take on fresh meaning.

On one particular day I remember my late wife Trudy mentioning at breakfast that our youngest daughter, Amy, then 18 months old, was fussy and running a temperature. I went to work and called home during the morning hours to see how Amy was doing. Trudy reported that her condition was worsening and her temperature was nearly 104° F. By mid-afternoon we decided that Trudy should take Amy to the emergency room of a nearby hospital.

When I came home from work, I parked my car in the driveway and was just getting out when Trudy drove in behind me and lifted Amy from her car. Amy's face was beet red and contorted in pain, and she was screaming at the top of her lungs. I asked what the doctor had said and Trudy said, "There's good news and bad news." "Well," I said, "What is the good news?" She answered, "The good news sounds bad, but is actually good." I responded, "What does that mean?" She said, "The doctor said that Amy has an infection in both ears, which is creating great pressure and that is what is causing all the screaming." She went on to say, as she held up a bottle, "He gave me a prescription for these antibiotics which he says will knock out the infection and take away the pain, so we don't need to worry." I asked, "What's the bad news?" She sighed and said, "The bad new is that it may take up to 12 hours before this antibiotic will work to reduce the pressure that is causing the pain."

Trudy followed me into the house and headed upstairs with Amy. As she went up the stairs she said that dinner was in the oven and asked if I would serve it to our other three children while she took care of Amy.

We finished dinner and the children helped wash and dry the dishes. Then I did what I could to help with their homework. About 8:30 the children and I turned on the television and became engrossed in a program. I must confess that I had forgotten about Trudy and Amy upstairs. It was not like me, but I had forgotten.

About 9:00 p.m. a door upstairs opened and I could hear Amy screaming. The screams got louder as Trudy brought Amy down the stairs. I jumped up and met them at the landing. Trudy turned and looked at me, with tears running down her face and said "Oh, Hal, I can't handle this crying any longer, I've been walking this baby all day and she won't stop."

I was really embarrassed by what she said, because I hadn't even offered to help. So, I reached over and lifted Amy from her arms and put her on my shoulder and said, "You go to bed Dear, right now, and if need be I will stay up all night with Amy." Walking crying babies was among my least favorite parental duties. But having had four children, I have done my fair share of it.

By midnight Amy was finally asleep, although fitfully, so we headed up to bed. I was reluctant to put her in her crib in a room away from our bedroom. Then I remembered that we had a canvas bassinet on a metal frame that we'd been given to bring one of our children home from the hospital. It looked something like a hand-carried shopping basket. The bassinet was equipped with four telescoping legs that created a raised canvas bed, somewhat wobbly, but stable enough for a newborn infant. It was really too small for Amy, but I got her tightly tucked in and brought her into our bedroom, where I positioned her along the foot of our king size bed. Trudy remained asleep and I lay down across the end of the bed so my head would be near Amy's little body. Within minutes I fell asleep.

About two and a half hours later I woke with a start. Unlike anything I've experienced before or since I woke up sitting on the edge of the foot of the bed, stiff backed, straight up and absolutely wide awake. My first conscious awareness was an overwhelming feeling of dread — actually terror. I hadn't had a nightmare, but I was alert beyond belief and as the feeling of apprehension floated over me, I threw myself to my left, landing on my left elbow. I pivoted my body and reached down into the bassinet with my right arm, literally scooping Amy up and out of the make-shift bed. Her small head and her feet caught on the frame, and she felt as limp as a rag doll. We deduced later that she must have had a convulsion and stopped breathing. I pulled her body up to my face and pressed my ear to her chest to listen. She had stopped breathing. She was gone. I screamed to Trudy, "Something has happened to Amy. Call the police."

Back then we didn't have 911 to call in an emergency. You had to call the local police if you needed emergency help. At the time the phone company had just introduced a phone called the Princess Telephone that had an illuminated dial. I had taken indelible ink and written the police number on top of the dial. Hearing my cry for help, Trudy spun around in bed and pounded in the number. Apparently they answered on the first ring and I heard her say, "Something has happened to our baby!" She gave our street address and hung up. Miraculously, a patrol car had just called in from our block. The dispatcher called the officer in the patrol car. He said the patrolman would be at our front door by the time we made it downstairs.

I couldn't bring myself to tell Trudy what I knew to be true, that our Amy was gone. I do remember following Trudy down the flight of stairs and seeing her ahead of me with her bathrobe billowing out behind her, and through the glass on the top half of the front door I could see the blinking roof light of the police car in the street. When Trudy pulled the door open I could make out the silhouette of the patrolman coming up across the lawn, a spotlight trained on his back, illuminating his way to the front door. When he got to the storm door he burst in and grabbed Amy from my arms, turned and ran down the sloping lawn. Trudy followed him. I instinctively knew that I would have to stay because of our three other sleeping children.

The front door slammed and my best guess is that I fainted. I must have fallen backwards and struck my head on the stairs. I don't know how long I was unconscious. When I regained consciousness, I remember hearing a ringing phone and not knowing where I was. In the darkness I tried to move toward the sound of the ringing, but was blocked by the handrail of the stairs. I made it to the landing and on to the entry hall and moved toward the sound of the phone on my hands and knees. I grabbed the phone and put it to my ear. At the other end was Trudy's voice. In the background I could hear a screaming baby. My heart leaped into my throat as I instantly knew the sound of my Amy's cry. She was alive!

In the days that followed we re-thought the events of that day. Amy, we concluded, had been perspiring profusely. Her clothes stuck to her body and in turn to me as I held her in my arms. Outside that night it was 10 degrees below zero. We surmised that when the patrolman opened the storm door, the wind caught the door and slapped it back against a restraining spring where the wind held it open. The patrolman reached in, took Amy into his arms and turned directly into a blast of freezing air and her small body reacted spasmodically. She drew in a breath of air and began to breathe. It was a miracle. She was brought from the near side of death back to life.

I can assure you that in the years that followed I tried never to think of that night again. It was the worst night of my life. The horror eased when I came upon the material regarding the RAS. I began to wonder, *What did I hear that night that woke me up?*

I suspect it was silence. You might ask, "How can you hear the absence of sound?" The RAS in our brains normally filters out background noise in our environment, but it also detects information of importance. While we are not consciously aware of other peoples' breathing, our brains hear it and record it. So when Amy stopped breathing, my RAS was on the job, sounding the alarm!

If you find it hard to believe we can detect the absence of sound, try this simple thought experiment. Imagine yourself on an airplane. The plane is cruising at 35,000 feet and you have fallen asleep. While you are asleep, all engines on the plane stop running. Notice how fast you wake up. The absence of sound is quickly detected by the RAS and the conscious mind is alerted to the change in the environmental sound.

Conversely, sounds that are not important can be tuned out. My wife Sharon and I live in a cottage on a bank of the Ohio River. Not more than 50 feet from us, at the very edge of the river, three sets of railway tracks carry most of the freight entering and leaving the greater Pittsburgh area. We have lived here for years and were astonished to learn recently that every twenty-four hours about eighty trains pass our cottage. Thanks to our RAS, we seldom hear them.

### *Information of Value Gets Through*

Once you learn about the RAS, you'll see many experiences in a new light. For example, I reflect on my bed-time rituals 30 some years ago. I remember that Trudy and I would head up to bed at the end of the late evening news. Trudy would get in bed and almost instantly be sound asleep. I would turn on a small bedside TV to catch the opening monologue of one of the evening late shows. I remember one evening Trudy went to sleep quickly, as usual, and, as if on schedule, began to snore. Normally, the snoring would last 5 to 10 minutes, followed by quiet, peaceful sleep. During the late show monologue the volume of Trudy's snoring would grow louder and louder and as it did, I had to turn up the TV volume to compete. On this particular night, all of a sudden, the bed began to shake. As I turned to see what was making the bed shake, I saw Trudy lurching towards the bedroom door. At one point she bumped into a dresser and fell back onto the bed, regained her balance and lurched toward the door again. As she left the room I called out, "What's wrong?" Her mumbled response was, "the baby, the baby." As I reached over and turned off the TV, I could hear the faint sound of a baby's cough coming from the next bedroom.

This story reveals yet another facet of the role and functioning of the RAS, namely that it is the importance of information that activates the RAS. It is not the volume of the sound that matters; it is the importance of the information to the listener that controls the RAS. Trains and street noise may be so loud that the important information appears to be drowned out in our conscious minds, but that is not the case. The RAS allows information of value to get through to alert us.

It would be reasonable to ask why Trudy didn't wake up instead of me on the night Amy stopped breathing. While I have no way of really knowing, my belief is that when I told Trudy to "go to bed and get a good night's rest and if need be I will stay up all night with Amy," Trudy's mind turned down her RAS receiver as her conscious and unconscious mind responded to my adoption of parental responsibilities.

## *Finding Four-leaf Clovers*

In the early years of my "Pathways to Greatness" workshop series, one participant, Ann Brown, felt that understanding the RAS might explain her unusual ability to see four-leaf clovers. Ann related that she had an older sister. When she was little, as you might expect, a sibling rivalry developed between the two for the attention of their parents.

One day Ann found a four-leaf clover and brought it to her mother, who made a big fuss over her find. Her mother called neighbors to brag about Ann's four-leaf clover and when her father came home he made an equally large ado about Ann's find. Ann instantly became the center of attention and she loved it. Sometime later she found another four-leaf clover and presented it to her father, who took it to his office to show his associates. When his friends from work came to the house to visit, they always asked if they could meet the "four-leaf clover girl." For reasons we will never know, those childhood experiences in Ann's life permanently conditioned the reticular formation in the base of her brain. Today as Ann goes through the world she sees nearly all the four leaf clovers within the field of her gaze, wherever she walks.

After meeting Ann, I was invited to put on the "Pathways to Greatness" program for a business group of CEO's called The Management Policy Council. These CEO's were all from companies with sales in excess of a billion dollars. I wanted to tell them the remarkable story of Ann's ability to find four-leaf clovers. I called Ann to ask if I could identify her by name to this group. She agreed and then volunteered to bring me four-leaf clovers for workshop participants. I told her that while her offer was generous it was probably unrealistic. I would need over 100 four-leaf clovers, because the wives of the CEO's would also be in attendance. I then added that I would be leaving my office in about an hour and it would be quite impossible for her to collect and deliver that many four-leaf clovers. Her response was, "No problem. I will walk across the lawn from my office building to yours and pick four-leaf clovers as I go." Within the hour Ann was in my office with a shopping bag filled with more than 150 four-leaf clovers.

Try this yourself. How many four-leaf clovers can you find in Fig. 8-2?[10]

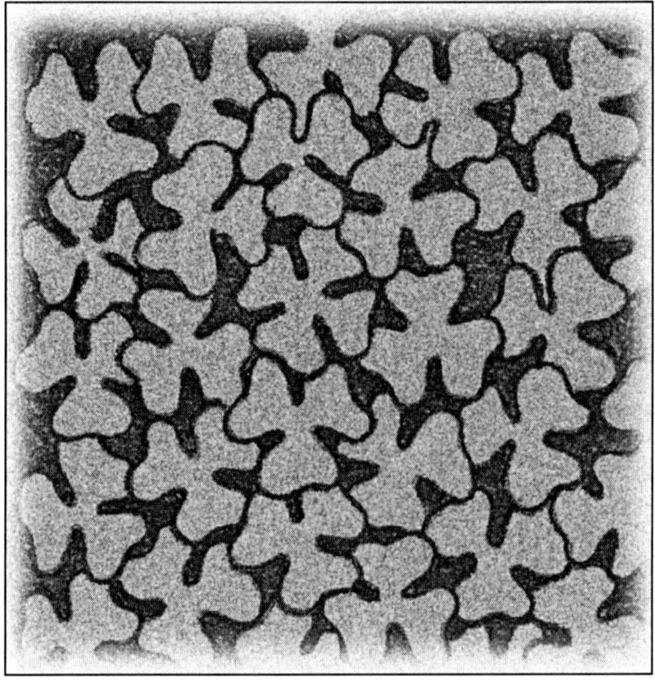

Fig. 8-2 Four leaf clovers

## *Summing It Up*

We now know that we miss sensing and identifying information in our environment until we complete a neural circuit that matches incoming information with previously stored information. Seeing the young woman/old woman picture illustrated this phenomenon.

We are also aware that we do not see with our eyes; we see with our brain and it is our brain and its neural circuits that compare incoming information with information embedded in neural circuits of our cerebral cortex. A problem arises when a neural circuit somehow blocks the match. When this happens we can miss information. This phenomenon was demonstrated by the F box exercise.

You will recall that all data from one's senses rushes in through the base of the brain via the brain stem. For us to be consciously aware of it, the data coming in must get to and be processed by the cerebral cortex. We know that the cerebral cortex of our brain can only consciously process data in a sequential manner, one thought at a time.

Wouldn't it be wonderful if you could go through the world and never miss anything of importance to you either because you failed to complete a circuit or because you had a neural circuit in place that blocked your perception of the information you valued?

In Chapter 12 you will find instructions that will allow you not to miss important information. The key resides in using a few simple techniques daily to mentally condition the RAS to recognize what is important to you.

# 9

# *Gestalt and Cognitive Dissonance*

## *Our Minds Want Completion*

I first came upon the word "gestalt" as I began to read books on thinking, and the operation of the brain. I did not know its meaning. First I tried to figure out its meaning by the context in which the word appeared. Have you ever come upon a word you don't understand, gone to the dictionary only to discover that the definition doesn't help because it uses more words you don't understand? You figure you may never get out of the dictionary! Well, that's what happened to me. I first consulted a small pocket dictionary, which provided a definition that didn't shed much light on the meaning of the word "gestalt."

The next time I came upon the word, I went to a bigger dictionary. The big dictionary was very helpful, because it defined gestalt in terms of "configuration," a word I understood because of my engineering background. In engineering the term "configuration" was used to describe the overall appearance of some object. For example, a biplane is a plane that has a two-wing configuration, one wing above the other. When we use the term "configuration," we are not talking about the material that goes into an object or its color. We are simply describing its overall appearance.

"Gestalt" might be thought of as the overall impression you get when viewing an object or thing. In other words, mental objects come as a complete form or "configuration," which cannot be split into parts; e.g. a square is perceived as a square rather than as four distinct lines.

Another way to think about the concept of "gestalt" is to treat it as the mind's need for completion. The mind appears to strive for completed wholes, especially when that which is being perceived is incomplete. This need for mental completion is more a psychological than a neurological, or physical need.

You may ask, "How does this need for completion express itself in our daily lives?" At a subconscious level the mind is always asking the following question: *What am I looking at?* Our mind rarely responds to this hypothetical question with: *I don't care.* It is always trying to make sense of what we're looking at, comparing incoming sensory data with our stored memories of everything we have ever seen or sensed, as well as our thoughts about what we have seen or sensed.

This need to gain closure on all sensed information appears to be an automatic function over which we have no conscious control. No matter how little information we receive, our minds always arrive at some judgment as to what we're perceiving. The judgment may be: *I have never seen anything like this before.* Or: *This is very similar to such and such.*

### *Let's Experience Gestalt*

Here's a simple mental exercise designed to allow you to experience gestalt, the mental need for completion. Please quickly glance at the next simple illustration, Fig. 9-1, and just as quickly return to this page for more instructions.

Now ask yourself: *What was it that I saw?* Some people instantly identify the subject of the illustration. More commonly the response is: *I am not sure.*

The reason for uncertainty is that the lens in the front of your eye focuses an image on the retina in the back of the eye. When the object under examination is relatively near the eye, such as is the case when you are holding this book and looking at the illustration, the image of the illustration falls upon a central portion of the retina called the fovea centralis. The fovea centralis sends an acutely sharp image of the illustration to your brain to be compared with previously recorded images. The fact that you did not find a match means that the sharp image that came from the center of the eye included so much detail it didn't match any previous image recorded with less detail.

Now hold the illustration at arms length or better still have someone hold it for you to see from across the room. What happens?

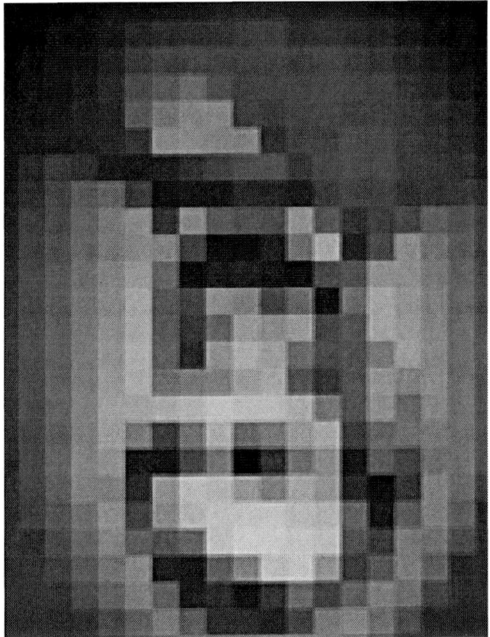

Fig. 9-1 What do you see?

Do you now see Abraham Lincoln, albeit upside down? Most people do. Is it really a picture of Abraham Lincoln? Only roughly, not a photograph or a portrait. When your mind tells you it is

Abraham Lincoln, you have just experienced the phenomenon of "gestalt," i.e., the mind's need for completion.

If you had never seen the image of Lincoln would you have identified the image as that of a face or perhaps seen only a misshapen pear? In one of my workshops a young man from China, in the United States only a few weeks, was dismayed when everyone in the room decided the image was the face of Abraham Lincoln. He interrupted the workshop and asked, "What is an Abraham Lincoln?" The young man from China had little or no exposure to images identified as Abraham Lincoln.

## *Dissonance — the Invisible Mental Motivator*

Many brain functions are automatic and require no conscious mental effort to initiate. One such automatic mental function is "cognitive dissonance," which was described in 1957 by Leon Festinger, a highly regarded social psychologist.11

It is cognitive dissonance we experience when we realize we are twenty pounds overweight, and we are committed to being healthy and fit.

> Defined in terms of neural circuits and thoughts stored in them, cognitive dissonance is a feeling of mental discomfort that people experience whenever a thought, belief or perception is introduced into the mind that in some way conflicts with a thought, belief or perception previously recorded in the brain's neural circuits.

When people experience cognitive dissonance, they are motivated to reduce the dissonance because of the psychological discomfort it causes. The discomfort can be relieved by changing either beliefs or behaviors or both, to eliminate the dissonance. We can be motivated by cognitive dissonance, or we can adapt to it.

A good example of the motivating power of cognitive dissonance is my own early experience described in Chapter 1. I wanted to be a regular, normal kid who would measure up to being a "Williamson", but I was diagnosed as retarded and then I heard Mr. Blake, an adult I looked up to, say I'd never amount to anything. I spent most of the rest of my life trying to prove them wrong in order to get rid of the cognitive dissonance those experiences created in me.

### *The Joys of a New Car*

Cognitive dissonance operates in both life-changing and every day situations. Here's an every day example with which most everyone can identify.

Assume you decide to buy a new car and, after weeks of shopping and research, you purchase the car of your dreams. You gleefully bring your new car home and find it difficult not to just stand around admiring its good looks. In fact, you are so taken with the beauty and utility of your new car that you wash it once or twice a week during the early days of your ownership, just to spend time with it, to look at it and touch it and keep it beautiful! While you are not consciously aware of it, as you wash your car you are visually recording every structural feature of your new car in the neural circuits of your visual cortex. Your new car is very important to you. You also want to reaffirm its value, because you will be paying for it for years to come.

To your surprise and eventually to your dismay, after you've driven your new car for a few days, you notice something about other cars on the road with you. There are lots of cars just like yours. When you bought your car, you never dreamed that you would come upon so many cars just like your own.

You note as you are driving down the highway at 60 miles an hour and see another car traveling at 60 miles an hour in the opposite direction (which means you are closing in on each other at the rate of

120 miles an hour), that it is the same make and model as yours and has the same wheel covers as your car! This awareness is not cognitive dissonance. It is simply your reticular alerting system (RAS) detecting information you value.

The next experience I want you to imagine occurs maybe four weeks later, when you leave the grocery store. As you unlock your car in the parking lot, you notice that some lout has parked next to you and banged a car door into yours, severely dinging the body of your new car.

How do you feel when you see the ding in your car? Most people I poll after presenting them with this scenario tell me that they feel upset, mad or angry. This distress is caused by cognitive dissonance.

Let's apply the definition to the scenario just described. Our previously recorded visual perception of our new car, the gestalt we hold in our mind, is that of a perfectly flawless, new car. When we look at our now badly-dinged car, our mind compares the gestalt of the dinged car with the recorded image of a perfect car and we feel cognitive dissonance. It's not the ding itself that bothers us. It's the changed gestalt of the whole car.

Most people have experienced this type of mental discomfort, if not with an automobile, then with some object or comment or belief asserted by another person that conflicts with the beliefs recorded in their brain's neural circuitry.

After six months, does the ding in the car bother you as much? No. Why is this so? Think about it for a moment. After the ding in the car is first noticed, every time you see the car with the ding in it, your brain overlays the stored image of a ding-free car with an image of a car having a ding. Every time you look at the car you strengthen the neural circuit image of the car, but now it is a new gestalt, that of a car with a ding in it. Six months later when you look at the car with a ding in it, the image does not conflict in any way with the dinged car image now recorded in your brain's neural circuits. The gestalt in your head has changed.

The simple explanation of why the ding no longer bothers you is usually attributed to the fact that you have "grown used to it." As startling as it may be for some individuals to believe, humans can grow "used to" a remarkable array of environmental and mental conditions without conscious awareness of the lessening of mental discomfort over time.

This is a good thing, to a point. Good if we can stop ourselves from being bothered, all out of proportion, by events and situations.

### *A Frog in Boiling Water*

When is the ability to overcome cognitive dissonance not so helpful? It is the old frog in boiling water story. Put a live frog in a pot of boiling water and he will jump out immediately. However, put a frog in a pot of room temperature water, then gradually bring the water to a boil. The frog will adapt to the slow change in temperature and end up cooked!

Fig. 9-2 The Old Frog Story

As people grow used to changes in their environment, their belief in what is fair, good or bad may not change. What does change is their familiarity with the mental or physical context in which they find themselves enmeshed.

Examples of this are legion. Have you ever known someone who has been involved in an abusive relationship, has courageously ended it, only to find themselves in a new abusive relationship? It may be a stretch to say that they got used to being abused. But it may be said that the abusive behavior they experience in the new relationship matches their previously stored perceptions of intimate relationships. The fact that the new experience matches in many respects their previously recorded bad experience is paradoxically absent new feelings of mental discomfort. It seems odd to say that being abused is psychologically comfortable. Familiar is a better word. It may be counterintuitive, but people who have been abused sometimes feel psychologically uncomfortable when they are treated with love and respect. (Often with reframing or therapeutic intervention they can learn to both expect and enjoy respectful, loving treatment.)

It is also true that when we violate our own value systems over time, the cognitive dissonance may diminish. If a person steals something, even if he feels guilty, stealing again will be easier. When people have been unfaithful in a marriage relationship, it is easier to be unfaithful again. The shame and guilt decrease with each violation, as the new situation becomes practiced and familiar. In the same way, if you tell a lie repeatedly, neural circuits form in your brain and for you the lie becomes the truth. You may be genuinely incensed when challenged. You have come to believe your lie and the challenge causes you cognitive dissonance.

## *Reacting To Cognitive Dissonance — It's Automatic!*

In appreciating cognitive dissonance, we need to understand that it does not occur because of exposure to inherently wrong thoughts, beliefs or perceptions. A normal human response to the feeling of cognitive dissonance is to attribute the discomfort to the thoughts, beliefs or perceptions themselves. The fact is that the new thoughts, beliefs or perceptions are not inherently problematic. They are just different from what's already in our head.

It is common for people to overreact to cognitive dissonance. They may say or do things that seem disproportionate to the situation. Our overreactions are induced by a strong sense of mental discomfort that we do not know how to deal with at a conscious level.

> It is a spiritual axiom that every time we are disturbed, no matter what the cause, there is something wrong with us.[12]

In the light of what we know about cognitive dissonance, this axiom might be restated as follows.

> It is a spiritual axiom that every time we are disturbed, no matter what the cause, there is present in the neural circuits of our brain, thoughts, beliefs or perceptions that conflict in some way with the information that disturbs us.

An essential attribute of cognitive dissonance is that it is an automatic response over which we have no instant conscious control.

### *Charlie's Story*

One day Charlie was looking for a somewhat expensive and fragile electronic device that he had always stored on the top of the mantle above the fireplace, out of reach of Max, one of his small children, then about five years old. As he approached the mantle he noticed a chair had been pushed up against the fireplace just below the place where he knew the device to be. He glanced at the mantle and saw it was missing. A scan of the room revealed the device on a coffee table. A wooden mallet used to break nuts in a bowl on the coffee table was lying next to it. The device, which had a number of buttons and dials, was smashed and broken. His instant response was anger. He carried the broken device to where Max was playing and accused him of having ruined it. Max did not respond, but averted his eyes and looked guilty.

Charlie was not proud of his actions that followed. He shouted at Max and asked if he had done the damage. Max nodded yes. Charlie told him that his failure to respect his dad's property was unacceptable behavior and there would be consequences for his actions. Charlie gave him a few swats on his backside, which resulted in a loud wail and many tears.

Even though Charlie had made a pact with himself never to spank his children as he had been spanked as a child, he had lost control. More than that, he had given Max two more consecutive swats on the backside even as he burst into tears. Charlie quickly took him into his arms and feebly tried to explain away his behavior by suggesting that the boy's actions made his dad physically discipline him. As Charlie looked back on his spontaneous response to cognitive dissonance, he was aware that abusive and inappropriate behavior may often flow from feelings of cognitive dissonance.

When Charlie told me this story, he added that, interestingly, the inappropriate striking of Max in no way relieved his sense of dissonance. When he came upon the damaged device the following day, he became upset the moment he saw it.

I can't resist this opportunity to make a point about the power of neural circuits laid down in childhood. Imagine a slightly different scene when Charlie discovers his damaged device. Max is in the backyard and Charlie calls to him, "Hey, stupid, get in here." Max responds, "Yes Dad, what do you want?" In this situation Charlie doesn't spank him but begins to tell him he must be the stupidest, dumbest kid on the planet. He had been told not to touch any of Charlie's things and if he cannot understand that simple instruction he was incapable of learning anything and that he was bound to grow up and be nothing but an incompetent nothing of a person. Charlie may have been talking like this to Max since he was two or three years old. Max loves his dad. Charlie never hit him. He takes him fishing, plays ball with him, and takes him hiking. For Max, the sun rises and sets on his father.

A year or so later Charlie sends Max off to school. How do you think he will perform in school? If you surmise that his academic performance will be sub par you will more than likely be correct.

Because he is a young child, Max has not developed the ability to push away his father's highly charged negative judgments. Charlie is, in real time, driving neural circuit development in Max's brain that will affect his self image and academic performance at a subconscious level for many years to come, possibly for the rest of his life.

I once learned of a study of children ages three to seven in which each of the children had a micro cassette recorder secured to their clothing. The recorder remained turned on all day to record what was said to the child and how the child responded. Fresh batteries and recording tapes were provided, as needed, over the course of the day. At day's end the tapes were transcribed and studied to determine what percentage of the comments made to the child were negative or restrictive in nature.

It may not surprise you that 80% of the comments were negative or restrictive. What is more interesting is the fact that 80% of the negative comments came from the children's parents. Amazingly the people who love them most were responsible for the limiting neural circuits that would likely operate at the subconscious level in the minds of their children for the balance of their lives.

Nearly everyone who reads this book has hard-wired in place a host of beliefs and perceptions put down in neural circuits during their childhood that directly affect their ability to accomplish whatever it is that they want in life. People sometimes become despondent when they learn that much of the person they are to become in life finds its origin in neural circuits laid down in their early years.

> The good news this book brings is the reality that you can learn how to rewire your brain to overlay old negative circuits with life-enhancing circuitry. This will allow you a choice of behaviors and a fresh awareness of the world. Ultimately it means you can get what you want in and out of life.

### *Harry's Story*

Returning to cognitive dissonance, a striking example of an individual's inability to prevent the automatic response to cognitive dissonance is described in the following story.

As mentioned earlier, I had been invited by Harry Stonecipher, the CEO of the company I worked for, to share the "Pathways to Greatness" program with him one-on-one in the company's boardroom. We had just been through this material on cognitive dissonance. As I was completing the section, I asked him if he believed that cognitive dissonance is an automatic mental response over which people have no conscious control. Harry responded by saying, "If you say so, Hal." That was not the answer I wanted. I interpreted his response as the gentlemanly way to say he did not agree. This was a problem for me because, at a later point in the curriculum, the acknowledgement of the reality of this automatic response is crucial to enabling individuals to accomplish remarkable things.

I turned to Harry and said, "You know, Harry, what I need to do right now is say something to you that will instantly produce cognitive dissonance."

Harry smiled, folded his arms across his chest and said "Okay, Hal, take your best shot at me." I know what he was probably thinking. "What can this character say to me that will cause me to be mentally uncomfortable, especially since I know in advance what he is trying to prove?"

I must confess that Harry's, "If you say so," response came as a complete surprise. I have no idea where my next words came from. I said, "Harry, do you realize that in the United States virtually all Americans believe that it is morally wrong for the CEO of a company to receive an annual income that exceeds ten times the pay of the company's lowest paid factory worker?"

Harry responded by abruptly storming out of the room. He did not come back right away and I realized that my comment was probably in poor taste, given my awareness of his recent heated exchanges over head count reductions among factory workers to improve the company's bottom line at the same time he was receiving increases in his compensation package from the Board of Directors.

I began to gather my presentation materials together, sensing that I had just blown the only opportunity I would have of getting Harry to support my desire to have all 6,000 of the company's employees attend the "Pathways to Greatness" program.

But to my surprised delight, Harry returned and as he entered the room he said, "I now understand what you meant when you said cognitive dissonance causes an automatic response. Let's get on with it."

## *Using Cognitive Dissonance*

The most powerful antidote to feelings of dissonance is first to become consciously aware of the rising level of mental discomfort that always accompanies cognitive dissonance. Some people begin to feel hot, others feel agitated. By observing yourself, you can learn your own body's cues. With practice, this awareness can trigger you to consciously delay responding to the experience that is causing the discomfort. The age-old maxim: "whenever you feel yourself becoming disturbed, you should count to ten before responding" has a sound basis in the neurophysiology of your brain. In my own life I have found this advice profoundly useful in keeping my discourse with others non-confrontational. (See Chapter 4.)

Chapter 17 returns to cognitive dissonance — how its ability to motivate can result in achievement — or greatness!

# 10
# *Staying Comfortable with Ourselves*

In this chapter you will learn why neural circuits cause human behavior to favor activities that allow the brain to maintain itself unchanged, thereby maintaining current reality.

## *Comfort Zones*

It is interesting to note that while many of us talk about wanting excitement, adventure or change, the truth is that people are most content when there is little or no change in their environment. Most people choose to behave in ways that maintain this "current reality," also sometimes called homeostasis.

Current reality is the world as you know it. It could also be defined as the *conscious awareness produced in the mind by the sum total of all neural circuits in the brain.* The neural circuits that form as a result of people's sensory experiences apparently lead them to place themselves in physical and emotional circumstances where new sensory experiences will closely resemble the old.

This phenomenon is also referred to as our "comfort zone." The term "comfort zone" can be ironic because the prior physical and emotional circumstances may, in fact, be emotionally unhealthy or physically unsafe. However, whenever an individual senses that the physical and emotional environment being experienced at the moment matches one that he or she already recorded in the neural circuits of the brain, it feels familiar. Changing that environment entails unknown risk, which we often avoid. The ironic comfort zone is often experienced by people in early recovery from alcoholism. As lousy as the life of active addiction had become, at least it was familiar. Recovery — staying sober — is unfamiliar and uncomfortable at first.

Sociologists call one of the most common comfort zone experiences "nesting." Nesting occurs in many situations, including the familiar scene when we attend a gathering that will be meeting in the same room a number of times. When we first arrive at the room and select a seat, any of a number of choices is available. For example, we may have a preference for sitting in the front, in the back or near the door. Once we have taken our seat, we are not consciously aware that the neural circuits in our brains are busily recording everything being processed by our senses, including the layout of the room and our physical relationship to all the structural features in the room. As the class proceeds, we are not consciously aware that as we glance around the room we reinforce the neural circuits forming right then in our brain. These circuits-in-formation are not being consciously tagged as they are being formed.

When we return to the room the next time, we find ourselves going back to the same seat. Why? The answer is simple. We will feel most comfortable when we sit in the same seat and the world around us matches the world recorded in our neural circuits. Our mind, resident in the neural circuits of our brain, is uncomfortable with changes in our surroundings. This mental discomfort finds its origin in the cognitive dissonance we experience when there is a mismatch between what we perceive with our senses and what we have recorded in our neural circuits.

There is a small subset of people who do not "nest" as described above, but seem to get comfort in constant change instead. They may infuriate you by sitting in "your" seat after even a short break!

### *Curt Gets Comfortable*

In 1989 I was having my home remodeled and I shared with a group of acquaintances my distress at having run out of funds to complete the painting. The following Saturday Curt, a dear soul who had heard my paint and money problem, simply showed up and said he loved to paint and would be glad to lend a hand. I thought the paint job would be done in a weekend.

As the weeks turned into a month and then a second month, Curt and I painted and conversed on a wide range of subjects from spiritual matters to our hopes and concerns regarding family members, our work and our roles in the community. Curt was bright and hard working. He'd had a difficult life, which included humble origins and too much drinking. Now he was sober and had a steady job.

My late wife Trudy kept us well fed as we worked and soon we called his wife Carol to join us at our meals. We cooked over our outside barbeque grill because the kitchen was not finished. We sat on boxes and make-shift tables of construction material. In short order we became fast friends. It took two months of steady weekend work to finish.

Once the job was done, Curt and Carol were our first dinner guests. They were honored guests. That evening we set the finest table we could, with our best china, finest linen, our silver service, candelabras and crystal glasses. Bouquets of fresh flowers decked the tables.

Curt showed up in a suit and tie, the first time I had ever seen him dressed up. As we sat at the table, joined hands and said grace, Curt's face flushed with color and he said "Hal, I cannot describe how immensely uncomfortable I feel sitting here. Are these feelings I am experiencing because of the cognitive dissonance thing you shared with me?" Curt went on to say that he had never in his whole life experienced this kind of fine dining. The dissonance Curt experienced was because he was out of his comfort zone

It took only a few more dinners at our home for Curt to announce one evening that the cognitive dissonance was gone. He had come to feel quite certain that this type of dining was appropriate for him!

### *Sales Techniques Pull Us Out of Our Comfort Zones*

An understanding of comfort zones and an appreciation of the neural circuits involved will soon allow you to sense why new car advertisers want you to take a free test drive. This is especially true if your car appears to be running just fine and you have had it for years. They need to make your current reality less comfortable. Simply getting behind the wheel of a new car will create dissonance that might result in a sale. The new car even smells fresh — like a new beginning. Driving the new car creates a wider cognitive dissonance gap. You can almost hear sparks in your brain's neural circuits as they compare the smooth glide of the new car to the feeling of driving your old clunker.

## *Self Image and Stories We Tell Ourselves*

Each of us has a self image, whether we are consciously aware of it or not. A positive self image is an important part of self esteem and self acceptance. Over the course of our lives all of the thoughts and feelings and beliefs we have about ourselves are laid down in our neural circuits. The fascinating thing is that the self image we carry in our brains may or may not actually be true. For example, your self image may include, "I am not creative at all." This may be true, or it may be that you have defined "creative" narrowly, or have not been trained or yet found your creative outlet.

Another way of describing the thoughts, beliefs and feelings that make up our self image is to say that they are the stories we make up to explain our own experience to ourselves. We all believe the stories we tell to support our beliefs are true and factual and that to suggest otherwise is to question our integrity. I have had the experience of being with my siblings and remembering a shared event in the past. The memories we hold are so different it is hard to believe we are talking about the same event. Once again we detect the presence of cognitive dissonance.

### *Maintaining Self Image — a Whole Brain Activity*

Much has been written about self image, with explanations of just what "self" is or is not. We will highlight a few.

Rene Descartes, the 15th century French philosopher, said that humans are comprised of a body and a mind/soul. The body is simply a physical machine that moves through the world under the control of the mind. Upon the death of the body, the mind/soul, which have no physical substance, survive forever.

Some religious beliefs suggest that the eventual destiny of the soul is either in a state called heaven, which is close to the love of God, or a state most removed from the love of God, called hell.

There is a school of thought that says we are simply complicated machines and the idea of a mind in the brain suggests that there is some sort of ghost in the machine that directs the physical behavior of the machine.

This book does not take sides in the philosophical debate of mind/soul and self. What we will do is view the brain and body as a system that is an interconnected whole comprised of multiple organs that all function in an interdependent manner. In this view, the mind is resident in the brain and electrochemically responsive to every bodily function we experience, such as breathing, sweating, digesting food and sleeping.

### *Wherever I Go, There I Am*

As we go through the world, we drive neural circuit development that records all of our experiences, as well as our thoughts about our experiences. I would suggest that these circuits, when taken as a whole, represent a "core self." This core self is comprised of my self as I believe I am, the self I would like to be and the self as I believe others see me. Our self image is therefore a composite of the three selves just described.

Let's play with this notion a little. We want to observe how the "core self" responds when taken from its normal and regular environment and placed in a totally foreign place and culture. So imagine yourself the recipient of an all expenses paid, month-long home-exchange vacation in a remote region of an undeveloped country. Your living quarters have been selected for you and food will be provided. Imagine next that the vacation site is in a rain forest village and your housing is a structure of bamboo and broad leafed plants with a thatched roof and no door. There are openings in the walls, but no glass. Flying insects come and go, as well as mice and occasional dogs. The floor is swept dirt. The toilet is a covered hole in the ground, a precursor to the outhouse, several feet behind the house.

The plane that brought you here will return in thirty days. What will you do? As you stand in the hut, your seeing, hearing and smelling senses deliver messages about the environment which are decoded by your brain and filtered through your beliefs, attitudes and values. The actions you will take spring from attitudes, beliefs and values resident in the neural circuitry of your brain.

Do you think that you could live comfortably in that hut for a month? I have asked this question to countless workshop participants over the years. Without exception people respond that they would enjoy being in the rain forest and would work to make the living space more habitable by their familiar standards. Even though not one of them had ever experienced a living environment such as I described, each and every one acknowledged that they would be out of their comfort zone and that doing nothing to cover the floor and keep the animals out would conflict with their self image.

You learn that the family with whom you are trading homes has just arrived at your home. I asked these same individuals what kind of experience they thought the indigenous family would have in their exchange home. Everyone thought that the family would have a similar difficulty adjusting to an unfamiliar environment.

I then asked them the following question. "If you came home and found your home in some disarray, would you think there was something wrong with the exchange family?" Their instant response was, "Of course not. Nothing in their culture prepared them for the modern environment they would experience in our house."

## *Active Participation Drives Neural Circuits*

If we think back to our childhood years we may recall the incessant admonitions by our teachers to wash and dry our hands after using the toilet. Most of us had no appreciation of the role harmful bacteria could play in our overall health, but we did as we were told, and in time this behavior became part of the person we are. As adults most of us wash our hands, without conscious thought, before leaving the bathroom. So our experiences and our thoughts about our experiences drive neural circuit development and create our comfort zones.

# 11
# *Getting Inside: Useful Models of the Brain*

Let us turn now to examining some models of the brain that help us understand how we think. Most simply stated, the human brain is divided into two hemispheres that form the whole brain. The hemispheres are designated "right" and "left" and are associated with the right and left sides of the body. However, the right side of the brain controls the left side of the body and the left side of the brain controls the right side of the body.

## *Effort, Learning and Preference*

To pull together what we've learned in the preceding chapters, a further elaboration of some basic mental principles will be helpful. Some typical childhood experiences provide good examples. Small children have many physical tasks to learn. Some seem easy, some seem hard. Many children find it easy to climb up stairs even before they can walk. Some physical tasks like guiding a loaded spoon into the mouth seem difficult at first but with practice they become easy and soon require no mental effort at all. In contrast there are some tasks that become easier to perform but never become quite effortless.

Remember learning to tie your shoes (before the advent of

Velcro®!)? Our hands and fingers had to work together, as we concentrated to remember just how each lace was supposed to relate to the other. Initially, the tasks required our focused, conscious attention as the fingers of both hands cooperated with the laces to form loops that became bows when the loops were formed into a simple knot. Early efforts may have produced loops and bows that were uneven or incomplete or so loose that they quickly came apart when we walked. In time we no longer had to think consciously about the task. Eventually we were able to tie our shoes even in the dark without so much as a conscious thought directed to the control of our fingers or hands. In other words, we moved from being consciously incompetent to unconsciously competent at tying our shoes. I am told that today's robotic computers cannot be programmed to do this simple task.

You may ask, "Are there any tasks, physical or mental, that we perform almost effortlessly right from the beginning?" In the physical realm, the answer is yes. We seem to develop simple preferences in the use of our hands, arms, legs and feet. If I ask you, "What is your dominant hand?" you know the answer immediately, even without a definition of the meaning of the word dominant. Most people respond either "right" or "left." Some people will respond that they use both of their hands equally, whereas some tasks are always performed by one of the hands. These people are referred to as being "mix-handed." Individuals who can write and do other tasks equally well with either hand are called "ambidextrous."

When I ask right-handed people why they consider their right hand to be dominant, they often respond that the hand and fingers have more dexterity than the left hand and fingers. Left-handed people may say their left hand is somewhat stronger than the right, or that they can write with the left but not the right. Still others may offer the opinion that one of their hands is virtually worthless when it comes to performing most tasks other than simply grasping an object.

Humans are bilateral in nature. This means that parts of the body, limbs and organs, reside on either side of a center line up and down the middle of the body. This is evidenced by eyes, ears, arms, hands, legs, and feet as well as such internal organs as the lungs, the kidneys, and the brain, to identify a few.

Physical dominance arises as infants make constant and continual choices as to which of their limbs or organs to use in a given situation. Because there are always two organs, limbs, or body parts available, the child may continuously choose one over the other. This preference, which evidences itself in people being considered right or left-handed, right or left-eyed, is a natural consequence of living in the world. A preference or dominance simply implies that over time, in order to act spontaneously without conscious thought, humans develop preferences that allow this to happen.

Imagine, if you will, a contest between two individuals, one right-handed and the other left-handed. The contest involves a puzzle that requires manual dexterity with the fingers of one hand. In this contest the person who fully assembles the puzzle first wins a cash prize! However, there is a single condition to the contest. The right hand of each individual will be tied behind his back during the contest. If you are one of the contestants and you are right-handed, how do you feel? Who has the advantage? Who do you think will win? Most right-handed individuals protest that the contest is unfair, because it pits their non-dominant left hand against the dominant left hand of their opponent. They generally concede that they will be more likely to lose to the left-handed contestant.

The moral of this story is simple. Humans have preferences in the use of one of a pair of limbs and organs of their bodies. These preferences manifest themselves by the ease and spontaneous manner in which the body parts are used by the individual. The use of the preferred limb or organ is unconscious and by its very nature responds quickly when called upon to practice and learn a new skill.

## *Are You Right-eyed Or Left-eyed?*

Because they seem so natural, most people don't realize that, in addition to handedness, they have other preferences. For example, you have a dominant eye. Here is a simple self-test to determine your eye preference. Take your dominant hand and bring your thumb and index finger together to form a small circle. Now extend the hand to arm's length with the thumb and finger still forming a circle. Next select a small object or a small, structural detail of a large object fifteen to twenty feet in front of you. With both eyes wide open, move the circle made by your thumb and finger to locate the object or structural detail within it. At the moment the object or detail appears to be in the middle of the circle, alternately close one eye and then the other. You will become aware instantly that only one of the eyes sees the object or detail in the circle of the thumb and finger. The eye that sees the object in the circle is your dominant eye.

If you are right-handed and right-eyed, you will find this useful in activities when you need to align two objects in space, for example, shooting a shotgun at clay targets catapulted into a space before you. To hit the flying targets, you place the stock of the shotgun against your right shoulder, allowing the right side of your face to rest against the gunstock. Your right eye is now aligned with a small sighting bead near the end of the gun barrel. The object of the sport is to move the gun so the bead on the barrel lines up with the clay target as it flies through the air. You pull the trigger and the gun fires a pattern of shotgun pellets at the moving clay target. When the shooter is right-eyed and the bead at the end of the barrel lines up with the clay target, pull the trigger and the clay target will be history....every time!

An inherent challenge of the sport is the quickness required by the sportsman in raising his gun, aiming at the moving target and pulling the trigger before the target is out of range. This speed requirement forces the shooter to fire the gun with both eyes wide open. What does this mean for a sportsman who is right-handed but left-eyed? His left eye directs its focus on the bead of the barrel to line it up with the clay target. Unfortunately when he pulls the trigger, the pellet pattern will pass either ahead of or behind the target. The direction the barrel of the gun takes, resting on the right shoulder, is different when the left eye is dominant. It is not unusual for individuals who are right-handed and left-eyed to give up the sport. Yet others will learn that if they consciously keep the left eye closed, they will consistently hit the target, because now the right, non-dominant eye controls the pointing of the gun barrel's bead on the target.

You may wonder, "Does anyone benefit from being right-handed and left-eyed?" The answer is, yes, especially in sports such as golf and baseball. In the case of baseball, when batting right-handed, the left-eyed batter can easily keep his left eye on the ball from the moment the ball leaves the pitcher's hand until he brings the bat around to meet it. A right-eyed, right-handed hitter can accomplish a similar visual contact with the ball, but it is harder and less natural, requiring the batter to twist his head towards the left to bring his right eye into a position with a clear view of the pitcher's release of the ball.

Other right-handed, right-eyed batters simply lift their left foot off the ground slightly and rotate their torso to the left, which brings their head and right eye around to better track the flight of the ball. The problem with this movement is that when a batter changes his stance to enable his right eye to track the ball more accurately, less power is delivered to the ball on impact.

Instead of opening their stance, some right-handed, right-eyed batters close the left eye to keep visual track of the ball with the right eye. This can work, but is not natural, and usually results in a fairly low hit rate.

Right-handed, left-eyed golfers find it easy to keep their left eye on the ball as they swing the putter into contact with the ball. With the head still, the left eye looks directly down on the ball. When preparing to hit the ball with the putter head, the golfer needs only to shift her eye slightly to assure that the path the ball will take is directly toward the hole.

## *What Does Dominance Have to Do with Greatness?*

You might wonder, "So what role, if any, will knowledge of physical dominance play in identifying elements of natural greatness in me?"

The answer lies in noticing what comes easily. Activities that come easily, whether physically or mentally, are free-flowing. These are always activities that call upon our natural preferences, as illustrated by the baseball player and golfer noted above. This leads us to reflect on the impact natural preferences might have when it comes to thinking.

Wouldn't it be wonderful if the life we wanted to live seemed to happen automatically and with ease? People differ in what seem to be their natural abilities. Some people excel in mental activities that involve analysis, math and logic. Other people seem naturally organized in their thinking and planning. Some people enjoy being with others, are naturally empathetic and comfortable in company. Other people are highly creative, naturally synthesizing ideas and looking at the big picture.

## *Dr. Roger Sperry's Work*

In the 1970's Dr. Roger Sperry and a team of researchers at the California Institute of Technology were working with individuals who suffered from untreatable epilepsy. When everything they tried had failed to stop the unwanted discharges of electrical signals from the brain that caused seizures, he and his colleagues did the unthinkable. In each patient, they operated to split the brain by cutting the giant nerve fiber bundle (the corpus callosum) that connects the two hemispheres (Fig. 11-1).

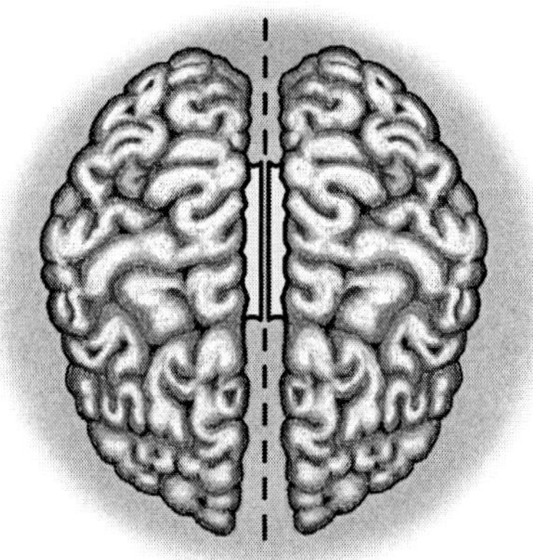

Fig. 11-1 Split Brain

Amazingly, the patients lived and their seizures diminished significantly or were controlled by medication. Sperry became famous for experimental studies of how brain circuits are formed and for research on mental activities in the right and left hemispheres of the brain. For this work Dr. Sperry won a Nobel Prize in Science in 1982.

Studies and experiments involving these split-brain patients revealed that right and left hemispheres appear to handle different types of thought processes. The nature of these differences may be appreciated by even a casual study of Fig. 11-2, which has been derived from the published work of Drs. Roger Sperry and Robert Ornstein.

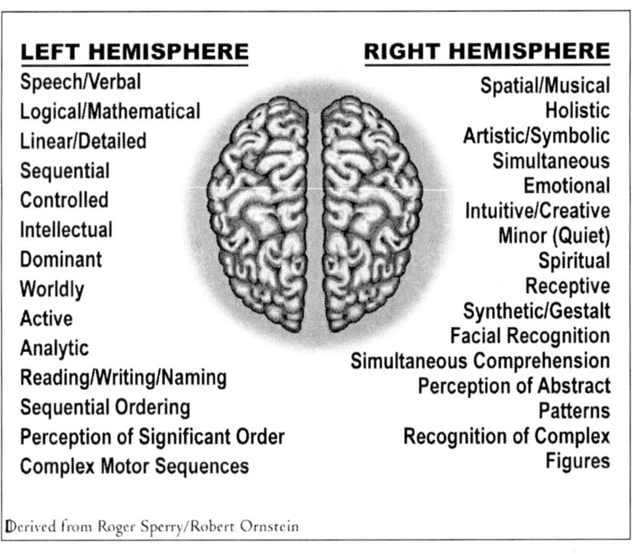

LEFT HEMISPHERE
Speech/Verbal
Logical/Mathematical
Linear/Detailed
Sequential
Controlled
Intellectual
Dominant
Worldly
Active
Analytic
Reading/Writing/Naming
Sequential Ordering
Perception of Significant Order
Complex Motor Sequences
RIGHT HEMISPHERE
Spatial/Musical
Holistic
Artistic/Symbolic
Simultaneous
Emotional
Intuitive/Creative
Minor (Quiet)
Spiritual
Receptive
Synthetic/Gestalt
Facial Recognition
Simultaneous Comprehension
Perception of Abstract Patterns
Recognition of Complex Figures
Derived from Roger Sperry/Robert Ornstein


Fig. 11-2 Thought Processes by Hemisphere

The left hemisphere appears to process information in a linear, sequential manner. It's no surprise that speech, reading, writing, logic, math and analytical reasoning appear to take place there.

The right hemisphere involves mental functions that require the simultaneous processing of incoming and stored data/information. These include holistic, artistic, creative, intuitive and synthetic processing, to name a few.

It appears that the left hemisphere can process data at incredible speed, but is constrained to doing so in a linear, sequential manner, whereas the right hemisphere processes vast quantities of information simultaneously. Hence the right side of the brain will process, in real time, more information than the left.

## *Ned Herrmann and the Four Quadrant Model*

About the time of Dr. Sperry's split brain research, Ned Herrmann, who was employed by The General Electric Corporation's

Executive Educational Center in Crotonville, New York, became fascinated by the divergent thinking styles he observed in individuals attending his workshops and training programs. Herrmann was attracted to the work of Sperry because it appeared to offer insights into human thought processing.

Determining which specific part of the brain does what has turned out to be more and more difficult. Researchers have discovered that simple right and left brain categorization of brain processes is not wholly accurate, as the operation of the brain is far more subtle and complex than right/left implies. Herrmann took Sperry's physiological explanation of brain processes as a jumping off point for creating a metaphorical model, Fig. 11-3.

In this model the left hemisphere includes quadrants "A" and "B", and the right hemisphere includes quadrants "C" and "D". Note that Herrmann has clustered sets of thought processes adjacent to each quadrant.

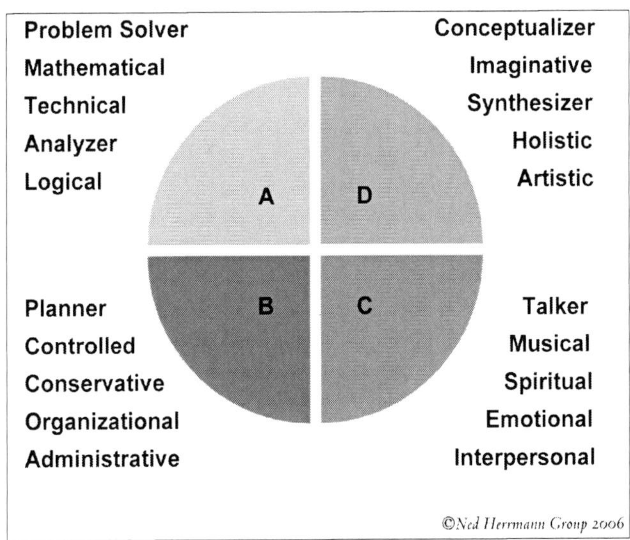


Fig. 11-3 Herrmann's Whole Brain, Four Quadrant Model

## *Whole Brain Technology*

Could there be a correlation between your thinking style preferences and living a purposeful life that readily allows you to get what you want out of life? Given the bilateral nature of the brain and the apparent clustered thinking style processes derived from Sperry's work, Herrmann asked, "Might people have preferences about which thought process or processes to apply in a given situation?" To determine the answer, Herrmann created a paper and pencil survey instrument that included a series of 120 questions. The questions were designed to elicit responses indicating a preference for one or more of the thinking styles. Herrmann called it a survey instead of a test, because there are no right or wrong answers. It is a set of questions used to graphically display the way an individual likes to think. The questions are designed in such a manner that the scoring of the instrument provides a numerical score for each quadrant. This instrument is now called the Herrmann Brain Dominance Instrument (HBDI™).

Herrmann determined that indeed a case could be made for four very different types of mental processes, and that we individually prefer to use some of these more than others (Fig. 11-4).

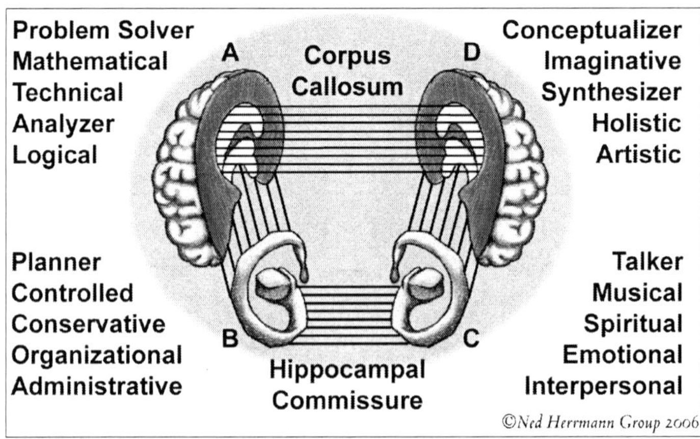


Fig. 11-4 Herrmann's Whole Brain

Shown in another way, this model describes our four different selves (Fig. 11-5).

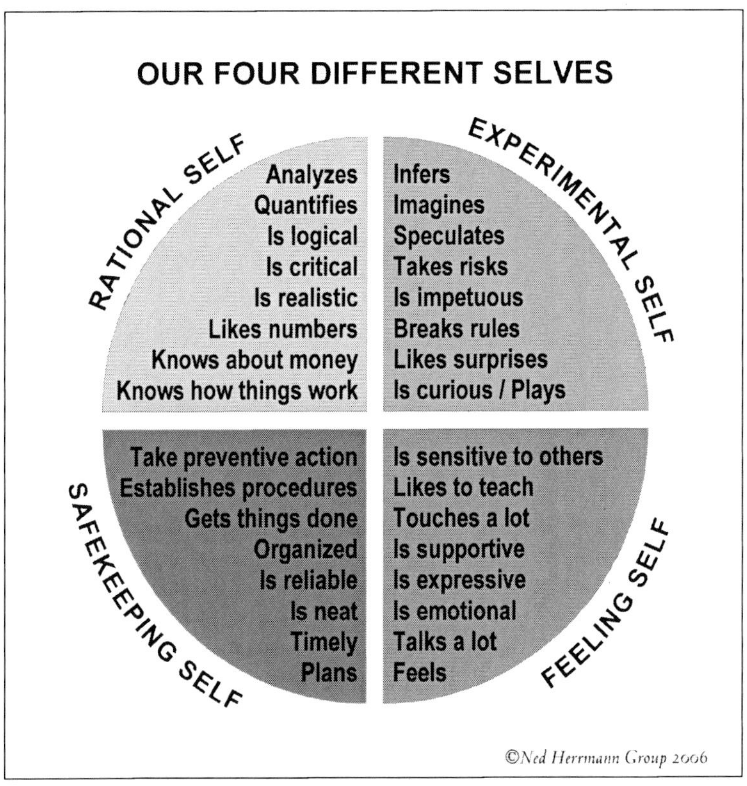


Fig. 11-5 Our Four Different Selves

The score of a completed HBDI™ survey is plotted in the four separate quadrants as shown in Fig. 11-6. The larger the score in a given quadrant, the stronger the person's preference to use mental processes of that quadrant. If the score falls within the innermost circle, the individual probably does not like, or may actually avoid, the use of the mental processes of that quadrant, even if they have developed some skills in that quadrant.

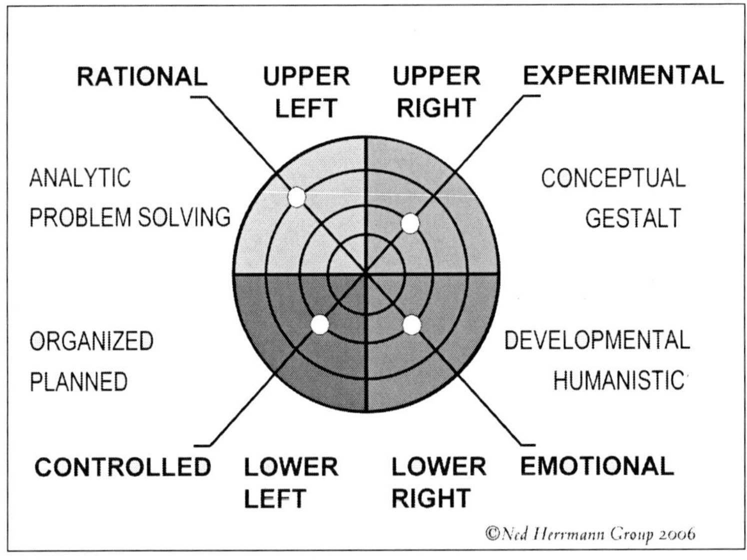


Fig. 11-6 Plotted scores

An HBDI™ Profile is created by connecting the four dots, Fig. 11-7.

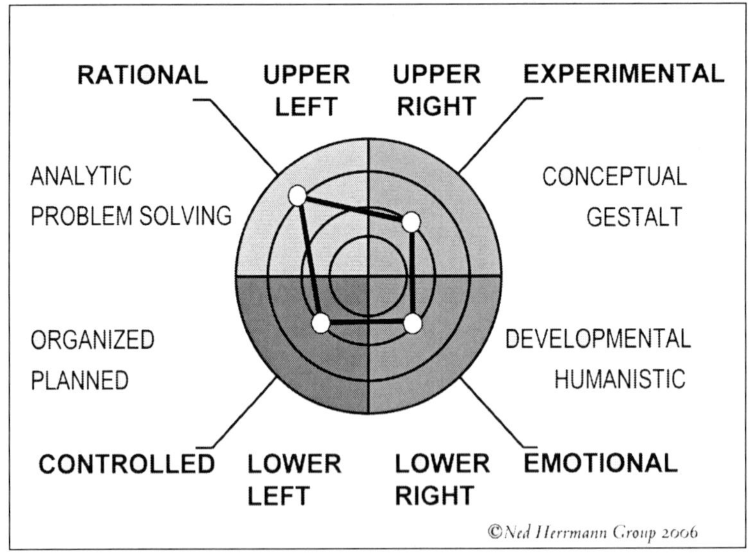


Fig. 11-7 Emergence of HBDI™ Profile

Each profile is a geometric figure that may be one of a variety of configurations. Fig. 11-8 shows two very different thinking style preference profiles, one preferring to use the clusters of thought processes in the upper left quadrant, the other preferring to use the clusters of thought processes of the upper right quadrant.

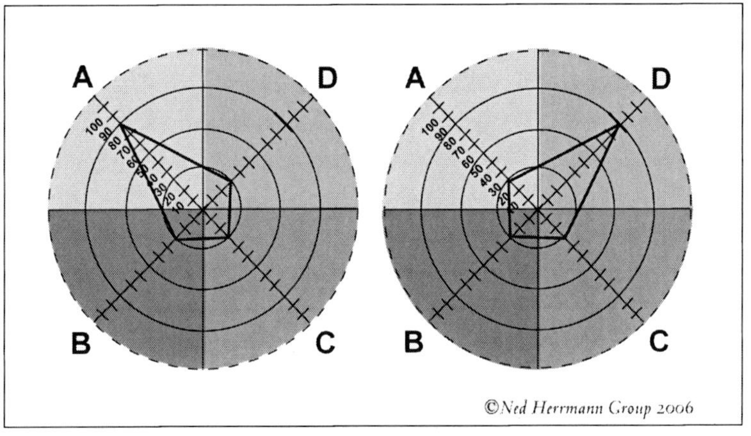


Fig. 11-8 Thinking Style Preference Profiles

Question: Do these survey results mean that the person whose profile is in the upper left cannot use the thought processes of the upper right quadrant? The answer is obviously no. While the profiles created were initially referred to as brain dominance profiles, Herrmann also calls them thinking style preference profiles. It is important to note that the Herrmann model talks about preference, not competence. A person can become competent using any quadrant. Just as a right-handed piano player also uses the left hand effectively, a person who prefers to use his right brain can become competent in left brain activities with practice. But here's the rub. Working in a non-preferred quadrant is effortful, while working in a preferred quadrant is fun! Knowing our thinking style preferences helps us understand ourselves and make important decisions about where to spend our time and energy.

A major reason to know your profile is this: Working in a non-preferred quadrant drains you, while working in a preferred quadrant makes you feel energized and smart!

The Hermann Whole Brain Model™ is enormously useful in analyzing the thinking styles essential to performing the duties inherent in a variety of careers. Fig. 11-9 shows pro forma thinking style profiles devised by Herrmann that suggest the mental processes called upon in the daily performance of a number of professions.

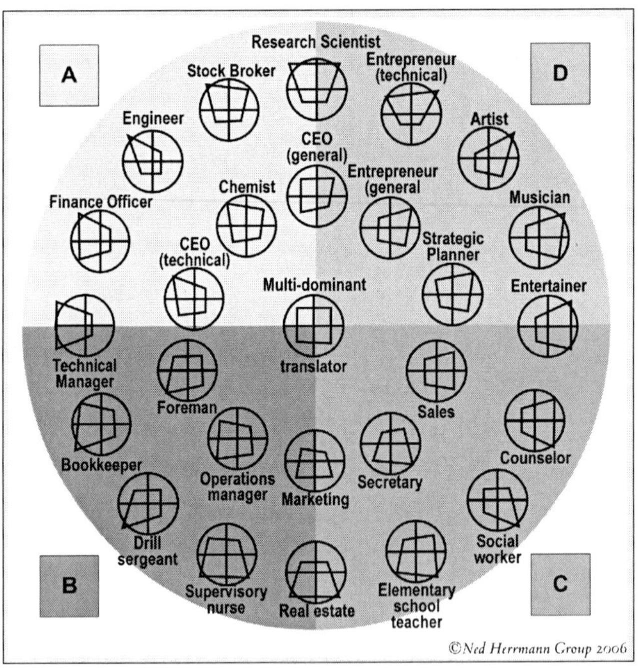


Fig. 11-9 Professions and Profiles

As you look at these profession-related profiles, what do you think about your own? What sorts of mental activities fill your day?

I had the opportunity to complete the Herrmann Brain Dominance Instrument™ in the mid-1980's and was dismayed to discover that my profile, shown in Fig. 11-10 on the right, did not match that of a patent attorney's work, shown on the left. I silently wondered if I had chosen the wrong career!

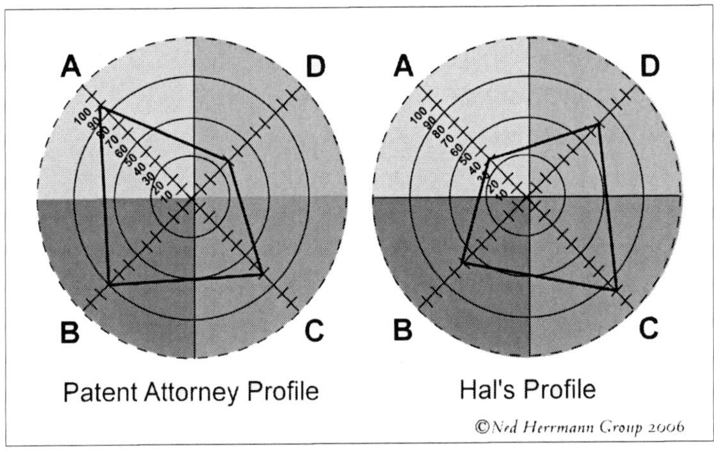


Fig. 11-10 Patent Attorney Profile & Hal's Profile

I began to think back on my high school years and my difficulty with math. I envied my classmates who sailed through their math lessons. I required a much greater study effort to achieve a similar level of mastery. On the other hand, I felt at ease verbally sharing my thoughts on almost all matters and subjects that caught my fancy. Public speaking came easily to me. I was fascinated with all branches of science and voraciously read magazines, books and periodicals that provided summaries and overviews of science past and present. When equations were offered in the articles as a mathematical explanation of the principles described, I would simply skip them and continue reading the explanatory text.

I decided to become an engineer, even though it would require many years of math study at the university level. I would have to study harder than the engineering students who found math easy.

Few of my contemporaries in engineering school were aware of the midnight oil I burned and the weekends I spent cloistered in the library developing mastery in math. While my learning was painfully slow, once I had mastered an understanding of the theory and mathematical principles, I performed well on exams.

Law school was not easy. It did, however, heighten my analytical and logical reasoning skills, which were not natural to me.

At this point in my life I believed that being average in anything was unacceptable. To be average was to be the best of the worst or the worst of the best. But, without knowing it, by my choice of college major and career path, I was setting myself up to fall short of the best. This was to become the taproot of a growing sense of inadequacy in all of my endeavors. The feelings of inadequacy were present even when my efforts and accomplishments were being applauded.

I became a successful patent attorney, working in the corporate world. Over time I found myself energized by oppurtnities to teach engineers how to identify and disclose invention in their work. Invention disclosures poured in; patents covering their inventions began to issue at record rates.

> So how about you? What comes easily and naturally to you? Could you redesign the way you work to fit your thinking preferences more, as I did? Could you find someone who likes to do what you dislike and work together? Live your natural greatness and see how your life improves!

As I look back on these events now, I see that I had transformed my job as a patent attorney, writing extensive legal descriptions of technical subjects, into a teacher who facilitated liberation of the creative essence in countless design engineers I worked with. I had figured out how to be a patent attorney using my right-brained thinking style preferences.

The most effective teams, in HBDI™ terms, are whole-brain teams, where the aggregate of the team members' profiles shows strength in all four quadrants. This is true in the workplace, in partnerships, in marriage. And one way to get the power of the "whole brain" is to become situationally whole brained yourself. Take a mental walk around the four quadrants to see any situation from all four perspectives. Questions to ask yourself are indicated in the Whole Brain Walk-Around Check List of Fig. 11-11.

| A | D |
|---|---|
| **Is your approach:**<br><br>Logical?<br>Rational?<br>Realistic?<br>Theoretically sound?<br>Data based?<br>Financially Sound?<br>Meet technical requirements? | **Is your approach:**<br><br>Conceptual?<br>Holistic?<br>Experimental?<br>Imaginative?<br>Forward looking?<br>Visionary?<br>Strategic? |
| **B**<br>**Is your approach:**<br><br>Organized and in sequence?<br>Reliable?<br>Tested and proven?<br>In control?<br>Operationally planned?<br>Scheduled?<br>Do-able? | **C**<br>**Is your approach:**<br><br>People oriented?<br>Communicative?<br>Sensitive?<br>Enabling or empowering others?<br>Aware of emotional issues?<br>Responsive to team needs?<br>Rewarding and recognizing?<br><br>*©Ned Herrmann Group 2006* |

Fig. 11-11 Whole Brain Walk-Around Check List

# 12

# *How to Get There From Here*

## *Visions and Goals*

Today, it is common to find companies, countries, organizations and individuals all trying to craft a "vision statement" that describes an image of where they want to be and what they want to look like at a certain time in the future. A quick search on the Internet revealed 1,120,000 companies and organizations that have posted their Vision Statements.

The distinction between a goal and a vision is not clear to most people. People often use the terms "goal" "objective" and "vision" interchangeably. But they are profoundly different.

Many people were first exposed to the concept of a vision statement when, in May of 1961, President Kennedy described a vision in language he termed as a "goal." The now-famous quote is as follows.

> I believe that this nation should commit itself to achieving the goal, before this decade is out, of landing a man on the moon and returning him safely to the earth.

That year the National Aeronautics and Space Administration (NASA) officially published the following Vision Statement in a reworded form as Kennedy's "goal," but it was truly a vision.

A man on the moon
and return him safely
by the end of the decade.

## *Baking a Loaf of Bread*

Let us use an imaginary scenario to examine the difference in mental processes called upon to bring a goal and a vision to fruition.

Imagine that you are one of two people I invite to my office to participate in a challenge. One of you, for purposes of this example, prefers to use the left side of his brain, while the other prefers to use the right. (We're going to make the left-brainer a man and the right-brainer a woman, but choose to be whichever you want.)

Remember that the left side of the brain is involved in linear, sequential processing that involves logic, reasoning, analysis and planning. The right side is involved in simultaneously comprehending and processing various kinds of data, such as images and pattern recognition to name a few.

When you enter my office, you notice a white board displaying the following statement:

**A FRESHLY BAKED
LOAF OF BREAD**

I point at the statement and advise you that the first person who returns to my office with the freshly baked loaf of bread will receive $5,000. You both enthusiastically accept the challenge.

Imagine the mental activities that might take place as you and your competitor move into the challenge.

The internal dialogue in the left-brained person probably sounds something like this:

*Before I can create a step-by-step process to produce a freshly baked loaf of bread I will need to determine what ingredients are required, what ingredients I have on hand, and what ingredients I must buy. Second, I will need to purchase the missing ingredients. Third, I will need to follow the instructions in the recipe closely. Fourth, I will bake the bread. When I have done all of these things as quickly as possible, I'll have the freshly baked loaf of bread and win the money!*

The thought process described above is graphically shown in Fig 12-1.

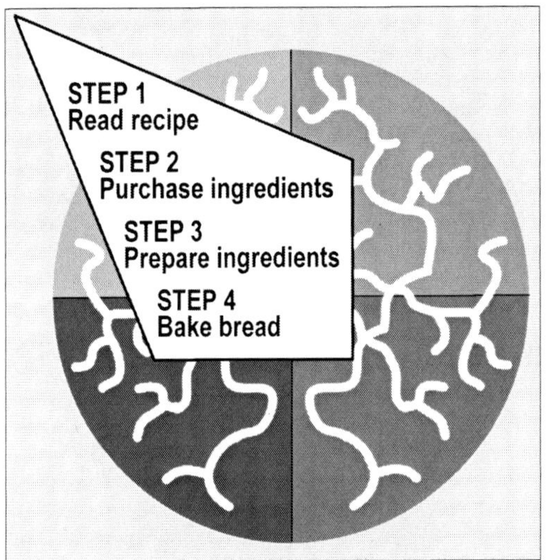


Fig. 12-1 Left Brain Plan To Win Contest

Now let us imagine the mental activity that might take place in the right-brained competitor's mind.

*I have a mental image of a freshly baked loaf of bread just out of the oven (a vision). The image is so real that the aroma of warm bread right out of the oven is there with the picture.*

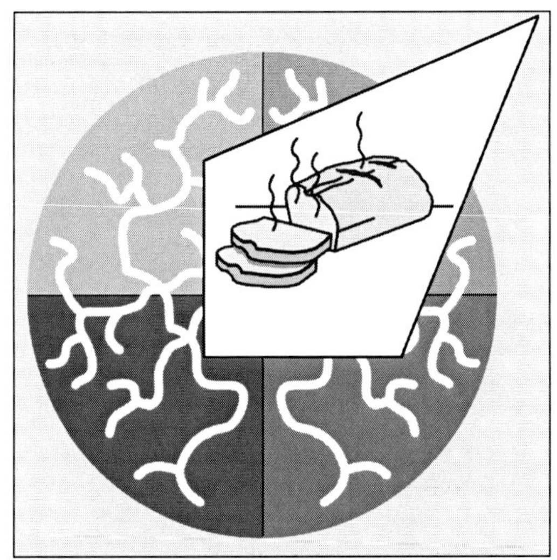

Fig. 12-2 Right Brain Vision to Win Contest

Fig. 12-2 conveys how the right brain is sensory — tied in this case to both vision and aroma. Fig. 12-3 shows the two competitors side by side, vying for the $5000.

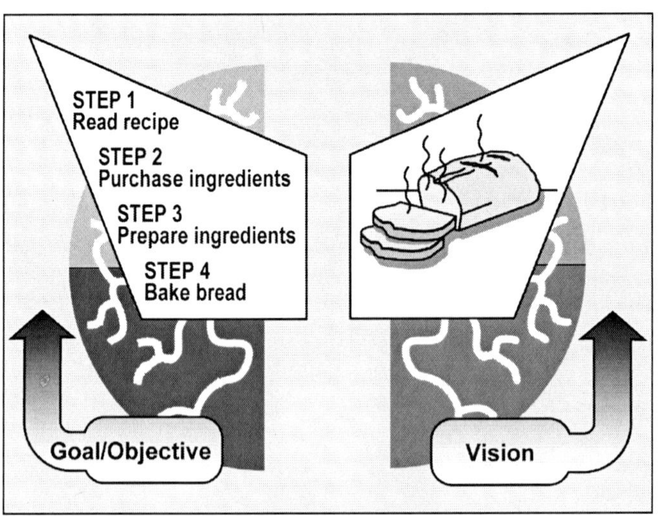


Fig. 12-3 Goal and Vision for Winning the Contest

Fig. 12-4 summarizes the neurological bases of a goal and a vision, depicting goals and objectives as left brain mental activities and vision as a right-brain mental activity. You can see that goals and vision together become a whole brain activity.

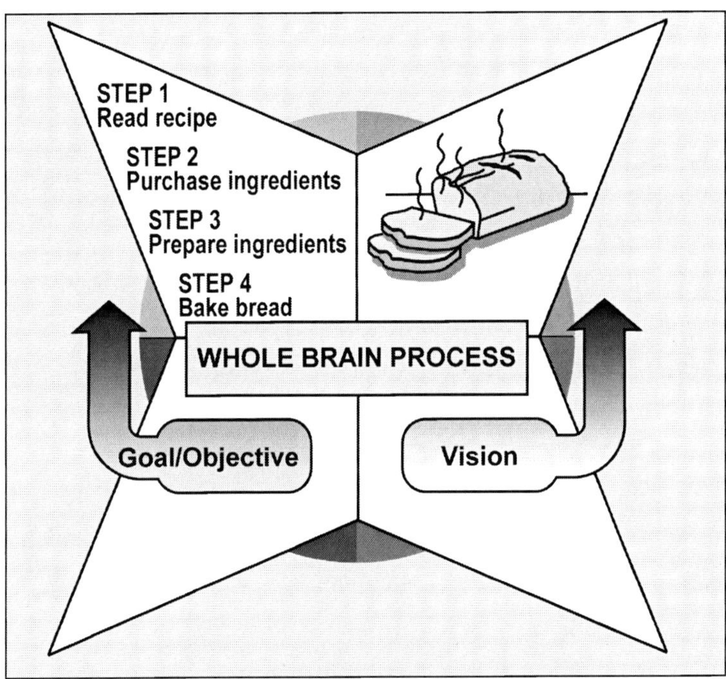


Fig. 12-4 Whole Brain Strategy

We will now go back to the scene where the left-brained, goal-seeking participant is figuring out how to get a quick, freshly baked loaf of bread. He has never baked bread in his life, so he calls his wife, tells her about the contest and gets a list of ingredients not on hand at home. As our left-brainer heads to the store, he reflects on how much he dislikes shopping. Motivated by the thought of the $5,000 prize, he begins to consider how he might speed up the entire four-step plan he has laid out in his mind. He knows that when he gets into the store, he does not want to waste any time looking at his list of missing ingredients, so he memorizes them by repeating the list: "milk, butter, salt, sugar and yeast," "milk, butter, salt, sugar and yeast," until he has them firmly in mind.

His keen analytical mind reflects next on the nature of the layout of almost all the food markets he has ever been in, with aisles disposed perpendicular to the front entrance of the store and the checkout stations. He also recalls that it is a common practice for food markets to locate signage listing commodities found in that aisle near the ceilings at the head of each aisle.

With the list of ingredients firmly in mind his task will be simple. He need only enter the store and fix his gaze on the signage most remote from where he is and then move visually in a sequential manner from sign to sign until he has matched in his mind which aisle has one or more of the needed ingredients.

Let us now revisit the scene where we left our right-brained contestant sitting thoughtfully. As she reflects on her mental image of a freshly baked loaf of bread she asks me, "May I look at the yellow pages of your telephone book?" When I ask, "Why?" she responds simply, "I am going to call some bakeries."

She calls several bakeries and discovers that all the bread they have for sale has been baked the night before. She asks me whether last night's baked bread meets the test of a freshly baked loaf of bread. I reply, "No."

After 20 minutes on the phone calling all the bakeries in town, it dawns on her that she will simply have to bake the bread herself. Off to the store she goes.

When I was creating this scenario in my mind, I was living in Rockford, Illinois, a community that had the most successful supermarket in the state of Illinois. It was known as the original Logli store on State Street. I had come to know a great deal about the operation of the store from my youngest daughter, Amy, who worked as a check-out clerk at Logli during summer vacations from college.

At an evening meal she asked: "Did you ever notice that on the back wall of the store there is a large sign that reads **BAKERY** in two foot high, block letters?" I had. She went on to say, "I was surprised to find that there is no bakery back behind the bakery counter and displays." She went on to inform us that the only baking equipment the store had was a large pizza oven which was turned on every day from 6:00 a.m. to 12:00 midnight. The only baking done in the oven, she told us, involved about a half dozen loaves of bread baked every hour or so.

On my next visit to the store, I checked it out more carefully. As I passed the Bakery sign directly above the oven, I became aware of a large vent hood with a fan that sucked up the heated air and the aroma of the baking bread and exhausted it into a duct that traveled above the ceiling tiles to the front of the store. There the air was directed down on customers as they entered the store, literally enveloping them in the warm aroma.

This was only one of the store's clever marketing strategies. Another was the position of the bakery, down stream of the traffic flow past the deli counters. I noticed that there always seemed to be a half dozen or more warm loaves of bread in paper bags easily reachable by customers passing through the delicious-smelling baking area. I asked Amy about the warm bread that was always on display. She advised me that this was brought about by moving cold loaves of bread from the bakery area to the front of the store and replacing them in the back with freshly baked loaves of bread every hour.

Keeping this description of Logli's in mind, let us now rejoin our left-brained contestant as he enters the store. In accordance with his action plan, the instant he enters the store, his gaze locks on the most remote ceiling sign listing items stocked in that aisle. As his mind and gaze fix on the sign, he is enveloped in the aroma of the freshly baked bread. Do you think he smells it? Most likely not.

Remember the lesson of the young woman/old woman image which provided us with the insight that we can only consciously process a single thought at a time. Our left-brained contestant is so focused on his needed ingredients as he speeds through the store, there is no chance he will smell anything! He completes the task and dashes out to his car heading home to bake his loaf of bread.

Our right-brained contestant is dismayed to see the left-brainer driving out of Logli's parking lot as she pulls in. She notes in passing that his car is piled with shopping bags, probably containing all he needs to finish the task of baking the bread and claim the $5,000 prize. But all is not lost, she thinks, because he may live a long distance away from the store and this may allow her to make up some of the time she lost searching for bread on the phone.

Unbeknownst to her, she is about to discover an attribute of the neural circuit wiring present in all human brains that will allow her to act in a highly advantageous manner.

Let me now refresh your recollections regarding the role and function of the reticular activating system, or RAS. (Chapter 8) The RAS is located in the brain stem and acts as a filter, allowing information of value to pass at any instant through the brain's limbic region to the cerebral cortex where it can be consciously acted upon. Remember that prior to birth there is a massive set of neurons in the RAS that have sprouted nerve fibers that have driven their way through the brain and into the right cerebral cortex. Neurons in the cerebral cortex have also sent nerve fibers to the RAS. So the connection is strong! It appears that when our minds hold a mental image in the right cerebral cortex, the neural circuits electrically influence the RAS to select information directly related to that mental image, as shown in Fig. 12-5. When our right-brained contestant enters the store and is enveloped by the aroma of the baking bread, do you think she smells it? You bet she does! And she literally follows her nose to the bakery section, grabs a freshly baked loaf of bread, pays for it, proceeds to my office and claims the $5,000 prize.

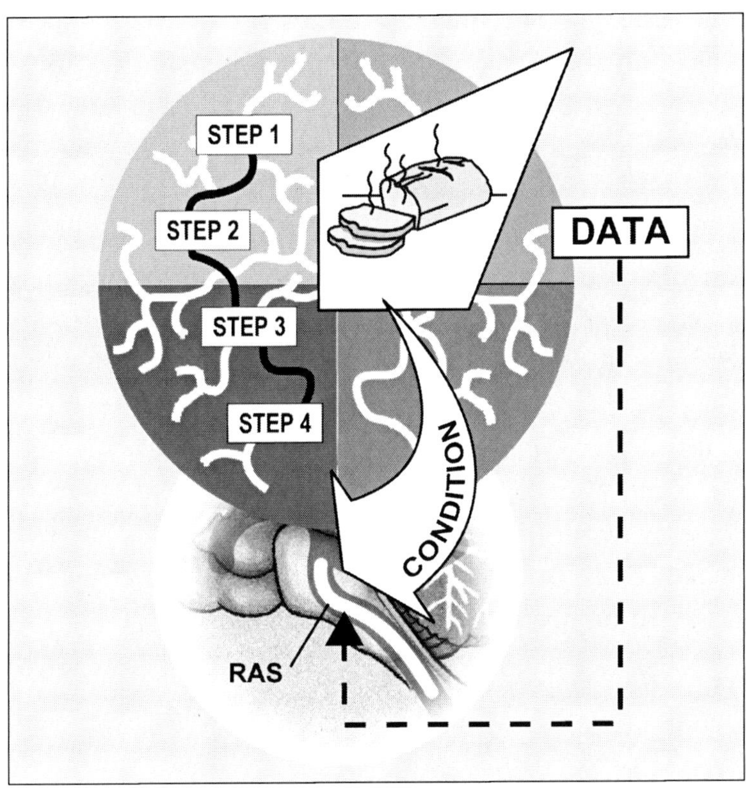


Fig. 12-5 Conditioning the RAS

Our left-brained contestant is feeling confident that he has the lead in the contest, because he noticed his competitor arriving just as he was leaving Logli's parking lot. Living only a block from the store, within minutes he is studying the recipe, preheating the oven, making the bread dough, and putting the dough in the oven to bake. All the while this is happening his wife is much taken with the speed at which he moves through each step. She consults the *Guinness Book of Records* and is delighted to report to him that he is about to break a world record for the fastest baking of a loaf of bread. He heads off to my office with the freshly baked loaf of bread under one arm and the *Guinness Book of Records* under the other.

When he gets to my office and discovers that the $5,000 prize has been picked up long before, he is stunned. He wonders to himself, "How can you break a world's record and lose?"

In the early 90's I was conducting the Pathways program for a small group of senior executives. Among this group sat a vice president who appeared to be quite agitated as I described the actions of the man and woman involved in the hypothetical contest. She interrupted me and said, "Just one second, Mr. Williamson. That right-brained person cheated!" "In what way?" I asked. "She was supposed to *bake* the loaf of bread." I asked her where she got that idea. All I asked for was "a freshly baked loaf of bread." I never did persuade her that there was no cheating involved.

## *The Power of Pictures*

On several occasions when presenting this material, I have had seminar participants suggest to me the reason that Asian people, especially those from China and Japan, are highly effective competitors is that they are mostly left-brain thinkers. I have no awareness whatsoever of the thinking style preferences of Asian people. I do, however, believe that they may inherently have an advantage derived from the very nature of their languages. What does their written language look like? Ideograms or pictures. This may provide a clue as to why many Asians are such able competitors. Think about it. The written languages of these people are made up of images that are processed by the right side of the brain. Repeated reference to images of that which they wish to accomplish strongly conditions the RAS to pick up information of value as they move through the world.

## *Whole Brain Teams*

I would submit that our Asian contemporaries have no inherent neurobiological competitive edge. A whole-brained team of men and women, that is, a team with strength in every quadrant is the most powerful team there is, regardless of culture. We lead workshops teaching the concepts of Whole Brain Technology, where all participants have completed the HBDI™ and we have their scores. In these workshops, we often have participants do an activity in small teams. We intentionally design the teams by thinking style preference. So, for example, when it is a big group, we have "A" teams, with people with a strong preference in the "A" quadrant, B" teams, "C" teams, and "D" teams. When the group is smaller, we have primarily left brain and primarily right brain teams. In both cases, we also structure a team or two which is clearly whole brain, including people with varying thinking style preferences, representing natural strength in all four quadrants. Each team is given one large nail pounded into a block of wood and eleven more big nails they are asked to balance on the head of the one nail. In the many years we've done this, with only one exception, the whole brain teams have solved the puzzle first. It is fascinating to watch them work. The right and left brain teams often get stuck on one idea, whereas the whole brain teams try many different approaches. It is common to hear a whole brain team jump from physics to out-of-the box creativity and back again, while coming to the solution. A whole brain team is spontaneously pulled by a vision and pushed by goals and objectives.

> A whole-brain team is more than a match for any competition.

## *Goals and Visions — the Real Distinction*

In the early 90's as a senior executive of Sundstrand Aerospace I was privileged to be invited to the company's annual New Year's management function, where Harry, the CEO you met in Chapters 6 and 9, detailed the accomplishments of the past year and offered strategies for the future. The evening program opened with the CEO getting the attention of the executive leadership team, which numbered about one hundred. "I want to share with you my Vision for this company: We are going to double sales, increase the global content of sales by 50% and we will do it in five years."

A month later I was with Harry in the company's boardroom, introducing him to the Pathways curriculum. At the time Harry had presented his vision to his staff, I observed something in the audience reaction to his statement that piqued my curiosity. I asked Harry if he remembered what happened moments after he shared the vision. He said, "No, should I?" I said, "Yes, you should, because of the first question that came from the floor." I asked him if he remembered it and he said, "Frankly, no." I followed with the comment, "You never answered the question. In fact you beat around the bush and never directly answered the question." This charge by me that he was not responsive and possibly evasive in his response did not go over well. In fact, he responded, somewhat indignantly, that he thought my recollection of that evening was clearly off the mark.

Let me ask you, the reader, for your educated guess as to what the question was that came from the floor. Before you respond you should know that 90% of the executives were engineers or scientists.

In Fig. 12-6, the four quadrant model is shown with the statement "Current Reality," which represents the state of mind of the engineers and scientists as they heard the CEO's "Vision."

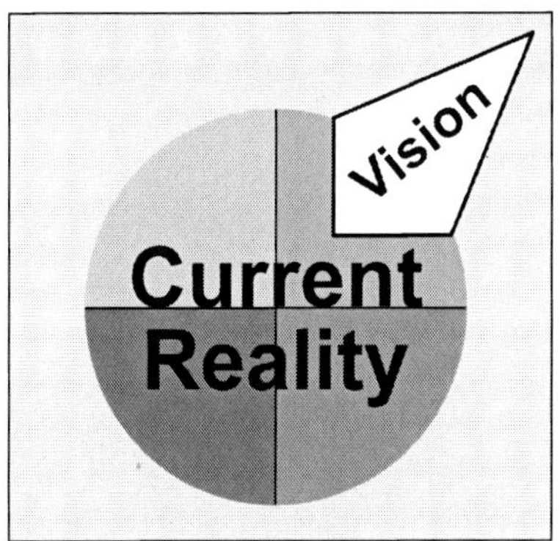


Fig. 12-6 Current Reality/Vision

Fig. 12-7 shows the question that came from the floor, which Harry did not answer.

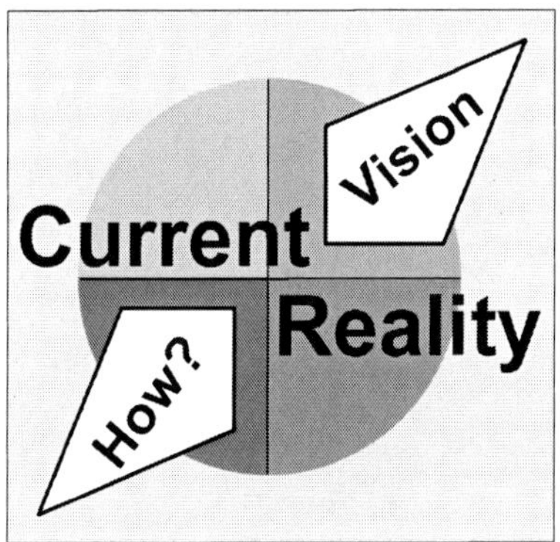


Fig. 12-7 How?

When I shared the "How" question with Harry, I asked, "Isn't it true that you don't know how?" He did not respond immediately. In that instant I knew that what he had shared with us was truly a vision. One of the most powerful qualities of a vision is that you don't know how to realize it. It is something desired. It is a stretch.

> What is a vision but a description of something desired in the future, when you don't know how to get there? A goal, by contrast, is a desired outcome, where you can devise a plan that you can implement to attain the goal.

Harry turned to me with a puzzled look on his face and said, "I said it was a vision. Are you suggesting that most of the people in the room thought I was talking about a goal or objective?" I asked him to reflect upon the probable thinking styles of his engineering and scientist management team, most of whom were undoubtedly left-brain thinkers. He appeared dismayed by the possibility that few of the management team appreciated that he was proposing a powerful vision to pull the company into the future.

Another story from the same company will illustrate the power of vision. I had become intimately familiar with the company's technology and I discovered there, in the engineering staff, the most incredible collection of creative men and women that I have ever seen in my life. I remember sharing the following thought with the other patent attorneys I worked with in the early1980's.

> You don't realize what we have in this building. So much creativity! If only half of the disclosed ideas were patented, this company would rank in the top 20 U.S. companies, in terms of patents issued each year.

How they laughed at me, because they knew we ranked 877th with respect to patents issued each year.

In 1984 I made that same comment again. "You don't realize what we have here." When they laughed, I walked away, went into my office and shut the door. By then I knew what I know now. I had a vision. I took out a large piece of cardboard and I wrote at the top "My Vision for Sundstrand: In the Top Twenty Companies in the U.S." And underneath it I wrote the date, December 31, 1991. I made the cardboard sign in 1984, and I listed the probable top twenty U.S. companies and who was number 20? The Sundstrand Corporation.

Shortly after the Christmas shutdown in 1991 I called Washington D.C. and spoke to an old friend who still worked in the Patent Office. I asked if she could find out how we ranked in the matter of patents issued for 1991. Do you know what she told me? She said, "Hal, I am pleased to tell you that Sundstrand just moved into the top twenty U.S. companies." I told her the number I put on the vision chart back in 1984. She said "Well, you beat it by three patents."

In my work with management teams and individuals in the years since my experience with Harry, I have found only a handful of people who grasp the conceptual (and physiological) distinction between a goal and a vision.

We will continue to explore visions and goals and their role and function in the system dynamics of the human mind in the next chapter. Applied to an individual, these concepts are key to understanding and developing "personal mastery", one of the five primary disciplines described by Peter Senge in *The Fifth Discipline.*

# 13
# *Systems, Goals and Visions*

This chapter explains the nature of systems that fashion our current reality. When our world is viewed as a system, a sound scientific basis arises for understanding why goals and visions are equally powerful. Yet very different mental tools are used to accomplish our goals and to realize our visions.

## *Systems*

For purposes of this book, a system will be defined as a set of at least two interacting elements that function as a complex whole. An example is a wind-up clock, a mechanical system where all the elements of the system interact with each other in some way. When we speak about interacting elements we are not necessarily limiting the nature of interaction to that which is physical. The solar system, with planets orbiting the sun, is a system. The interaction between the sun and a planet is defined by the gravitational pull between the sun and that planet, as well as gravitational forces of other planets on each other.

A key characteristic of a system resides in the inherent tendency of a system to reach a condition of balance between opposing forces, influences or actions. We describe this balance as a state of equilibrium. In other words, if we leave a system alone in an environment that does not change, in time the system will reach a state of equilibrium.

### *Getting a System to Work*

In order to get work out of a system you must unbalance the system. In the clock example the spring is manually tightened, storing mechanical energy in the spring. This stored energy is released slowly via the interconnected parts of the clock. The hands on the clock face are connected with the inner workings to provide a visual representation of the passage of time, as the system moves back to equilibrium.

Humans are living systems and differ from non-living systems in that we maintain ourselves at a resting state we term homeostasis. The nervous system alone cannot bring about the state of homeostasis (see Chapter 10). The nervous system must work in concert with the endocrine system. Briefly stated, the endocrine system is the chemical coordinating system. The endocrine glands produce hormones. Some of these glands are located in the cranial cavity, such as the hypothalamus, pineal and pituitary glands. Others are located in the body, such as the thyroid, parathyroid, thymus, adrenal glands, pancreas, ovaries in women and testes in men. All of these glands release hormones into the blood stream or lymphatic system. The endocrine glands release hormones that induce emotional states (fear and flight) as well as sexual functions and a host of other bodily functions and mental states. The nervous system coordinates many functions of the body by means of electrochemical signals.

Homeostasis involves the maintenance of normal, internal stability or balance in an organism through the coordinated response of the endocrine and nervous systems that automatically compensate for environmental changes. In other words homeostasis can be thought of as a steady-state condition.

The primary residence of the human mind is in the brain in the cranium. The nerve fiber connections provided by our nervous system interconnect the networks of the brains in our gut and heart to the brain in our head, establishing a complex whole that provides mental processes we describe as the mental activity of our mind. (See Chapter 2). This mind controls the entire living organism or system.

Now let's go back to where we started. In order to get work out of the human system, the system must be unbalanced. One way to unbalance the human system is for the mind to set a mental goal or objective to be accomplished. However, the mental activity of setting a goal or objective is little more than a wish, until the person setting the goal notes the gap between their current reality and the goal. When the mind perceives such a discrepancy, a tension in the system results. If the mind focuses intently on the goal, then the individual, who is positioned in current reality, will move toward the goal. When the goal is reached, the tension is reduced to zero and there is a return of balance in the system. It follows that if mental interest in the goal is weak and the mind focuses mental activity on current reality, the tension between the two will pull the system back toward current reality and the original goal will never be attained.

It should be kept in mind that equilibrium is attained not only when current reality is brought to the attainment of the goal but also when the goal is pulled back, unaccomplished, to the original current reality.

The mental tension that pulls toward the attainment of the goal is greatest when the goal is initially set. It is like the tension in a rubber band. The tension is the greatest when the band is stretched, but decreases to zero as the rubber band is allowed to return to its normal, unexpanded state of equilibrium.

### *Try It*

I want you to have a simple experience of unbalancing a system by mentally setting goals and then sensing the mind/body responding as a system.

To this end I invite you to locate a rubber band of a size that feels secure, not loose, around both hands, when one hand is placed on top of the other as shown below.

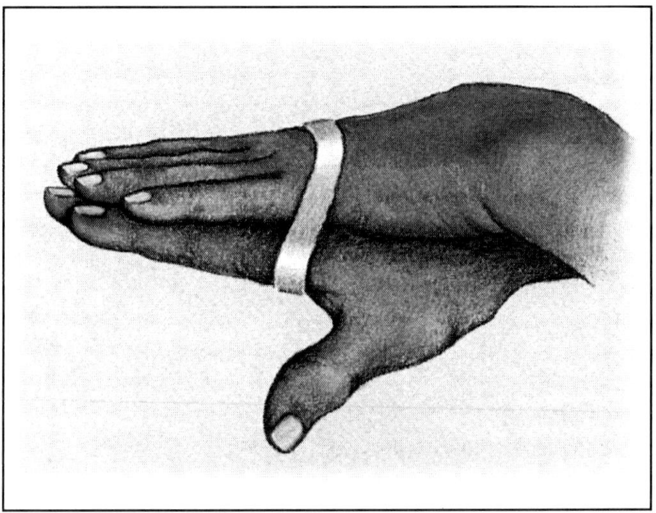

Fig. 13-1 System at Rest

With your hands and the rubber band positioned as shown, you have introduced a new structural component into the mind/body system. How do you know that the rubber band is now part of your system? Simply perform the following physical action. With the lower hand resting on a surface, call upon your mind to command the upper hand to move up away from the lower hand, which you hold steady. Think of the lower hand as representing current reality. As your upper hand begins to move, you will sense increasing tension created by the rubber band as it is stretched. This is the experience of physical tension in the mind/body system I wanted you to experience.

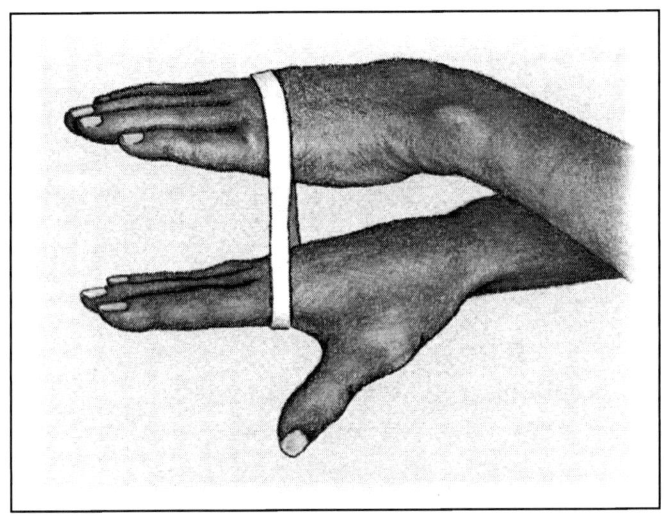

Fig. 13-2 System in Tension

Imagine next that you set a goal represented by moving the upper hand up and away about six inches from current reality where the lower hand is positioned. As you move the upper hand towards the goal of six inches, what do you notice about the tension? Is it increasing as you move towards the goal? When you reach the goal of six inches, does the tension in your mind/body system that now includes the rubber band disappear or stay constant? Even if you do not actually employ a rubber band and you treat these instructions as a thought experiment, you will probably answer the last question, "The tension remains constant in the mind/body system as long as my upper hand remains at the goal height of six inches above the lower hand state of current reality."

If I ask you to hold your hands apart for the next four hours, what do you think will happen to the position of the upper hand? Most people respond by saying that the upper hand will tire and return to where it started. Or, if they use lots of words like I do, they might say that the mental/physical effort to keep the upper hand at the goal height would begin to weaken and the upper hand would be pulled down toward the lower hand, as tension in the rubber band overcame the strength of the mental/physical instruction to keep the upper hand at the goal height of six inches.

The return of the upper hand to its original, current reality state, resting on the lower hand, comes as no surprise in this experiment. What may be overlooked is the inherent nature of a system-over-time to return to a state of balance, a state of rest.

In the just described experiment the mental/physical effort to maintain the desired goal of six inches up was not strong enough to overcome the inertia of current reality, represented by the lower hand. Had the strength of the mental/physical effort been strong enough, what would have happened to the lower hand, given the inherent nature of a system's need to reach a state of equilibrium?

If the effort to maintain the goal is stronger than the inertia of current reality, then the system tension in the rubber band will resolve itself by causing the lower hand to move up towards the upper hand or the goal level of six inches. When both hands are at the goal level, we have reached a new state of equilibrium. We have also achieved the original goal and established a new current reality.

It is also possible that progress toward the goal may diminish over time, as the importance of the goal decreases or the effort to continue overwhelms. In this case equilibrium may be established in some new place, short of the original goal. The question is, "which is stronger, the pull-back of current reality or the pull-forward of the goal?"

Let us now go back to the lower hand, representing current reality, which is being drawn by tension in the rubber band towards the goal. As the lower hand approaches the upper hand, what happens to the intensity of the tension in the rubber band? Is it the same as when the hands were six inches apart? The obvious answer is that the tension pulling one from current reality to the goal continuously diminishes as the attainment of the goal approaches.

There is another important lesson to be learned here. No matter what goals we set in life, as we move toward their attainment, our drive and energy diminishes. Evidence of this system reality is present in the lives of individuals who have set a goal to lose weight, for example ten pounds by the end of the month. Many dieters find that the first few pounds come off easily, followed by an automatic adjustment of their basic system metabolism to maintain their weight given a reduced caloric intake. People frequently find themselves a few pounds short of the goal weight for what seems to be forever. When this happens dieters often reduce the mental effort to attain the goal weight and settle for a current reality that is a few pounds short of their goal. The new equilibrium has been established at a midpoint between the original current reality and the original goal.

### *Implications for Successful Planning*

Almost all anyone wants out of life can be attained by conscious planning. This planning needs to include the development of a series of doable steps that will take us from where we are to where we want to be. One of the most frequent stumbling blocks to attaining life's goals arises during the execution of the plan, when an individual decides to fully accomplish each step of the plan before launching into the next step. This approach may prove useful if you simply want to gather ingredients you need for an evening meal. Living life, however, is far more complex. More often than not, any given step in the plan calls for a multiplicity of coordinated individual activities that fuel the accomplishment of the next step in the plan. The entire effort may lose momentum if the planner insists on completing each step before going on to the next. (This is a distinct danger for left-brain thinkers who are most comfortable when their activities are linear and sequential.)

Remember that systems nearing a state of equilibrium experience a diminution of the energy that exists because the gap between current reality and the goal is narrowing. Highly successful people recognize this phenomenon and have figured out a way to sustain momentum. As they approach the accomplishment of a goal, they switch their mental focus to the next step of the plan. By doing so, they experience an energy boost to complete the preceding step of the plan. In the weight loss example given earlier, as attainment of the goal weight is approached, the simple mental step of increasing the original weight loss goal by five pounds may increase the tension in the system to pull one to the initial weight goal. (Of course, as my dietitian friend reminds me, this works only if the weight loss goal is reasonable.)

## *Goals or Visions?*

I have frequently been asked which is the more powerful approach to get what we want out of life, setting goals or creating visions? Is success best accomplished by having clearly defined goals and objectives that lend themselves to cause and effect, action-oriented planning or is it best accomplished by creating a detailed, time-specific vision of what the world will look like to you once your vision is a reality? There is no simple answer, as the next few paragraphs will show.

The primary purpose of having a goal, a vision, or both resides in the fact that no mental or physical activity will be initiated unless there is some tension in the system. The *Fifth Discipline Field Book*[13] notes that "The central practice of personal mastery involves learning to keep both a personal vision and a clear picture of current reality before us."

The power of holding a time-specific vision comes from the fact that holding a mental image in the right side of the brain strongly conditions the RAS to pick up incoming information of value passing through the brain stem on its way to the cerebral cortex to be recorded and acted upon. In other words, a vision points you mentally toward a future destination, all the while conditioning the RAS to pick up information that will help you attain the vision.

The power of a goal, which involves left brain mental activity, is in the mental push it gives the goal setter to move through the steps of the plan toward the goal. The inherent power of goal setting resides in the action that flows as a result of the tension experienced in the human system as each step of a plan is executed and the presence of a next step pushes the goal setter forward.

### *Goals May Not Lead To the Desired Result*

People love setting goals and then filling their lives with activities they think (consciously and subconsciously) will get them the results they want. The downside of goal setting is that people often discover, after the plans are executed and the goal attained, it doesn't give them all they had hoped for. A woman may decide that what her family needs in order to be happy is a bigger house. So she sets a goal of buying a three bedroom, two bath home in a nice neighborhood, within two years. She plans all the necessary steps, finding the neighborhood, saving the money, talking with realtors, going to Sunday open houses. Finally the perfect home is found, finances are arranged and the family moves in. However, if there are tensions in the relationships or other problems, the home may not make the family any happier than it was before.

## Vision Sets Direction

The power of vision is that by its very nature it provides a direction to the mental activity of goal setting. This direction may be thought of as a vector. Let's look to the world of sailing for a metaphor. In sailing there is a point or destination on the horizon that the sailor is trying to reach. The sailor sets the sails and the rudder to take the sailboat towards the destination. A sailboat cannot sail straight to the destination, unless the wind is directly at its stern. Instead it must make a series of tacking maneuvers, changing directions repeatedly in response to the wind across a line of sight from the sailboat to the destination. Think of each tacking maneuver as representing a fresh set of intermediate steps to reach the destination. In this metaphor the sailor who visually focuses on his destination (vision) automatically conditions his RAS to pick up visual cues of changing wind and weather patterns that may affect his tacking and sailing strategy. He is quite literally being pulled toward his vision. Those who are considered gifted sailors have conditioned the RAS and practiced repeatedly, so that they pick up changes in the water surface imperceptible to the rest of us. They are also consistent winners in competition.

## Integrating Visions and Goals

Goals will always get you somewhere. However, when you arrive there, it might not be where you really need to be to achieve your deepest desires.

Visions that are not time specific are not much more than wishful thinking. Visions that are time specific create a sense of urgency. That urgency dissipates, however, without an accompanying goal-setting action plan.

Here's the question we started with, Which is more powerful, goals or visions? The answer is: We need both.

Visions are pull structures. Goals are push structures.

Visions and goals working together engage your whole brain to optimize the attainment of what you want in life.

# 14

# *Systems Resist Change*

Our minds have been defined as the consciousness that originates in the brain and directs mental and physical behavior. "Consciousness" is defined as mental awareness of one's own existence and environment. Humans are living systems controlled in large part by the mind that is resident in the brain.

## *System Control — Autopilot*

I cannot count the times I have heard individuals announce New Years resolutions by which they intend to change their behavior. They announce them with great certainty. To their own surprise, no matter how determined or resolute their initial intention to change, they often fail. Why this happens is readily explainable by examining the basic nature of system control.

Let us first examine an electromechanical system under the control of a human. Think of the device we call an automatic pilot (autopilot), that is part of conventional aircraft flight control equipment. Now this is not exactly the way autopilot works, but for the sake of this metaphor let's agree that the role and function of the autopilot is to keep the plane level and on a predetermined heading automatically.

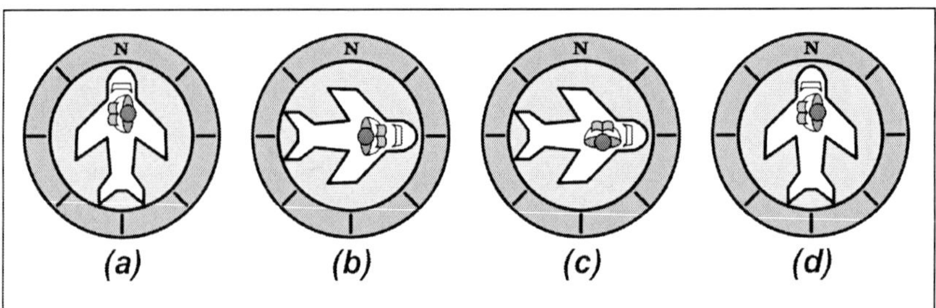


Fig. 14-1 Airplanes

In Fig. 14-1(a) the airplane is heading due north. In the nose of the aircraft there is an autopilot device. The autopilot has been electronically set to maintain the airplane's due north heading with no aid from the pilot. Positioned just below and behind the autopilot is the human pilot of the aircraft. The schematic representation of the pilot is intended to convey that the pilot has turned in his seat so that the steering column of the plane is adjacent to his right shoulder. In his lap is a set of navigational maps he is studying, while the autopilot flies the plane for him. The airport where he plans to land is due north of the current position of his plane, as shown and just described.

As the plane continues in a northerly direction, the pilot receives a radio message from the tower of the airport he is headed toward. The message advises him that a line of thunderstorms has suddenly materialized and he is instructed to turn the plane sharply to his right, that is, due east and to hold that heading until further notice, in order to avoid the storm. In response the pilot turns in his seat and grasps the steering column with both hands, turning the plane so it now is heading due east, as is shown in Fig. 14-1(b). Once the plane has been turned to a due east heading, he again releases the steering column and turns in his seat to study his maps as shown in Fig. 14-1(c).

Assume next that all he has done to control the direction of the airplane is to override the autopilot by physically gripping the steering column and turning it so that it is heading due east. Once you override a modern autopilot, it's like cruise control. You have to re-engage it to get it to work. But for the sake of this metaphor, assume that once the pilot settles back to study his maps as depicted in Fig. 14-1(c) the plane goes back to its pre-set northerly heading, as shown in Fig. 14-1(d) in the illustration.

Think now of the wiring of your own brain. You can't even feel all those neural circuits which, over your lifetime, have become embedded with all of the behaviors that allow you to engage the world in a free-flowing manner, without any conscious mental effort on your part. These neural circuits are your autopilot.

For many years I drove to work on the same route every day. My office was in the suburbs, just off a parkway that went on through to the center of the city. I was promoted and my new office was in the center of the city. In the years that followed, there were a number of occasions when I found myself in my car, parked in my old parking space at my earlier job site. I had been driving to work, deep in thought, on autopilot. It was always slightly embarrassing to find myself backing out of my old parking space and waving at the company security guards as I exited the property only moments after having arrived and parked.

Knowing what we know about neural circuits and the behaviors they produce, we find it easy to explain my unintentional trip to my old place of work. At any given time, there are lots of neural circuits that were used in a previous stage of our lives but are not called upon in our present lives. Thankfully many new neural circuits have been laid allowing new behaviors in our lives and because of their repeated use, they dominate our inward thoughts and outward behaviors. We've reset our autopilot.

## *How We Resist Change*

By now you would probably agree that mind is a system resident in a brain which has a generally spherical shape. Imagine a sponge rubber ball about the size of a human brain. The sponge rubber ball is a system of interconnected resilient matter that exhibits classic system behavior when acted upon by external forces. In a system sense, the ball is like the human mind. Imagine that you place the ball between the heels of your hands with the fingers of both hands interlocked. Squeeze the ball between the heels of your hands. As you squeeze, what do you notice about the pressure of the ball on the heels of your hands? The harder you push on the ball, the harder the ball system pushes back. When you place the ball between your hands, the sponge rubber ball is in a state of rest. There are no unbalanced forces in it. Pressure on the ball by the heels of your hands unbalances the resilient internal structure of the ball, creating system forces that you sense in your hands as a push-back force. The harder you push on the ball the harder the ball pushes back.

Do you think you could hold the ball in its compressed condition, squeezing it with your palms, for a few hours? Probably not. The ball wants to get back to its original position and so do your hands. If you leave an unbalanced system long enough, it will return to a state of equilibrium or rest.

> The simple take-away lesson from this experiment is the following: Whenever you push on thought, thought pushes back.

What evidence is there that thought is pushing back? Whenever we are pushed mentally, the natural human response is to feel anxious. This is evidence of the mental push-back. You will recall that the presence of cognitive dissonance and its associated mental discomfort was best described as a feeling of upset or anger.

Psychologists tell us that when we are pushed, we mentally resist by pushing back with behaviors that keep the mental pressure in balance, subconsciously hoping that the party or parties applying the pressure will relax their efforts and allow us to return to long-established patterns of behavior. (Ironically this is true even when the push is internally generated. We want to change, but oh, how much more comfortable it is not to change.)

People in situations where there is an unrelenting mental pressure to change tend to respond subconsciously by slowing down. We see this in union movements when management pushes the workers to perform at levels and ways the workers consider unfair. Workers typically fall into patterns of behavior that strictly follow agreed-upon work rules. This activity is described by management as a work slow-down.

In manufacturing facilities where management pressure to perform is excessive, it is common to find mentally distracted workers, which results in manufacturing errors, scrap and the need for rework. Management points to the scrap and the rework as evidence that the employees are involved in active sabotage of the manufacturing process. In the same way that it is difficult to determine which child started a fight, it is difficult to determine the cause of a work slow-down or a defective work product. The cause may seem to be workers, but may actually have its origin in actions of management.

In your own family life you may experience this type of slow down when you demand that your children "Hurry up." If you don't have children, ask some member of the family to go shopping with you and when they agree to go, announce that you are going to the car. The instant you get in the car, begin to lean on the horn. The response of many family members will be to slow their pace of movement towards the car. Others may hurry, but be so annoyed by the blowing horn that they will blame you for anything they've forgotten or that goes wrong in the next few hours.

All human systems, because they are systems, inherently seek equilibrium and shake off external pressures whether those pressures are mental or physical. When this urge to return to equilibrium is recognized as a normal function of the mind, it becomes easy to understand why any change, whether perceived to be good or bad, produces feelings of anxiety.

This normal resistance to change, which is part of the human system, explains why it is so difficult to get individuals, let alone large numbers of people in teams and organizations, to change. It was recognition of this fact that led Sharon to become a personal and executive coach. She noted that participants were often energized by a training program, but usually went right back to doing things in their old, habitual ways. Regular coaching sessions over several months drive the development of new neural circuits and help people integrate new ways of thinking and behaving into their lives.

## *The Subconscious System*

This section further elaborates on the powerful notion of the subconscious mind begun in Chapters 2 and 5. The section on neural circuit development explained that as we go through life, we establish neural networks that record all of our sensory experiences. I find it helpful to think of this mass of neural circuits as our "subconscious system" in which all of our experiences and our thoughts about our experiences are stored in an interconnected manner. These include our attitudes, assumptions, beliefs, stories we tell ourselves, etc. It is this subconscious system that defines the state of current reality for each of us.

We are not consciously aware of current reality until we run into something that doesn't match our expectations. As long as our experience matches the contents stored in our subconscious system, we don't notice our surroundings. In other words, our external environment matches the reality that is recorded in our subconscious mind system. For many individuals this match appears to others as a state of contentment. Individuals who have all their health and survival needs met may be quite contented even though they live in circumstances others may view as unacceptable. When we realize the reality of this last statement, it is not hard to appreciate the truth in the statement, "Be it ever so humble, there's no place like home."

The subconscious system of each individual is unique. This can cause problems even in intimate relationships — when you assume your partner needs the same set of circumstances you do to feel contented. What is stored in his or her mind about the requirements for contentment may not match those stored in your mind!

Any outside stimulus that opposes the equilibrium state of the mind's subconscious system will cause the mind to push back and resist it. The resistance is experienced as a state of internal discomfort.

## *The Future Subconscious System*

Within the human mind/brain/body system we have a huge set of neural circuits that have captured our accumulated thoughts about the future. These include our goals, visions, plans and the way we want or expect our future world to be. These goals, visions, plans and the state of our future world are by-products of our imagination.

Imagination is defined as the process or power of forming a mental image of something not real or present. I like to think of the neural network containing our thoughts about the future as the mind's "future subconscious system."

In a systems sense we can illustrate the subconscious system and the future subconscious system embedded in the context of the mind/brain/body system, as in Fig. 14-2. The arrows represent the interconnected systems.

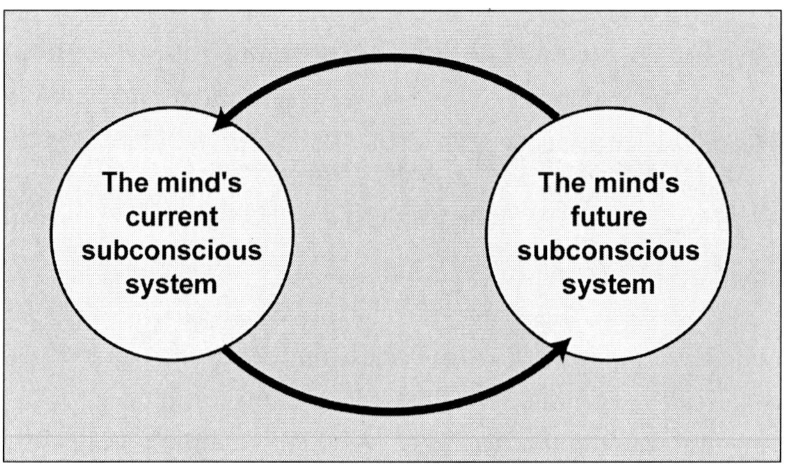


Fig. 14-2 Mind's subconscious systems

## *Now*

Fig. 14-3 represents past (contained in current reality), present and future system states. Until recently I have explained my understanding of how the mind works with a simple model that included one neural circuit system accounting for past experiences and thoughts and another neural circuit system that embraced plans, goals, and visions of an imagined future (Fig. 14-2). My study of Eckhart Tolle's book *The Power of Now* has prompted me to modify my model to include a mental state I have labeled as "NOW" (Fig. 14-3).

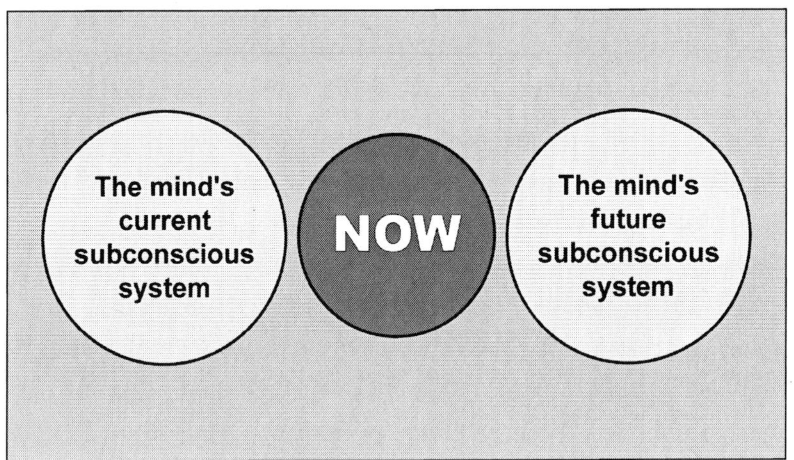


Fig. 14-3 Three States of Mind

Whenever we can disconnect from the current subconscious system, which finds its roots in the past, and the future subconscious system which finds it roots in our imagination, we will find ourselves in the bliss state of "being" Tolle describes as the NOW.

Eckhart Tolle did not discover the mental state he calls the NOW. Ever since the dawn of time, philosophers, gurus, prophets, sages, shamans, and theologians have identified a state of "no mind" as a desirable mental state. When one is in the NOW state there is a mental disconnect between the past and the future. There is no past or future. There is only present.

It is interesting to note that we have only one word in the English language for time, while the Greeks have two. *Kronos* is time as we usually talk about it, measured time passing, past and future. The second, *kairos*, is very different. It is participation in time, time that so engrosses us that we lose track of it, timeless time, moments when the clock stands still, nourishing, renewing, creative time, the time Tolle calls NOW.

## *The Dynamics of Change*

We have said that thoughts our mind creates that are inconsistent with our experiences, habits, attitudes and beliefs are consciously experienced as mental pressure by the subconscious. The subconscious system pushes back in an effort to maintain system equilibrium. This response from the subconscious arises without regard to whether we really want to change, we tell ourselves we *have* to change, or some source of pressure outside us demands that we change. Both inside mental demands and external demands for change evoke the same feelings of anxiety and an attendant equilibrium-seeking system push-back against the perceived demands for change.

When we decide to change, it is normal to experience both positive and negative emotions, and I hope that this discussion has given you the reasons that is true. Many of us would like to change but we dont get around to it in the push of life and all the things we "have to do."

Truth be told, we don't "have to" do anything during our life on this planet. We don't have to eat, sleep, drink, get an education, get married, have children, or pay taxes to name a few. The only thing that is certain is that we have to die. Even as you are reading these words I can sense your mental muttering, "What do you mean I don't have to eat, sleep, etc?" It is vital that you accept the reality that you don't have to do anything. There are, however, consequences for the actions or inactions you choose.

## *You Choose Your World with Your Attitude*

You may live in the world of past memories and cling to the impossible wish to recreate the good old days. You may live in a nether world where the mantra of current reality is "ain't it awful" and that of future reality is "the world is going to hell in a handbag."

The good news is you have more freedom than most people reconize. You have a choice to frame each decision you make and each action you take as either "have to" or "want to."

Imagine how vital your life will be when you begin to engage the world with a like-it, love-it, want-to attitude. Those who see life as a grand adventure inherently cloak the dynamic state of their mind/body system in a pull structure. The choice is yours.

# 15
# *The Science Behind Affirmations*

## *Affirmations*

What is an affirmation? An affirmation is a declaration that something is true. It is a statement of fact. When tagged with emotions, affirmations create strong, new neural circuits. These new circuits have the capacity to alter old, unwanted behaviors in favor of new, desired behaviors.

People have been practicing affirmations since the dawn of time. In recent years affirmations have been recommended by many self-help movements, usually without a scientific explanation for how and why they work. I realize, in retrospect, that the passage from the basic text of The Fellowship that I repeated every day for years (Chapter 1) was an affirmation. Countless people have testified to the power of affirmations in altering their lives in positive ways. Although the anecdotal evidence is legion, only in the recent past has research in artificial intelligence, neurobiology, cognitive psychology and systems thinking provided insight into the probable scientific explanation of why and how the affirmation process works.

> Repeated, identical, conscious thoughts physically enlarge the neural circuits that contain them. As a result they have a stronger effect on the subsequent behavior controlled by these neural circuits.

Many people have trouble with the notion of affirmations, thinking they sound a little woo-woo, like a magical incantation of some kind. We will now introduce the concept of affirmations and their use in conjunction with visualization, and talk about both why and how they work.

I was first exposed to affirmations in 1985 at the weekend retreat I mentioned in Chapter 1. In addition to introducing me to the concept of brain dominance, Dr. Henry, the speaker, shared a set of affirmation principles he had learned from Lou Tice's internationally acclaimed program, *Investment in Excellence*®[14].

Dr. Henry gave us instructions for crafting positive statements of fact that were to be repeated in the morning upon arising and in the moments just prior to going to sleep. These statements were to embody some change we wanted in our lives. As we mentally repeated the affirmations, we were encouraged to imagine in our mind's eye how the world would look from our eyes if the change we wanted had already happened. We were told to hold in our mind, at the same time, a positive emotion we could recall from some earlier event in our lives. We were counseled to continue the twice-a-day affirmation process, holding the image in mind and re-experiencing the positive emotion, until the change we wanted to achieve was realized.

I must confess that my educational background, steeped in physics and the sciences of mechanical and electrical engineering, made me skeptical. Quite simply, I was doubtful about the affirmation process and its alleged benefits. At the same time I was quite impressed with Dr. Henry's sincerity and conviction that it worked. However, I left the weekend with no intention of actually using affirmations. I was ambivalent and so made no positive commitment.

## *Skepticism Meets a Need — Weight Loss*

In the spring of that year I was beginning to take out my warm weather wardrobe. Every spring I wondered if last year's clothes would still fit. In the fifteen preceding years, my weight had stayed around 230 pounds. I must confess that I yearned for the days when I was a junior in college, on the wrestling team, weighing in at 180 pounds. I had long since given up hope that I would ever see that weight again. As I peered into my closet, I remember a fleeting thought, "Why not try that affirmation stuff and see what happens?"

I crafted a set of affirmations following the recommended model and did as Dr. Henry had suggested. In the first few weeks I did not even tell my wife that I was doing something as unscientific as repeating affirmations morning and night hoping that I would magically lose weight.

## *A Miracle*

Miracle of miracles, at the end of ten months I had lost 50 pounds and weighed 180 pounds. When people asked me how I did it, I never admitted the role affirmations played. In fact, I didn't know how affirmations were helping. They still seemed so unscientific! So I would simply respond, "I ate less and exercised more." The statement was true, but I did not know why I was eating less and exercising more.

Upon reflection I recall that during that ten-month period I found myself impatient with the elevator service in the building where I worked and would spontaneously run up the flights of stairs rather than wait for the elevator. In trips to the mall I found myself parking in the first open spot that I came upon rather than looking for a spot closer to the shops. For reasons unexplained, when helping with the family's weekly grocery shopping, I began to forget to buy ice cream, a weekly purchase I had routinely made in the past.

With my weight down to 180 pounds I stopped the affirmation process. My weight stayed within a pound or two of 180 for the next seven years. Then I began to gain weight. But I am getting ahead of myself. I will return to the issue of weight gain later, in Chapter 17. For now, the next step is learning how affirmations work.

## *The Invisible Power of Visualization*

Even though we cannot see thoughts in the sense we can see objects in space, thoughts have boundaries and shape.

Remarkable changes to neural circuit brain structure and behavior occur by utilizing what are called "affirmation visualization techniques," which are described in Chapter 16. In a sense, your mind is like an invisible magnetic field that links parts of the human mind/body system.

It is always difficult to understand things that we cannot see. For example, electricity moving along a wire cannot be seen. Although we may not fully understand electricity, we can see and appreciate its effect, such as the brightness of a light bulb. For most people it is a mental stretch to accept the idea that something we cannot see can have a shape or configuration.

## *Magnets in Action*

Back in elementary school I had a teacher who led me and my classmates through an experiment that I will never forget. The teacher wanted us to understand that magnets possess properties that extend beyond their physical shape. She first held the legs of a "U" shaped magnet beneath a flat piece of cardboard on which she had sprinkled a fine layer of iron particles. When she moved the magnet's poles back and forth, we noticed the iron particles move and seem to cluster around points above the ends of the legs of the "U" shaped magnet positioned under the cardboard. She explained the movement of iron particles by telling us that magnets produce something invisible called a magnetic field. It was this magnetic field interacting with the iron particles that caused the particles to move.

This experiment was followed by another involving what is called a bar magnet. A bar magnet is a bar of hard steel that has been so strongly magnetized that it holds its magnetism, thereby serving as a permanent magnet. In this experiment the teacher placed the bar magnet with its north and south poles at either end on a box in the middle of the classroom. Each student was given a small compass the size of a penny that had a tiny needle with a north and south pole. We were told to stand along the four walls of the room with our backs to a wall and the small compass held face up in the palm of one hand. The arrangement of the student-held compasses and the bar magnet is shown in Fig. 15-1.

Fig. 15-1 Bar Magnet

We were then instructed to start moving in a straight line from where we were towards the bar magnet. We were told to stop our movement if we noticed the compass needle beginning to move significantly from its initial position. When everyone had stopped moving, we had stopped at different distances from the bar magnet. The teacher explained that the compass needle moved as we entered the magnetic field of the bar magnet. The positions of the students in the "butterfly shape", shown in Fig. 15-2, were visible evidence that the invisible magnetic field of the bar magnet had a shape or configuration.

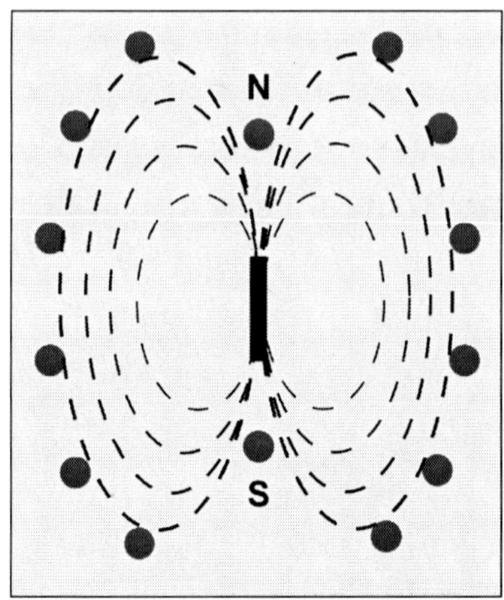


Fig. 15-2 Butterfly-shaped Magnetic Field

Next questions: Can you push on something that you cannot see but has a shape and configuration? How will you know that you have actually pushed on something you cannot see? What evidence will you have?

Some of you may remember the once popular black and white Scotty dogs mounted on small bar magnets. You could cause the magnetic field of one Scotty dog to push on the magnetic field of another Scotty dog, causing the second dog magnet to move. Let us use the Scotty dog magnets as a metaphor and ask similar questions about the nature of human thought.

## *Visualization — Developing Neural Circuits Through Imagination*

It has long been believed that anything a person vividly imagines produces changes in the brain as if what was imagined actually happened. Proof of the increased proficiency brought about by imagination and visualization has been demonstrated in many settings.

In 1969 Alan Richardson[15] reported on an experiment which improved success in shooting basketball free throws. One group was instructed to visualize the ball between their hands, then visualize delivering the ball on a trajectory that arced perfectly and swooshed through the hoop without touching the rim. The other group actually practiced shooting free throws every day on the court. At the end of six weeks, the results were that those visualizing shooting free throws improved by 23%. Those actually practicing on the court netted only one percentage point better, at 24%. Visualization is powerful.

The benefits of visualization have been acknowledged by coaches of every sport. It has also been known to backfire! When the kicker on a football team missed the extra point for the third time, he was sent to the locker room and told to think about what he'd been doing wrong. Do you think the next kick after he returned to the field was successful?

> The practice of perfection makes perfect.

How many of you have heard the admonition, "Practice makes perfect"? This statement is false in that it is incomplete. A truer statement would be, "The practice of perfection makes perfect." The only way you can practice perfection is by visualizing a perfect performance in the brain/mind/body system. The kicker sent to the locker room needed to think about kicking a perfect, right-in-the-middle-of-the-goalposts kick! Then his next kick may well have succeeded.

In 1993, the scientific community reported that by utilizing positron emission tomography they were able to record evidence of neurons sprouting and interconnecting to form neural circuits in response to repeated mental activity.

That same year Dr. Alvaro Pascual-Leone[16] reported on what he termed a key experiment. He taught healthy adult volunteers to play the piano and charted the resulting brain changes. He reported:

> We wanted to look at the changes that take place in the brain with the acquisition of a new skill. We taught a five-finger piano exercise, up and down the scales. The group practiced daily for five days.

His findings were swift and astonishing.

> There were tremendous changes in the size — very dramatic changes — in the brain's representation of hand muscles in the subjects who learned the piano exercise. They more than tripled the size of their brains' motor maps. And these changes paralleled their improvement in performance.

These brain motor maps are the neural circuit systems we have been describing in this book. We create neural circuit systems that contain instructions to send electrical signals to muscles in the body to bring about activity we describe as behavior.

Think now of Dr. Pascual-Leone's instructions to the first volunteer group. They were instructed to sit at a piano keyboard and practice five-finger exercises up and down the scale. As they practiced, neural circuits were established that resulted in electrical signals being delivered to their arms, hands and fingers. Once an initial set of circuits had been formed and the volunteers practiced daily for five days, it should not surprise us that these sets of neural circuits grew in size and became stronger. The stronger and larger these circuits became, the easier it was to initiate free-flowing hand and finger movements.

In this experiment there was also a second volunteer group. These people were instructed to simply sit at the piano keyboard and randomly strike the keys in any way they wanted. At the end of five days there were no discernable changes in the neural circuits in the motor cortexes of this group.

But the biggest surprise came from volunteers in a third group who were taught the piano exercises but were only allowed to rehearse them mentally, while looking at a keyboard. After five days, the brains of these people were identical to those who had manually practiced.

> *Scientific proof demonstrates that the same neural circuits developed by the mind to bring about the execution of a behavior are also involved in imagining it. Furthermore, any vividly imagined behavior develops the same type of neural circuits that develop when the task is actually carried out.*
>
> Dr. Alvaro Pascual-Leone

This discovery has profound significance for everyone in the world who would like to drive neural circuit development in their brains without actually physically performing the desired activity. This research provides the world with clear and convincing scientific evidence that people may create neural circuits of their own choosing by use of visualization techniques.

> We can create a neural circuit of anything we can imagine.

We will now explore how affirmation visualization techniques may be used to generate new neural circuits. These new circuits overlay old neural circuits, changing long-standing, unwanted patterns of behavior.

## *Why Do Affirmations Work?*

I was delighted to find in the story of Dr. Pascual-Leone's work a scientific explanation for why affirmations work. He had discovered that the same brain cell networks involved in executing a task are also involved in imagining it. The light bulb went on in my head! This means that anyone can establish in their subconscious system a neural circuit of what they have visualized. It follows that repeated visualizations of the same image will make the neural circuit stronger and larger over time. It suddenly dawned on me that once the visualized neural circuit is in place, the introduction of a thought, belief or perception that in any way conflicts with the visualized image will unbalance the system and evoke feelings of mental discomfort.

It will be recalled that systems are always in an active process of resolving internal tension to reach a state of equilibrium or rest. How does this work with the mind and behavior?

Within the vast circuits of the subconscious system there are neural circuits whose job it is to bring behaviors into play that keep the mind/brain/body system in a state of equilibrium. This state of equilibrium is present when the actual perceived image matches the visualized image. The selection of the behaviors that brings about this state of equilibrium may be thought of as the inherent genius of the subconscious.

### *Experience the Power of Visualization Using a Makeshift Pendulum*

I would now like to ask you to perform a visualizing exercise using a makeshift pendulum. Please get a piece of yarn or string and attach an object such as a washer, a button, or a heavy paper clip to one end. Hold the other end between your thumb and forefinger and rest your elbow on the surface of a table such that the object is positioned over an X on a sheet of paper. Now focus your visual attention on the object and lower the object until it just touches the paper at the center of the X. This should stop any movement of the object; the object should hang nearly motionless. Raise it slightly to free it from contact with the paper and then focus on the object and visualize it in your mind moving back and forth from side to side. Keep your attention focused on the object until it begins to move, first slowly then more strongly. If for some reason it does not move, change your mental image of the movement of the object from side to side to a back and forth movement in a different direction. Follow this by visualizing circular clockwise and then counter-clockwise movements of the object. If for some reason you can get no movement of the object in any direction, ask a friend to perform the experiment and observe.

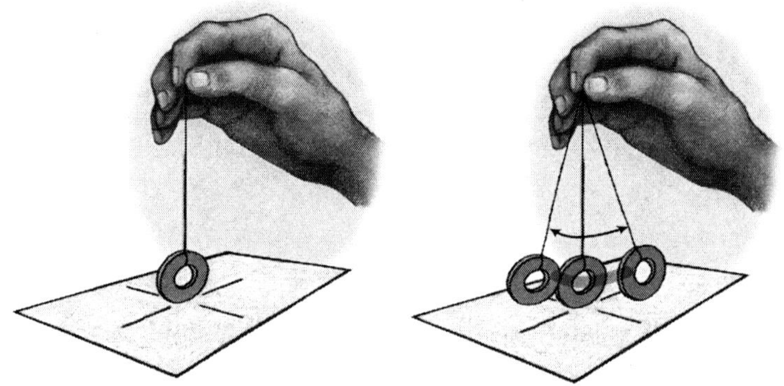

Fig. 15-3 The Pendulum Moves

I have witnessed more than a thousand people in one setting become amazed as they each make the object move by their invisible mental powers. Because we are so used to the linear, Newtonian world of cause and effect thinking, you may assume that when the hanging object moves, you have somehow sent mental energy waves toward it and these have caused the object to move. This notion is heightened when you carefully watch another person performing the experiment. You will not see any discernible movement in their fingertips.

To further prove this point, perform the experiment again. However, this time do not visualize, but consciously attempt to move your fingers and hands in a manner that will cause the object to move in the desired patterns. You no doubt will observe that it requires an almost counterintuitive, exaggerated movement of your hand or fingers to accomplish the desired movement.

In order to understand why the object moves when you visualize it moving, you will need to know that in the mind/brain/body/nervous system there are numerous motor muscle control systems that operate below the level of your conscious awareness. You can sense these systems when you want to pick something up. Your mind commands muscles to contract, causing your arm, hand and fingers to move in a coordinated manner toward the object. You are consciously aware of these movements because your eyes can see the movement.

Most people are unaware that there are innumerable fine motor control neural circuits in the fingers and especially the tips of each finger. Movement brought about by activation of these fine motor control circuits is virtually impossible to observe with the naked eye. We know they are there when these miniscule muscle movements are amplified by the length of the string from the fingertips of the thumb and forefinger to the pendulum object. We see these tiny movements made into large, amplified movements of the object.

This amplified movement is much like what we see as we watch the tip of the second hand on the wall clock sweep its way around the minute/second markings on the clock's face. The second hand is secured at one end to a shaft coming out of the clock face. Very small, rotary movements of the shaft are amplified by the tip end of the long second hand. What we observe is the second hand traveling from second to second, much as we have seen in the movement of the hanging object.

Let us now return to a study of the operating systems and subsystems of the mind/brain/body/nervous system. Fig. 15-3 depicts your brain visualizing the object moving. When you look at the object at the end of the string, your eyes deliver the image to your brain. In order to create the required equilibrium in the brain, the subconscious circuit that is visualizing the object moving will activate the fine motor control circuits at the tips of your fingers to produce the desired movement.

When the imagined movement and actual movement match, a state of balance or equilibrium exists in the fine motor control circuits of your brain. As long as you hold the image of the object moving back and forth, your brain's fine muscle motor control circuits will act to keep the object moving and the system in equilibrium.

Let us generalize what you have just learned.

- The same neural circuit networks involved in executing a task are also involved in imagining it.
- Over the course of your lifetime vast arrays of neural circuits have been established in what we have defined as your subconscious system. All the information that has entered your mind/body system has been recorded in these innumerable neural circuits. Because the greater bulk of this information was not consciously tagged when stored in memory, you cannot consciously call upon these circuits. However you can call upon the information stored in these neural circuits to affect your behavior as you move through the world.
- Because you are not consciously aware of the presence of these circuits, it seems almost magical when behaviors controlled by these circuits are activated. Movement of the object can be rationally explained only when you are aware of the presence of fine motor control circuits that are a part of the subconscious system.

This understanding may well help us appreciate why the affirmation process I embarked upon to lose fifty pounds worked without my having any conscious awareness of why I was losing weight.

Like most Americans, I have been bombarded with information

that repeatedly advises me that to lose weight I need to either reduce my calorie intake and/or increase my calorie burn rate by exercise. Upon reflection it comes as no surprise to me now that the creative, subconscious function of my current reality system brought into play the behaviors that led me to run up flights of stairs rather than taking the elevator, forget to buy ice cream and park some distance from mall stores. There were no doubt a fair number of behaviors of which I have no conscious recall that also involved diminishing my calorie intake as well as increasing my exercise.

As hard as it may be to imagine, your mind/brain/body system has a virtually limitless memory storage capacity. Every book we have ever read, every class lecture we have been exposed to, all our experiences and our thoughts about these experiences are recorded in neural circuit networks in our brains. Most of this information we cannot consciously access, because it was never tagged or coded for retrieval as it entered the mind/brain/body system.

Dr. Ben Carson is the Director of Pediatric Neurosurgery at Johns Hopkins Children's Center, a position he has held since 1984. He first received worldwide fame in 1987, as the principal surgeon in the 22-hour separation of the Binder Siamese twins from Germany – the first time that twins connected at the back of the head had been separated with both infants surviving. Here's what he has to say about the brain:

> The organ system of the brain is one of incredible complexity and power. It can process millions of pieces of information per second. It remembers everything a person has ever seen or heard. For example, by placing special electrodes into the parts of the brain that control memory, you can stimulate recall in an 85-year-old so specific that he could quote verbatim a newspaper article read a half-century earlier.[17]

All of this is good news! It means that whatever we visualize repeatedly drives the creative capacity of the subconscious to search for neural circuits that will evoke behaviors which work hard to bring about the very thing we have visualized.

You will remember that the object at the end of the string only moved in the direction you were visualizing for as long as you maintained the visualized motion. When you began to visualize clockwise or counter-clockwise motion, you no doubt became aware that there was a time lag before the newly visualized motion began. It was during this time delay that your creative subconscious was searching for and activating the fine motor control circuits required to change the motion of the object. Note that delays between an influence and a response are classic characteristics of the subconscious mind.

# PART 4

## APPLICATION

## *Changing Ourselves By Rewiring Our Brains*

# 16

# *Creating Affirmations That Work*

Here are three steps for creating powerful affirmations to produce a desired change in yourself.

1. Craft an affirmation that you will repeat mentally.
2. Visualize an image of the way the world will look as viewed from your own eyes, when the affirmed fact is a reality.
3. Simultaneously recall an event that triggered positive emotions and the visualized image in order to chemically tag the new neural circuit formed by the affirmation.

Positive results from practicing affirmations come from our natural urge to reduce the cognitive dissonance that is created when we compare current reality with the emotionally tagged image.

## *Step One: Craft an Affirmation*

To be highly effective, the words of the affirmation need to follow six basic guidelines:

- Be Personal
- Be Positive
- Use Present Tense
- Express Positive Emotion
- Be Realistic
- Be Specific

Let's investigate what is meant by each of the six.

### *Be personal*

Sometimes you may have a strong urge to write an affirmation about changing someone else. However, the only person you can change is yourself. (It may be comforting to remember that often when you change, others will change in response to the "new you".) So write your affirmation about yourself. Use words like "I am," and "me." It is your conscious mind that wants to create a new neural circuit. This new circuit will become part of your subconscious mind.

### *Be positive*

Instead of "I do not like being overweight," try "I have a trim, fit body." The neurobiological purpose of writing an affirmation is to generate an image in the brain of how the world will look after your desired change. Remember, whenever you hold a mental image in your brain, the presence of the mental image causes a neural circuit to form.

If the neural circuit includes the idea, "I can't do something," then the only behavior that can flow from it is a behavior that will ensure that the "something" does not happen. If we repeatedly tell ourselves that we are bad at remembering names, neural circuits form in response to these thoughts, which perpetuates the problem. The statement "I am bad at remembering names" is an affirmation. An affirmation is a statement of fact. In other words, when you affirm anything, you are declaring that the statement is true.

Henry Ford was reported to have summed it up this way: "If you think you can do a thing or think you can't do a thing, you are right."

### *Use present tense*

Make the affirmation in the present tense, as if the stated fact is already true. For example, "I am healthy." It is important to remember that your conscious mind speaks to the part of your brain that will record your exact thought in neural circuits. These circuits form what we call the subconscious mind. If you use such terms as "I will" or "I can," nothing will change in the present, because these are words referring to your potential and the future.

For example, "I can be rich." True, anyone can be rich, but most are not. Stated in the present tense, the affirmation is "I am rich because I own my own home and can easily finance my children's education." The objective of the affirmation is to create neural circuits in the brain, just as if the circuits were forming in response to experiencing current reality.

### *Express positive emotion*

Include an emotionally positive word in the affirmation you write.

- "I am *ecstatic* now that I am fit and trim and weigh 180 pounds.
- "I feel *energized* now that my basement is organized."
- "I am *content* in my marriage now that we talk about our relationship every day."

The emotionally positive word helps tap into the reservoir of emotionally positive experiences stored in your brain and conditions the limbic system to expect more positive experiences.

### *Be realistic*

The affirmation can represent a stretch for you, but it needs to be realistic. Successful practitioners of affirmations strongly suggest that for neurobiological reasons not fully understood, affirmations such as "I am a millionaire," when the person writing the affirmation is making $30,000 a year, do not change behavior. The problem may be the inability of the individual to visualize his or her life in vivid detail, as if he were already a millionaire. This prevents the unrealistic affirmation from producing the desired change.

### *Be specific or exact*

Use words that are detailed and precise in creating the affirmation. Don't write, "I am happy now that I make more money." If you are earning $2,000 a month in sales and you realistically believe that since other people in sales are earning $3,000 a month, you could also earn that amount, your affirmation might read: "I am happy now that I make $3,000 a month," while you visualize a bigger pay check in an amount that represents a $1,000 increase.

## *Step Two: Visualize*

The second step in the affirmation visualization process is to create a mental image of the way the world will look out of your eyes when the change you seek has happened.

It has been my experience in working with literally thousands of people that the visualization step requires the most mental effort. A common mistake is to establish a mental image that would result from a video camera focused on you if the change were realized. In my weight loss example from Chapter 15, this would mean I imagined myself in a movie, striding along at a svelte 180 pounds. The problem is that this is not the image I would see out of my eyes if I weighed 180 pounds. That video image is what someone else would see.

Some have asked me if it would be suitable in this visualization process to simply look at a picture of myself when I weighed 180 pounds. The answer is "no" for a number of reasons. First, the image of me in the photo is a picture of me in the past. In my own case, the idea that I might look as I did when I weighed 180 and wrestled in college is unrealistic because at that time when I weighed 180 I had a 32-inch waistline. At my more recent 180 pound weight, my waist measured 38 inches. Not fat-looking, but certainly not the sleek physique I had in college. Secondly, a picture of myself weighing 180 is not what I would see out of my own eyes when I again weigh 180 pounds.

The image that I have found most useful to employ in using the affirmation visualization process for weight loss is the image of the dial on my bathroom scale which will show 180 pounds when I stand on the scale and look down.

### *Step Three: Tag with Emotion*

A third step in the visualization process involves chemically tagging the circuit that is forming as a result of the visualized image. Find an experience in your past associated with a very positive emotion, so you can piggyback on the chemical traces it caused. It might be the day you graduated from school, the moment you learned of a promotion, the day you had a baby, or a time someone you care for accomplished something major, was publicly recognized and you felt proud. It doesn't matter whether it is recent or from years ago. What matters is that when you think of it, you re-experience that little lift. We will use this emotional memory to strengthen the affirmation.

The remembered emotion need not have anything to do with the change in behavior you are currently seeking in your life. Whenever you experience a positive emotion, or vividly recall a positive experience and feel your emotions lift in response, the limbic system in the base of the brain is releasing chemicals that cause this effect. At the moment the positive emotion chemicals are released, neural circuits that include traces of these chemicals form to record the information. These new circuits are said to be "tagged." These tagged circuits and the information they contain are then readily available to affect your conscious behavior.

This is a nifty system. You can tag and strengthen any neural circuit-in-formation by simply recalling an emotionally positive event at the same time that you are holding the mental image of what you want. *This is an important step often omitted when talking about affirmations.*

## *Caveat: Don't Forget Current Reality*

Simply repeating affirmations morning and night as recommended will not work to change patterns of behavior. The motivation to change and the behaviors needed to effect the change come into play only when the affirmation-visualization neural circuit is contrasted with current reality. This is described in more detail in the next section — the Lose Weight example.

## *Craft a Family of Affirmations*

Go back now to the issues you noted at the end of the Introduction. You will find it useful to craft several affirmations, representing different areas of your life, to keep your life in balance. If you're focused very strongly on a work-related affirmation, it would be useful to create one relating to your personal life at the same time. It would hardly be progress to become so focused on improving one area of your life that the rest suffered. If affirmations are coming to you easily, go ahead and write several right now. I recommend that you focus on only one or two initially, then, in order to keep balance in your life, focus on one in each category, repeating and visualizing morning and night for several weeks or more, while the new neural circuits form and your life moves in the directions you've pictured.

> This is the time to go back to the last page of the Introduction, to the issues you identified when you started this book. Determine how one or all of the techniques described in this chapter will bring you closer to your desired future!

## *Review*

> The three-step affirmation visualization process that will drive new neural circuit development is:
>
> 1. Craft an affirmation which you will repeat mentally.
> 2. Visualize an image of the way the world will look as viewed from your own eyes, when the affirmed fact is a reality.
> 3. Recall simultaneously an event that triggered positive emotions in order to chemically tag the new neural circuit formed by the affirmation and the visualized image.
>
> Comparing current reality with your emotionally-tagged vision in step 2 will create the dissonance that will bring the results to be described in Chapters 17 and 18.

The affirmation visualization process has enormous power. Some of the results you can expect to get by using it include:

1. Secure the quality of life you want by activating existing neural circuits to change your behavior and relationships with others.
2. Neutralize unwanted emotions, change attitudes and beliefs.
3. Eliminate limiting attitudes and beliefs.
4. Condition the reticular activating system (RAS) to detect information in your environment that is of special importance to you.
5. Solve problems by utilizing subconscious processes to search for untagged knowledge.

To help you experience the subtle ways the brain works to change behavior, remember what you learned from the pendulum exercise in Chapter 15. If you did not do the exercise then, I urge you to do it now. The purpose of that exercise is for you to experience how you can use the visualization process to produce behaviors, however unlikely it seems.

# 17

# *Experience the Power Of the Affirmation Visualization Process*

## *Repeat Your Affirmations Daily*

In Chapter 4 we described brain wave states. The low frequency, theta brain wave state was identified as being dominant in the moments prior to going to sleep and again upon waking. It is currently believed, although not clinically proven, that conscious thoughts embedded in theta brain wave signals easily move back and forth between the conscious functioning regions of the brain and the subconscious processing regions of the brain. Accordingly, the affirmation-visualization process develops neural circuits most powerfully in the moments before going to sleep and upon waking.

To get the most from practicing the affirmation visualization process, do it at least twice a day, ideally just after waking and again as you drift off to sleep. Whenever you do it, quiet your mind before starting. Take three or four deep breaths and slowly release each breath. Most people discover that each cycle of quieting their mind and

> Repeat your affirmation(s) at least twice daily — preferably upon first waking, and then just as you are drifting off to sleep.

repeating the affirmation-visualization process takes 30 seconds or less to accomplish. Each time the affirmation visualization process is practiced, the forming neural circuit gets stronger, until it is so strong it seems real. In the weight loss example, the imagined 180 pound scale reading gets stronger and stronger until it is as strong as the neural circuit of viewing an actual scale reading.

Some changes take a short time, others may take years. Writing this book has been a daily affirmation of mine for nearly fifteen years.

## *You Can Change Your Behavior — (Weight Loss Example)*

Back in Chapter 15, I described how my first encounter with the affirmation process facilitated the loss of 50 pounds from a weight of 230 pounds down to 180. At the time I lost the weight I had no understanding of why this method worked. Today I know why and I'm going to share with you exactly how the process produced the changes in my behavior that resulted in the weight loss.

Go back with me now to the point in time when I had lost the 50 pounds. Once the weight was lost, there was no further need to continue the affirmation process. I am pleased to report that my weight stayed within a pound or two of 180 for the next seven years. Then I sensed that I was gaining weight. Initially I sensed the weight gain because my clothes fit more snugly than before. At the end of that year I had gained 12 pounds.

As I began to gain weight I hoped that others would not notice. My wife, however, was a no-nonsense woman, and one day she said "Hal, you are getting fat. Why did that affirmation process stop working?" To be honest, I did not have the faintest idea why I was now gaining weight. So, I gave some feeble answer. Trudy laughed.

Before long I reached 197 pounds. I was regularly delivering "Pathways to Greatness" seminars in corporate settings. In late

December I had been invited to present the Pathways program in a day-long seminar to a group of twenty vice presidents and their wives. As I began preparing for the seminar, I decided that when I reached the affirmation section of the seminar, I would share with the group my earlier weight loss of 50 pounds as a result of the affirmation process and how, after years of holding my weight constant, I had gained 17 pounds.

In the seminar I would state my intention to craft an affirmation to restore me to my desired weight of 180 pounds as it would be obvious to them that my earlier affirmation experience had stopped working.

The truth is I had stopped working it! I no longer said the affirmation regularly. I had simply found bigger pants in my closet and I hadn't weighed myself in months, so I wasn't experiencing cognitive dissonance. My subconscious system was no longer pushing me to take the stairs instead of elevators. Trudy and I were not taking regular walks. Old habits and neural circuits had crept back into play.

I want to describe my affirmation visualization process in some detail so it will be very clear to you. The affirmation to return to my weight level of 180 pounds read as follows:

I feel ecstatic now that I am fit and trim,
weighing 180 pounds.

Let us now check this affirmation against the six guidelines noted in Chapter 16:

| Principle | Affirmation |
|---|---|
| Personal | "I" |
| Positive | am fit and trim |
| Present Tense | now |
| Expresses positive emotion. | feel ecstatic |
| Is Realistic | doable |
| Specific | 180 lbs. |

Remember the second step in the affirmation visualization process is to create a mental image of the way the world will look out of your eyes when the change you seek has come into existence. The image that I have found most useful to employ is the image of the dial on my bathroom scale which will show 180 pounds when I stand on the scale and look down. In Fig. 17-1 the conscious process is shown with the affirmation located in the upper left, and the image of the scale dial shown on the upper right.

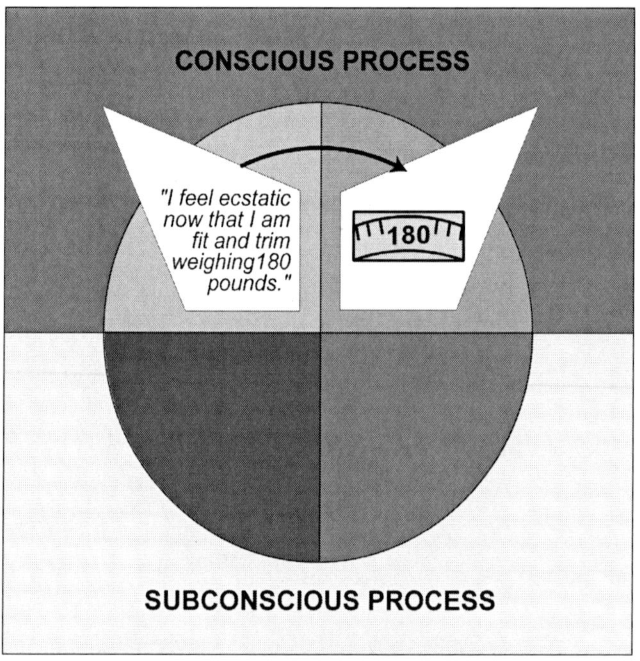


Fig. 17-1 Weight Loss Affirmation

The third step of the affirmation visualization process calls for chemically tagging the affirmation by recalling how you felt during some highly positive past event. In my case I found it easy to re-experience the joy I knew on the day I received my first bicycle. In Fig. 17-2 the picture of the smiley face with a thought bubble depicting a bicycle represents the re-experiencing of that positive emotion. I am holding the mental image of the way the world will look when the desired change has actually happened. Fig. 17-2 also shows the faint image of a neural circuit of the bathroom scale reading 180 in the subconscious region of the brain, next to the smiley face. The faint image represents a neural circuit-in-formation. It is not yet strong enough to change my behavior. I need to keep saying the affirmation and visualizing the bathroom scale at 180 and tagging them with positive emotion.

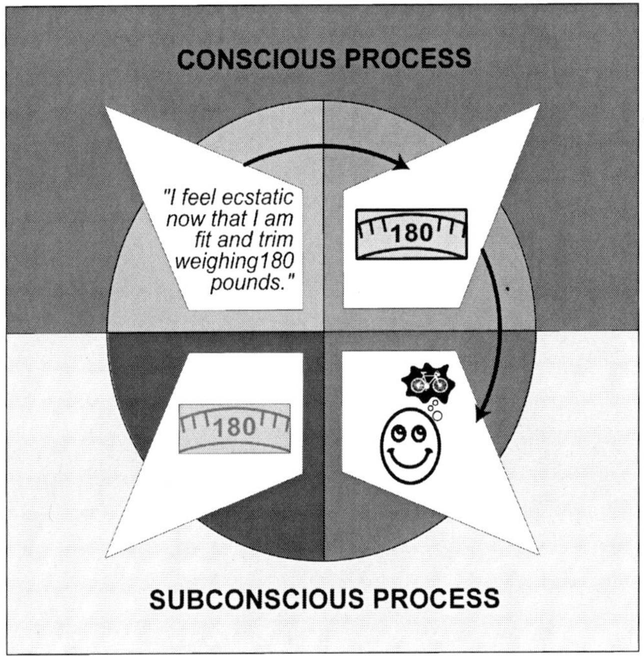


Fig. 17-2 Model of Neural Circuit-in-Formation

It just happened that the day following the Pathways program for the vice presidents and their wives, my company began its annual Christmas Week/End of the Year shut down. That year something unusual happened. For the first time since they'd left home, all four of my children came to visit over the Christmas holidays with their spouses and children. My wife and I grew up in a culture where this kind of family get-together called for "killing the fatted calf" to celebrate! My wife outdid herself cooking, and with the help of the children and their spouses every meal became a feast. It was a memorable week.

Even before the "Pathways to Greatness" program for the vice presidents and their wives, I had begun my new affirmation to change my behavior and lose weight. Faithfully morning and night I performed the affirmation visualization process. However, the one thing I never did was get on the bathroom scale.

On January second, I was getting dressed in the morning, running late, so I was pleased to note that I had a freshly dry cleaned suit still in its plastic cover. After putting on my undergarments, socks and shirt, I reached into the closet, removed my suit from the bag and extracted my trousers. I stepped into the trousers, pulled them up to my waist and was instantly dismayed to discover that between the button and buttonhole on the waistband was a gap of at least 3 inches. I couldn't believe my eyes and thought to myself, *The cleaners must have sent the wrong pants.* I quickly removed the pants, checked the fabric of the pants with the fabric of the jacket and was even more dismayed to discover there was a perfect match.

*What have the cleaners done to my pants?* I asked myself and instantly concluded that they had shrunk them. There appeared to be no other freshly pressed suit, so I would bite the bullet, put on the pants, pull in my stomach, pull the top of the pants together and button them. I was able to do it, but when I relaxed my abdomen the pain I experienced was huge!

As I stood there suffering the discomfort of pants too small for my too large waist and looking down at the pants where they came together, I remembered that most zippers have a lock on the pull tab that keeps the zipper in place anywhere along its path. All I needed to do was unbutton the top of my pants, let the waistband expand an inch or so, then apply the pull-tab brake. A belt with a large buckle would mask the gap. This, coupled with the judicious selection of one of my older, wider ties, would camouflage my ill-fitting pants. It worked well enough to allow me to finish dressing. I reached into the closet to grab my suit jacket and experienced utter consternation as the mechanical brake on the pull-tab failed to keep the zipper in place and my pants pulled apart enough that my shirt clearly showed between the zipper sides below my belt.

I was about to experience a moment of truth. I would have to weigh myself. As I headed to the bathroom, one hand gripping my pant top and my belt to keep my pants from falling, I thought to myself, *These pants are made of wool and must be very heavy. They may even weigh a pound or more.* As I looked down at my pants I couldn't help but notice my wing tipped shoes. *The shoes must surely weigh five or six pounds.* I sat down on the edge of the bed and removed my shoes and socks. As I stood to remove my pants, I pulled down my underpants as well. I could not have felt more foolish standing there in front of a full-length mirror, naked from the waist down. Having gone this far before weighing myself, it seemed logical that my true weight could only be measured if I got on the scale nude. With shirt and tie off, I headed into the bathroom only to note that I was wearing my large stainless steel diving watch which I figured must weigh five or six ounces. I removed it and placed it on the vanity next to the sink. As I did so, I looked into the mirror and observed that I was wearing bulky horn rimmed glasses. They would have to go as well. Now, with glasses off, I stepped on the scale and was dismayed because, with my nearsightedness, I could not read my weight on the dial.

I hunkered down as far as my abdomen would allow, squinted my eyes and made out the number. It read 210 pounds. I had somehow gained 13 pounds since starting the affirmation process a few weeks earlier. What had happened? The illustration of the affirmation visualization process and the conscious process/subconscious model shown in Fig. 17-3 sheds some light on this matter.

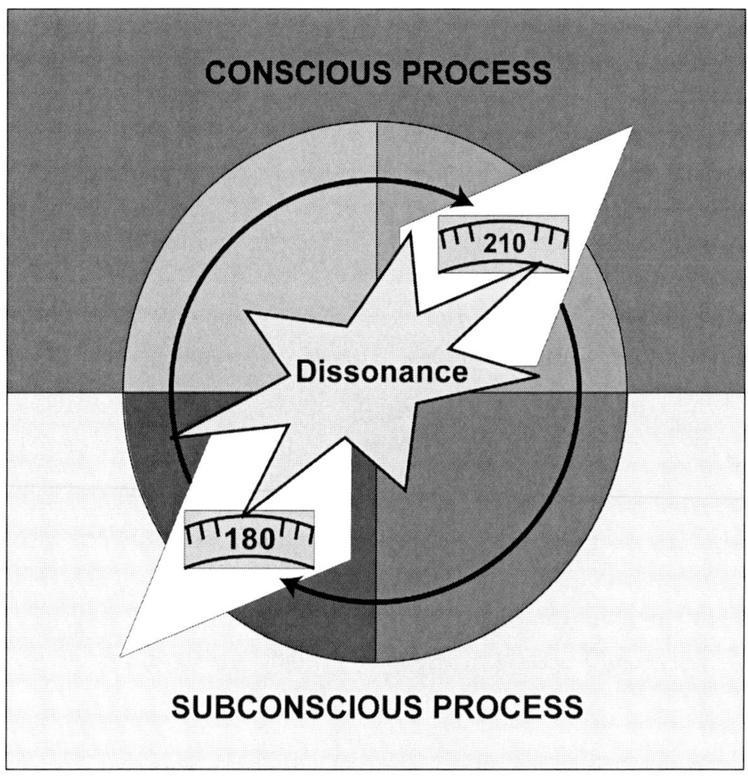


Fig. 17-3 Dissonance

When I looked at the scale reading of 210 pounds, the image was processed by the part of my brain that sees images. This is current reality! I now have in place at a subconscious level an image of a scale reading 180 pounds. What do I experience when these two images are present simultaneously in my brain? Right! Cognitive dissonance.

You will recall that cognitive dissonance is defined as a feeling of mental discomfort we experience whenever we have a thought, belief or perception wired into our brain, in the present case a scale reading of 180, and a thought, belief or perception is introduced that conflicts with it, in this case, the current reality of my actual weight of 210 pounds.

The mind/brain/body system is now in an unbalanced state because of the dissonance created by my practicing the affirmation visualization process. In accordance with system theory, if the system is in a state of unbalance, the nature of the system is to resolve the tension to return the system to a state of equilibrium.

If you never get on the scale and juxtapose the image of current reality with the vision imprinted image in the neural circuits of your brain, you will never experience cognitive dissonance. I hadn't weighed myself in months. I had gone back to wearing older, larger pants. (People avoiding the current reality of weight gain often become devoted to pants with elastic waists.)

> There is an important lesson here: the affirmation visualization process will produce no change in behavior if you avoid current reality.

How often have we heard people lament, "If I could only get myself motivated, I know I have what it takes to get what I want in life!" Motivation in its simplest system form arises when a system becomes unbalanced. The system is disturbed. Because of the system's inherent need to return to a state of equilibrium, the human mind/brain/body system automatically launches a search for neural circuits in the subconscious that will evoke behaviors that will, in the least effortful manner, allow the brain/mind/body system to achieve a balanced state.

Accordingly, when a person employs the affirmation visualization process to change behavior, the following caveat must be kept in mind: *Simply repeating affirmations morning and night as recommended will not work to change patterns of behavior. The motivation to change and the behaviors needed to effect the change come into play only when the affirmation visualization neural circuit in the mind/brain/body system is compared mentally with a current reality, and the current reality circuit conflicts in some way with the affirmation visualization neural circuit.*

If you are going to pursue a weight loss program using affirmations, I recommend you weigh once a week on the same day, at the same time. If you weigh every day, the dissonance fades as you become accustomed to the gap between current reality and desired reality. If you avoid weighing altogether, as I did, the gap never develops and subconscious behaviors like taking the stairs instead of the elevator never materialize.

Although it may be difficult to believe that virtually everything that you have experienced has been recorded in the many trillions of neural circuits in your brain, it should be a comfort to know the answers to almost every concern you have in life are stored in these circuits. Take the weight loss example just described. Even if they've never used the information themselves, I would imagine that almost everyone knows that to lose weight you should eat less and exercise more. Eating less involves avoiding high calorie foods and consuming smaller helpings of all foods. When these behaviors begin to operate at the subconscious level they bring the mind/brain/body system into balance.

I am often asked, "What if I don't have knowledge recorded anywhere in my trillions of neural circuits that will influence my behavior to bring about the changes I want?" Or sometimes the question is, "What will happen if, for reasons unexplainable, the knowledge that is needed in the neural circuits of my brain is simply not physically available?"

The good news answer to both of these questions is that once the subconscious has exhausted a search of all useful knowledge that can be retrieved internally, our mind's constant striving for completion (gestalt) and the motivating presence of dissonance will cause us to explore the world around us in an unconscious search for new knowledge that will be useful. We may find ourselves drawn to bookstores or our local libraries and wandering into a collection of weight loss books.

To summarize, we can activate existing neural circuits to change behavior in any area of our lives by

- Identifying the gap between current reality and desired reality
- Crafting an affirmation about what current reality will look like when the desired reality happens
- Using the affirmation visualization process, which includes visualization and emotional tagging
- Repeating the affirmation visualization process twice a day, morning and evening

## *You Can Neutralize Unwanted Emotions*

Some readers may well remember the seminal work of Dr. Norman Vincent Peale in his book *The Power of Positive Thinking.*[18] Millions of copies of this book have been sold in the U.S. and other countries. Peale urged his readers to craft affirmative declarations and repeat them frequently. The objective of these declarative statements was to counter feelings of inadequacy and instill a sense of confidence in the person who sought to neutralize feelings of inadequacy or lack of confidence. Peale, a Christian pastor, crafted many of his affirmations to include New Testament principles. For example: "I can do all things through Jesus who strengthens me."

### *Hal's Experience*

I remember reading Peale's book in my freshman year in college, in the fall of 1952. I followed Peale's instructions and found a fresh sense of confidence in my engineering studies. I had no idea why Peale's affirmations worked. As my confidence and competence increased, I drifted away from the affirmation process, since I was doing fine.

It was not until the mid 1970's that I ran into a serious career problem (See Chapter 1). I was caught up in a restructuring of merged companies and found myself unemployed after fifteen years with one company. With two children in college and no regular work for three and a half years, my material world began to crumble around me, as I faced financial insolvency and possible bankruptcy. My fortunes took a turn for the better when I landed an excellent position with pay that nearly doubled my last salary. But I had run up a great deal of debt trying to keep my children in college, maintain mortgage payments and recover from a failed business attempt. Even if I turned over my entire new paycheck to my creditors I could not cover the monthly installment payments on my debt.

The thought of personal bankruptcy drove me into a state of near despair. No matter how hard I tried to focus on the new job, thoughts of the dunning notices from creditors overwhelmed me with anxiety and dread. I tried some of the affirmations of the type Peale had recommended, but only half-heartedly because I could not imagine how they would help me pay my bills.

Fortuitously I came upon the book *Psycho-Cybernetic Principles*[19] by Dr. Maxwell Maltz and there discovered a fascinating explanation of control processes in biological systems. Dr. Maltz suggested that in situations where unwanted emotions arise in anticipation of a possible negative outcome, many people find relief in simply vividly imagining what life would be like if the dreaded circumstance came to pass. In my case, if I declared bankruptcy, I would not lose my job. Few, if any, people in my new community would be aware of my bankruptcy. I would have no past bills to pay. I would be earning more than I had ever earned in my life. Of course, I would have no credit and would not be able to obtain new charge cards for eight years. I could, however, keep a card or two that allowed only thirty-day balances to be maintained. Life would take on a fresh new look and feel.

Did I go bankrupt? No, I did not. Each time I began to experience the overwhelming emotion of apprehension regarding imminent bankruptcy I would say to myself, "Now that I have declared bankruptcy I pay all my bills on time and feel great about what life holds for me." I would visualize my checkbook and savings accounts with large balances and experience a sense of elation. The more I repeated the affirmation as a reflex thought to counter the anxious emotion brought about by thoughts of bankruptcy, the less distress I felt about my debts. I began to think rationally again.

I contacted all my creditors and told them that I wanted to make good on the principal amount owed each of them. I had a good job. I did not want to discharge my debts through bankruptcy. I then proposed a schedule of repayment. For some, the balances owed would be paid in a few years and for some it would take as long as eight years. I would agree in writing that should I default in any of the payments I would not avail myself of bankruptcy. The decision was theirs. Accept the principal owed with no interest or carrying charges or receive nothing at all if I were forced to declare bankruptcy. All of my creditors accepted the proposal.

During the eight years of debt repayment, there were no new cars or fancy vacations. As a family we enjoyed camping trips in the summer and cross-country skiing in the winter. Our life included a big garden in the back yard and we canned and froze produce in season for consumption year round. We had small holiday celebrations. We heated our home with wood burning stoves.

As strange as it may seem to some, life became an adventure for the whole family. Old Volkswagens I could repair myself provided ample transportation for the family, even for my teenagers who valued the freedom to travel at will. All members of the family worked in some kind of part-time job. Life was good.

Because I was able to remove my anxiety about a feared event, I was able to behave in a way that prevented the event. And, eight years later, with my credit restored and my debts repaid, I was able to enjoy a lifestyle that my rising income as a patent attorney naturally provided.

### *Jim's Story*

Another example is the story of Jim (not his real name), an unemployed executive who attended my "Pathways to Greatness" seminar at an uncomfortable time of his life, when he found himself entering a second year with no immediate prospects for a job in sight. Jim had worked for many years as an operations manager for a medium-sized company. He had become fascinated by the people part of management and decided to pursue a Master's degree in Human Resource Development, going to school at night. He did this and earned his degree while in his early forties. He loved this work. His company allowed him to do some training and apply some of his new learning. He continued to do his operations job, but felt energized by the new responsibilities, which he hoped to make his life's work in time. Unfortunately, the company went through a difficult time and began laying off employees, including Jim.

Without a full-time job, he found himself forced into long periods of time alone at home while his wife was at work and his teenage children were at school. Jim began to re-experience the uptight, anxiety-ridden feelings he had as an only child home alone. He had been a "latchkey kid" who came home from school every day to an empty house, and he had dreaded the hours he spent every day waiting for his parents to come home.

Now, nearly forty years later, his feelings of anxiety began to interfere with his efforts to carry out his job hunting in a focused way. The more anxious he became, the less he accomplished and the more desperate he felt. He developed severe irritable bowel syndrome (remember the brain in the gut?), requiring a colostomy, which added to his anxiety. In the language of systems, his mind was caught in a reinforcing loop that fed back on itself, creating a vicious cycle.

Jim is a Christian with a deep and abiding faith in Jesus. He came to me looking for some coaching in the crafting of affirmations that might neutralize his worsening state of anxiety. Here are two affirmations that appeared helpful:

> I am calm and content knowing that the spirit of Jesus lives in me
>
> The Kingdom of Heaven is within me and I know peace.

Jim was able to describe moments when he was in his church's sanctuary and feelings of peace and contentment would flood over him. I urged him to visualize and relive those moments as he repeated the affirmations.

I also reminded him of the example of the old woman/young woman image in Chapter 6, showing that he could only think a single thought at a time and that it was his thoughts that evoked the emotions he was experiencing. I encouraged him to repeat these affirmations again and again whenever he sensed even faint feelings of anxiety beginning to emerge. In time the neural circuits he was creating would automatically be triggered by any feelings of anxiety and these new circuits would produce the state of calmness and peace he desired.

Jim also described finding himself alone in his car as he ran errands and engaged in networking activities in search of job opportunities. These periods alone in the car with only his thoughts to keep him company provided fertile ground for anxiety.

Jim realized that it was his continually repeated thoughts that brought on the anxiety he experienced. We talked a lot about the fact that he was the only person in control of his thoughts. Jim told me, "I know you are right, Hal, but I can't seem to help myself."

In order to help him automatically generate anxiety-neutralizing thoughts while driving his car, I suggested the following:

- Select twenty-five or so of the general nature affirmations listed in Appendix A, which reflect a positive take on life.
- Tape record yourself reading each affirmation by reading each one out loud once and then, with the recorder still in the record mode, repeating the same affirmation slowly, silently, to yourself, to allow "blank" spaces between the spoken affirmations.
- Place the tape in the tape player of your car and turn it on the moment you get in the car. You will hear each affirmation in your own voice, and will be able to repeat the affirmations, each in turn, during the blank spaces.
- Today, if you are computer savvy, you can use a microphone to record these affirmations onto your computer. You can then burn them to a CD or transfer them to a portable media player such as an iPod®, allowing you to listen to the affirmations in a wide range of places.
- If you are uncomfortable repeating the affirmations aloud, it also works to repeat them mentally in the quiet time before you hear the next affirmation.

The anxious feelings Jim experienced as a home-alone child did not simply evaporate, and at times he was again overwhelmed by them. But, although it took time, this process was part of a path that ultimately led him to a life of great freedom and satisfaction.

*This affirmation technique does not require a visualization step and depends for its neural circuit building capacity on the conscious repetition of the affirmations.*

## *Yes, It Works*

You may ask, "Does the process just described always work?" The answer is, "Yes," although it may take a long time. The techniques in this process, pursued two or more times daily for a minimum of four weeks, result in a remarkable enhancement of one's outlook on life. Those who follow this process soon discover that the self-limiting thought patterns that were barriers to getting what they wanted in life simply fade away.

Keep in mind that the thoughts you think bring about the emotions you experience. Many people find The Serenity Prayer useful in neutralizing unwanted negative emotion.

*Serenity Prayer*

God grant me the serenity
To accept the things I cannot change,
Courage to change the things I can,
And the wisdom to know the difference.[20]

To neutralize unwanted emotions in your life:

1. Bring to conscious awareness the feeling of an unwanted emotion.
2. Find something positive in the negative emotion or imagine the worst case scenario actually happens. Then ask what positive outcome could come from it?
3. Craft an affirmation that you can trigger every time the negative emotion comes.

# 18
# *More Ways to Use the Affirmation Visualization Process*

## *You Can Change Your Limiting Attitudes and Beliefs*

By now you should clearly understand that our subconscious systems include a host of neural circuits that silently dictate our attitudes and beliefs regarding ourselves and the world we live in. Many attitudes and beliefs appear to prevent us from moving toward and securing that which we need and want in life. Fortunately, the integration of the affirmation process into our lives can profoundly affect the quality of our lives by neutralizing limiting attitudes and beliefs.

We know that we can only consciously think a single thought at a time and that the thoughts we are thinking determine our state of mind. One of the most common mental states involves a feeling of fear and apprehension that seems to come out of nowhere to interfere with our enjoyment of life. Let's tap into an experience shared by nearly everyone that will demonstrate how everything in the mind/brain/body system is interconnected.

## *The Challenge of Public Speaking*

When you were a young person in school, were you ever asked to come to the front of a classroom and give a presentation? Can you remember how vulnerable you felt when you moved from the comfort zone of your desk to the front of the room and realized that every eye in the room was focused on you? As you stood there, was there a rush of awareness that your appearance and your ability to connect thoughts into coherent sentences would be scrutinized by the class? You probably thought that if you did poorly the class would label you "stupid," or worse. Do you remember how the muscles in your throat tightened, making it hard for you to speak and how your diaphragm muscles tensed, making your breathing shallow so that your lungs barely produced enough volume of air to get your vocal chords and lips to work together to project the sound of your voice much beyond your mouth? Did your voice crack and your hands shake or knees shake? Did you experience fluttering movements in your abdomen or hear the pounding of your own heart?

Unless you were a born ham or had the rare, good fortune to be trained in public speaking by a knowledgeable, compassionate teacher, the neural circuits laid down in childhood experiences grow larger and stronger each time you have to speak in public. Even worse, your anxious imaginings drive strong neural circuits by re-experiencing again and again the enormous mental and physical discomfort brought on by public speaking.

It should not surprise anyone that in public polls which ask, "What do you fear most in life?" speaking in public is at the top of the list, ahead of dying. Most people spend little conscious time thinking about dying, as compared to time spent thinking of past bad experiences — real and imagined — involving public speaking.

Think back now to the autopilot airplane analogy (Chapter 14). The many neural circuits you have laid down in response to public speaking that evoke emotions of fear and bodily distress are just like the autopilot circuitry set to take the plane due north. You can, by an act of sheer will power, consciously override these neural circuits and force yourself to give a public presentation, but you will likely pay an emotional price for your effort.

There are a number of ways you can rewire your brain to form large, new neural circuits that strongly affect behavior in a positive way. The Toastmasters Club[21] is an excellent organization that provides a controlled environment in which participants learn by doing and watching fellow club members give talks. There is plenty of practice first with one and two-minute speeches and then with longer talks in a highly supportive atmosphere. There are few better ways to build neural circuits that neutralize nervousness and build confidence than participation in such a program.

Those whose schedules do not allow the Toastmasters experience can use affirmation techniques to greatly reduce the mental and physical discomfort public speaking may cause.

Using the affirmation visualization model in Fig. 18-1 has helped hundreds of people reduce the stage fright experienced before delivering a speech.

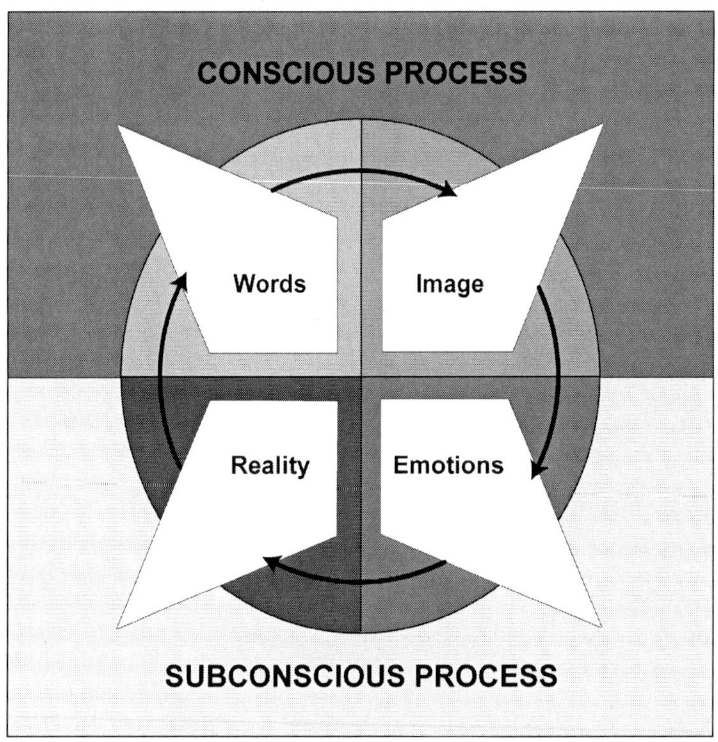


Fig. 18-1 Affirmation Visualization Process –
New Circuit of Desired Reality

Some people require a little coaching to do the visualization step with ease. Let's walk through the process shown in Fig. 18-1.

*Step one:* The words of a useful affirmation might be, *I feel confident and at ease as I speak in public.* Note that this affirmation is personal, positive and stated in the present tense. Often a family of affirmations, each with its own visualization, proves sufficient to neutralize negative emotions and nervous behavior. A couple of others might be, *I am relaxed now that I have prepared well* and *I find it easy to shift my gaze across the audience as I deliver my talk.*

*Step two:* Generate an internal image of what you will see out of your eyes when you are standing and speaking with ease to a group of people in a public place. We are not talking here about a video image of you standing in front of a group. We are talking about what you would see out of your own eyes, were you speaking in public. It's most helpful if you can actually see the space where you'll be speaking to an audience with ease. If you are on a podium and standing with a lectern in front of you, you will see the top surface of the lectern. On the lectern surface you might see the notes you are referring to as you speak. If there is a microphone secured to the lectern, a portion or the whole microphone will be visible. Beyond the lectern you will see the faces of your audience turned up looking toward you. This image of the room, the lectern, notes, microphone and audience looking back at you is the image you will want to visualize. Picture individual members of the audience smiling and nodding.

In my earlier days of public speaking I can recall getting to my church early and sitting in the front row. As the church filled up, I would stand and look back towards where the congregation was filling the pews. It soon became easy for me to imagine a large room filled with people. Even today after more than thirty years of public speaking to groups as small as four or five and upwards of fifty thousand, whenever possible I try to get to the event early enough to stand at the podium and gaze out into the room or hall. While standing there, I visually locate the entrances to the room and scan the empty seating arrangement. If there is a lectern present I place my hands so that they grip its outer edges. I turn my head and upper body to look back and forth in an arc that will duplicate my eye contact with an audience during the speech. I imagine the room filled with people, and I see them nodding in my visualization, indicating that they are following what I am saying and liking it.

*Step Three*: Tag the visualized image with an emotion. (See Chapter 16.)

*Step Four*: Do a great job! Fig. 18-1 calls it "Reality".

## *You Can Detect Information of Value to You*

The affirmation visualization process conditions your reticular alerting system (RAS) to detect incoming information that is of special importance to you. Earlier in this book I promised to teach you how to ensure that you never miss anything of importance to you in spite of the fact that you can think only one conscious thought at a time and you may be unable to detect information in your environment because of a neural circuit block.

To explain how this promise can be fulfilled, I am going to create a hypothetical scenario and ask you to be a participant. In this scenario you have just learned that you are the recipient of a real estate parcel at a mountain resort. All taxes will be paid on the property and any dwelling you build there, for the balance of your life. The house and property may only be sold upon your demise. For purposes of this story we are going to have you be a conservative, analytical, cautious, left-brain person. You do not find it easy to visualize much of anything. Your current plan is to begin a monthly savings plan that will provide you with a large down payment on the vacation/retirement home of your dreams in ten years or so.

You have read this entire book save this section which, for reasons unexplained, you skimmed. As you reflect on your savings plan, you remember something in this book that suggests you might discover information in your environment that could help you attain the house of your dreams more quickly and for less money than you had originally planned.

Since this is such a critical opportunity, you call to enlist my help to ensure that you understand every aspect of the process described in the book. I indicate that I would be glad to help you craft an affirmation that will do the job, if you come to my office and bring a picture of your dream home. The picture you have is that of a cedar-sided A frame. In response to my question, "Do you have any photos of your property you could bring with you?" you respond, "Oh yes, I have snapshots of some lovely, snow-filled winter scenes of the home site."

At my office I reduce the picture of your dream home in my copier so that it can be cut out and pasted on the winter scene picture you brought with you. You now have before you the image of your mountain property with the home of your dreams positioned exactly as it will appear when it is built on your site. Fig. 18-2 illustrates your affirmation visualization process.

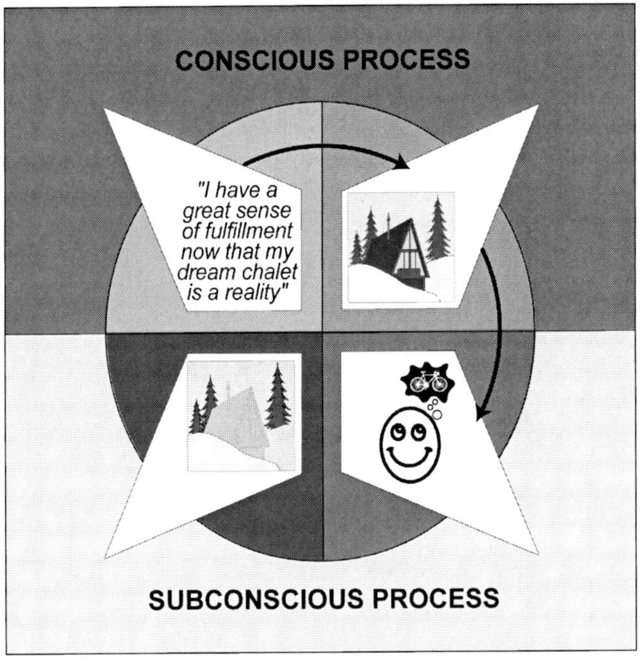


Fig. 18-2 Beginning Of the Affirmation Visualization Process

The beauty of being able to have the exact photographic image of the dream chalet on your home site is that it will take absolutely no mental effort to visualize what you will see out of your eyes when the affirmation realized is, "I have a great sense of fulfillment now that my dream chalet is a reality."

Next I remind you to chemically tag the neural circuit-image-information by recalling the gleeful feelings you experienced on the day you received your first bicycle, or some other joyful experience. In Figs. 18-2 and 18-3, you can see the faint neural circuit image being formed and growing stronger as a consequence of repeating the affirmation and chemically tagging it.

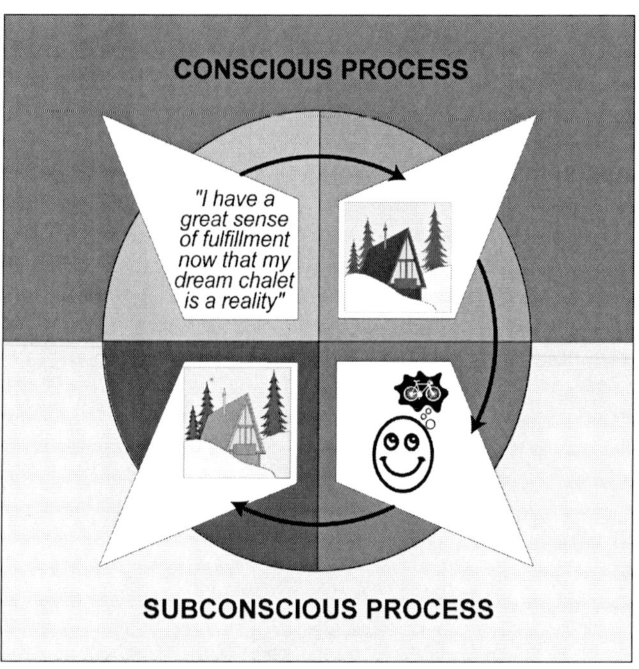


Fig. 18-3 Mental Picture Getting Stronger

Note that the background of the image, which represents the home site you have seen many times, is shown bolded, since that portion of the image has been seen many times in the past, whereas the dream home is shown more faintly.

Each day that you repeat the affirmation visualization process, morning and night, will result in the neural circuit image of the dream home becoming stronger and more vivid, until the neural circuit formed at the subconscious level is as strong as the image your conscious brain processes in the right cerebral portion of your brain. The illustration below is intended to represent the entire affirmation visualization process just described, after a few weeks of practice.

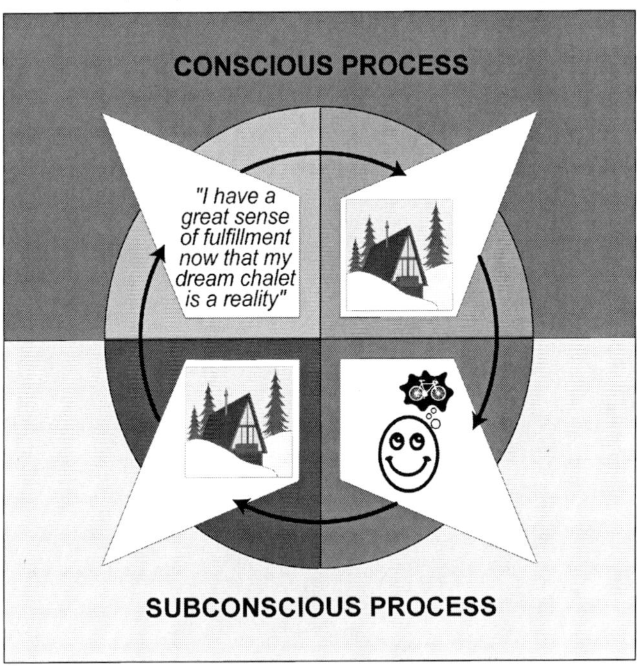


Fig. 18-4 Entire affirmation visualization process

Several months pass and you faithfully practice the affirmation, morning and night. Your wife notes that every morning before rising you sit on the edge of the bed holding a card with the image of the site with your dream home on it. She senses that you are mumbling something. You do the same thing at night before retiring and she begins to grow concerned with your seemingly pointless behavior. She asks you what are you doing and you tell her, "Hal said to do what you see me doing morning and night and this may allow us to get our dream home sooner and for less money." She laughs.

Months pass and you are beginning to suspect that the entire affirmation visualization process is a meaningless exercise. You call me and describe the growing sense of futility you are feeling. I ask if you have been up to the mountains to visit the home site recently. You reply that heavy snows have kept you from visiting. I suggest that the weather looks good for a trip the following weekend.

You and your wife go to the site, arriving midday on Saturday. The image of what you see is shown in the upper right quadrant of Fig. 18-5.

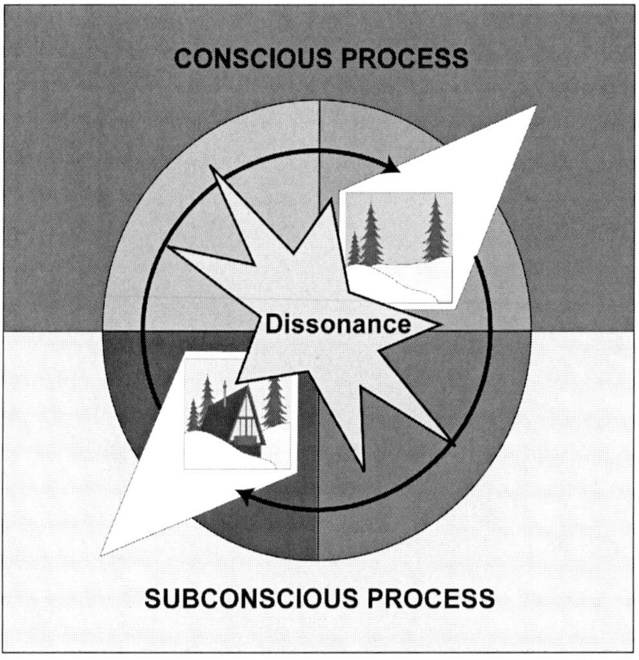


Fig. 18-5 Dissonance

When you see the vacant lot, what is your instant emotional response? Remember cognitive dissonance?

> Cognitive dissonance is the mental discomfort you experience whenever you have a thought, belief or perception wired into a neural circuit and a thought, belief or perception is introduced that conflicts with what is already wired in place.

When you experience this dissonance, your immediate thought is, *What has Hal done to me? I used to love coming up here and simply looking at the winter wonderland and imagining how lovely it will be to live here all the time.* The mental discomfort of the vacant site causes you to call me. "Hal," you complain, "What have you done to me? I used to love going up into the mountains to visit my home site and now I hate going there and seeing it in its natural state without a house on it."

I respond, "That's good. Keep up the affirmation visualization process; have faith in the process and stay in touch." You agree because you experience dissonance only when you are at the home site.

On a typical morning some weeks later, you are ritualistically reading the newspaper while drinking your morning cup of coffee. You routinely look at the sports section first, then glance at the headlines in the business section before studying the front page. Today, in large block print at the top of the first page of the business section, you see an announcement:

MAJOR CITY INDUSTRY TO SHUT DOWN

The large company you work for has been struggling for years and your first reaction is fear that it is your company that is shutting down, putting you out of work. You experience a sense of relief when you read further and realize it is not your company. You are holding the newspaper at arms length with your visual attention focused on the article you are studying at the top of the page. As you start to turn the page, something remarkable happens. In the lower right hand column of the business section, a few inches from the bottom, your attention is captured by the following small ad, which reads, "Local lumber company declares bankruptcy — is selling prefabricated cedar-sided A frames for ten cents on the dollar." Why do you instantly see the two small lines of print in a page of newsprint?

The answer resides in something you already know. (See Chapter 2, Seeing Circuits.) Let me refresh your memory. When light reflects off the surface of an object and passes through the lens of your eye, an image of the object is focused by the eye's lens onto the retina at the back of the eye. This image falls upon the 130 million photoreceptor cells (neurons), each of which has a nerve fiber extending from the rear of the cell where it joins the other nerve fibers to form the optic nerve. You will recall that the nature and intensity of the light striking the cells will be converted into electrical signals, which in turn are delivered to the visual cortex in the back of the brain, where an image is recorded in neural circuits.

> To detect information of value, condition the RAS to find what's important to you by using the affirmation visualization process.
> 1. Create an affirmation of what's important to you.
> 2. Generate an image in your mind of this important thing.
> 3. Tag the image with a positive emotion.
> 4. Repeat the affirmation at least twice/day, while bringing the image to mind and re-experiencing the emotion.
> 5. Be amazed when just what you need shows up!

Think back now to the lesson we learned when we studied the F box (Chapter 6), where we learned that we do not see with our eyes, we see with our brain. In the current example we have an image of the entire business page of the paper focused on the retina which in turn delivers the image of the entire page to the brain via the nerve fibers of the optic nerve. The brain then processes every word on the page. You will also recall that the RAS is hard-wired to the right cerebral cortex of the brain where we process images. Whatever we repeatedly visualize and deem to be important strongly conditions the RAS to detect incoming data relevant to that image. Remember Ann Brown and her ability to find four-leaf clovers? The reason you were able instantly to detect the single sentence in the page of newsprint that made you aware of the bankruptcy sale involves the same type of neural circuit that allowed Ann Brown to find four-leaf clovers.

You might well say to me, "Hal, the appearance in the newspaper of the bankruptcy notice was a convenient creation of your imagination that allowed you to make the point that the affirmation visualization process works to condition the RAS to allow you to pick up information from your environment that you would normally miss. What if over the next ten years there are no factual clues in my environment that can be detected and acted upon? Will I find myself staying away from trips to the mountains to avoid feeling dissonance when I visit my homesite and there is no dream home there?"

I respond that the point you make is a good one. In truth there is a price to be paid for those who are vision driven. For some people the mental discomfort that dissonance evokes is identified as an unpleasant mental state. For vision driven people the feeling of dissonance is a tension in their mind/brain/body system that they describe as a sense of adventure. Every day they wake up and wonder to themselves, *Is this the day? Is this the day I will come upon a key piece of the puzzle that will help me get what I want in life?* People being motivated by a vision often describe feeling excited and having increased energy. I feel this way almost every day.

If you are a person who is uncomfortable with this type of mental state, I suggest that you do not employ the affirmation visualization process. It may be that in systems language the pull structure of a vision is not for you. Life may be far more comfortable if you simply push in a linear, cause and effect manner through a step-by-step plan that will move you towards getting what you want.

But if you are willing to experience the tension of motivation and you want to detect information of value, use the steps of the affirmation visualization process. The RAS will be conditioned so it is working for you even when you are totally unaware of it. It happens behind the scenes. That's the kind of system I really like.

## *You Can Solve Problems*

There are basically two ways to solve problems: analysis and synthesis. Analysis requires taking the problem apart and fixing what's not working. Synthesis requires a good analysis and then creativity to fashion a new whole. Both methods are helped by using subconscious processes to search for untagged knowledge, information or data stored over a lifetime in the huge neural networks of your brain. The affirmation visualization process can help you solve problems.

The most common way to solve a problem is to begin by analyzing the environment in which the problem appears. By analyze, I mean dividing the problem's context into its constituent parts. For example, if some apparatus has stopped working, you find the problem that is causing the malfunction by simply taking the device apart and determining the role and function each part plays in the operation of the device. If you come upon a part that is defective in some way, you may well have found the source of the problem. The repair or replacement of the part will likely restore the operation of the device.

When large systems begin to experience problems, even

exhaustive analysis may not uncover the source of the problem. All of the parts may function perfectly when separated from the system as a whole, but not function well when fully assembled back into the system. This leads to a more sophisticated level of thinking called synthesis. Synthesis is defined as the creation of something new by the recombination of parts into a new whole. In this case the new whole would be free of the presenting problem.

It is at this level of thinking that we usually describe the solution of the problem as an invention. Before invention can take place, a person must thoroughly study the desired outcome. Invention in its purest state involves the combination of at least two means, components or systems that collectively produce a desired, beneficial outcome that was not previously obvious.

Whenever we speak of analytical problem solving we are talking about the use of the conscious mind operating in a sequential, logical manner. When we talk of synthesis and invention, we are describing an intuitive leap where we move from the conscious to the subconscious to synthesize a new whole, solving some identified problem in the process. The intuitive leap we call synthesis is a right hemisphere brain activity, whereas analysis is a left brain process.

Let's talk more about invention and the discovery of principles and ideas that find their origin wholly within subconscious processes. When I talk and write about subconscious processes and state that everything we have ever experienced in life is recorded, untagged, in the trillions of neural circuits of the brain, many people have trouble believing that all of our experience lives on in our brains and most people conclude that even if it is true, this information is not retrievable.

The evidence that all of our experiences are recorded in our brains is credible and mounting. Chapter 15 included a quote from Dr. Ben

Carson, who talked about how special electrodes placed in the brain could stimulate verbatim recall of a newspaper article read a half century earlier.

How do you retrieve the untagged information? You must consciously ask your subconscious mind for what you want. What most people don't realize is that if you are searching for untagged information in literally billions of neural circuits, the likelihood of the answer coming to mind the next day is exceedingly remote.

Some remarkably creative people such as Nikola Tesla, the inventor of the alternating current motor, received answers to conscious questions in the form of fully formed images of the invented product. The image was so complete he could actually visualize tests of his invention. This type of answer is quite rare. Most answers to conscious questions come in a visual form that is often described as a sign or a unique, sometimes symbolic, clue for solving the problem.

*A Problem Solved While Dreaming*

Elias Howe, the inventor of the first sewing machine, was initially stymied by the awareness that stitching two pieces of fabric together would require a needle with a sharp point at one end and an eye at the other, so that a thread could pass through the eye and the needle and thread could then pass together through both pieces of fabric and back to complete a stitch. As the story has it, Howe became obsessed with a search for a solution to this needle and thread problem. Howe reported that an answer came to him in a dream that had nothing to do with sewing. In the dream there was a scene which included a group of aboriginal natives, each holding a spear upraised vertically by one arm. The spears were noteworthy in that each had an opening or an eye near the very tip of the spear point. When he awoke, the image of the spears with openings near the tips was fresh in his mind. Howe realized that moving the needle's eye to the tip point of the needle would allow the thread to move through fabric and back without turning the needle around. Every person reading this book has benefited every day by the problem solving subconscious of Elias Howe.

*A Problem Requiring Invention*

Let me share another remarkable story that illustrates the problem-solving power of these principles. I clearly remember a late afternoon phone call from my company's number one research scientist, Tim Glennon, a man with more than a hundred patents in his name. He advised me that the company faced a huge challenge. If it wasn't handled successfully, it could well herald the end of the company's position as the number one worldwide supplier of power generating equipment for commercial aircraft.

Beginning in the early 1980's, the company had invented and successfully commercialized a hydromechanical device called a constant speed drive (CSD). The CSD was placed between an aircraft engine and an airplane generator. The function of the CSD was simply to connect the aircraft engine to a generator in such a way that no matter what the speed of the engine's shaft entering the CSD, the output shaft of the CSD that drove the rotary generator would remain constant. When the generator speed is constant, the frequency of the electrical signal leaving the generator remains constant. This constant frequency signal is crucial to ensure that all electrical equipment on the aircraft works efficiently. The combination of the CSD and a generator is called a variable speed constant frequency unit (VSCF).

In the U.S. electricity entering our homes has a frequency of 60 cycles per second. The electric clocks in our homes have motors that are designed to run on 60 cycles per second electricity, which allows clocks to keep nearly perfect time. If, for some reason, the frequency of the electrical signal delivered to your home fell to 30 cycles per second, your clocks would be slow and display one half of the real elapsed time since the slow-down. Variable frequencies in an airplane's navigational and operating systems would respond the same way as your clock, with disastrous results.

Now back to the call from Tim Glennon, the company's number one inventor. He reported that The Boeing Company was in the design stage of a new aircraft. They had requested proposals from the power generating equipment industry to provide constant frequency electrical power for the new plane. Their request for proposals specified that they would not accept any proposal that included a hydromechanical component in power generating equipment. Boeing was simply telling the world that they wanted someone to invent a black box that they could plug into the aircraft engine compartment that would deliver constant frequency electrical power.

Sundstrand had never manufactured and delivered a black box of this nature. At least one other company had just such a black box in service on one of Boeing's other planes. Our company belief was that our CSDs cost less and were more efficient and reliable than the solid state black box units of our competitors. The company quickly realized that if we did not win this proposal and all future Boeing aircraft called for black box power supplies, it would hurt our company. Obviously the company would have to invent a black box that met Boeing's exacting supply requirements and in every respect exceeded our competitor's already existing black box.

The company had faced these types of challenges before. A task of this nature would easily take eighteen months of diligent effort. We had to design and build a model that would provide evidence that the new design was feasible. As I listened on the phone, I was thinking to myself, *Why is this scientist telling me all this?* So I asked him.

He said, "Hal, we don't have 18 months to invent and propose the new power supply. We have 3 months to do it all. Management tells me that I can select a team of the company's top scientists and design engineers to work exclusively 24/7 on this project." He then said, "I want you to coach our design team, employing the principles you teach regarding problem solving using affirmation visualization, conscious and subconscious processes. We know what we want. We know what time frame we have to get what we want. Now tell us what you want us to do first."

I had great confidence in the process of helping them craft a vision of the product they wanted to invent and the subconscious processes that would be called upon to create a practical solution. The team was made up of thirteen individuals, most of whom had never worked with each other before. There were specialists in materials, design, solid state electronics, mechanical engineering and physics, to name a few. I was not concerned with whether their personalities were compatible. I knew the team represented extraordinary expertise, but I wondered, *Do we have a whole brain team?* Within a day we had the results of the HBDI™ survey instruments and I was delighted to discover that a composite of the team's individual profiles was almost perfectly balanced. We had a team that inherently possessed an optimal aggregate of thinking styles that would harvest the total capacity of the human brain to create a solution to meet the design challenge they faced. We were working with a whole-brain team!

One full day was spent in a seminar, during which the entire team learned about their thinking style preferences and many of the concepts in this book. The following morning the team got together at an off-site location to define a vision of the black box solid state power supply they were to invent, build and test in the next few months. The team expressed a concern that it was not readily apparent to them how they would create a vision of a product that did not exist. How would they know how it would look and perform? The answer was simpler than they had imagined. When a company such as Boeing publishes a request for proposals to meet a specific functional need, they provide a list of exact, specific, functional characteristics the product must include. By analogy you might think of an automobile manufacturer giving a design team the specifications for a new car such as required acceleration rate, fuel consumption, size, weight and passenger capacity, to name a few.

Once the team had defined a functional image of all the requirements, size and weight were the first to be addressed because the competition already had a solid state power supply in experimental service on a commercial plane. Given the known size and weight of the competitor's product, the team faced the challenge of coming up with a smaller alternative that would be so attractive Boeing would be driven to favor us in making their ultimate decision. The weight and size had to be realistic, given the known technology. Huge amounts of power passing through small components generate immense heat that would need to be accommodated. It took almost half a day to determine the theoretical limits of size and weight that would be substantially less than the known competition.

As the day progressed, the team defined, in functional language, the exact target values for every feature of the proposed power supply. Members of the team were assigned responsibility for each of the design specifications. Critical to the success of their efforts was their newly acquired faith that somewhere in their vast collective subconscious they would find the answer to every problem they faced. By the time the team had finished setting the values for every single functional requirement of the proposal, they realized they had defined a vision of a power supply the likes of which had never existed. The team's vision is shown in Fig. 18-6.

**THE VSCF VISION**

**Win of the Boeing 20/30 VSCF came easily to us because our proposed 20/30 VSCF includes the featues below:**

WEIGHT:
Air cooled converter 29 lbs + 2 lb TR
generator with fly by wire capability 31 lbs

NON RECURRING:
Original design reusable in subsequent VSCF programs

PRODUCIBILITY:
Low early hardware cost
NTE 200% of TMC $$

PERFORMANCE:
Meet spec in all respects

VOLUME:
Converter = 1,000 $in.^3$

MAINTAINABILITY:
20% better than spec

SYSTEM RELIABILITY:
Meantime between failures (MBTF) 20% better than spec

GENERATOR EFFICIENCY:
400 BTU/Min Heat Rejection

TMC = $$

CONVERTER EFFICIENCY:
93% at rated load @ unity power factor

Fig. 18-6 Vision of Power Supply

Albert Einstein was purported to have said "I never discovered anything with my rational mind." Einstein's famous equation E=mc2 elegantly related energy to mass and the speed of light. The equation E=mc2 seems like a pure, left-brain, mathematical statement. Story has it that the equation came fully formed to Einstein's conscious mind as he sat in a reflective state on a wall outside his dwelling. Some three weeks earlier he had imagined himself riding on a beam of light, at the speed of light, observing the passing universe. What he saw and the relationship he noted we will never know.

For many years he had been storing in memory, at the subconscious level, huge quantities of information about the physical universe gleaned from his studies. It is interesting that there was an equally large amount of information that, if he had known it, would have suggested the elegant equation was unfounded. Einstein was searching for a unifying principle defining a fundamental relationship that would be true and operate anywhere in the universe. Einstein's thought processes appeared to entail the use of his conscious mind to form a question to be answered by his subconscious mind.

Return now to the thought processes called upon by the team involved in the invention of a solid state power supply. They first created an affirmation of a vision statement, namely "The winning of the Boeing VSCF came easily to us because our proposed VSCF includes these features." Shown below the affirmation statement in Fig. 18-6, is a copy of the VSCF vision picture, including the features the finished product would contain.

Note that this affirmation is not time specific. When you are trying to create something entirely new, the addition of a time target often increases the tension that drives the subconscious to synthesize a new whole and fulfill the vision. In this case the team knew they had a three month deadline.

Directly beneath the VSCF vision in Fig. 18-7 is an arrow that passes through blocks representing the affirmation in a visualized form, indicating the delivery of the visualized vision statement to the subconscious.

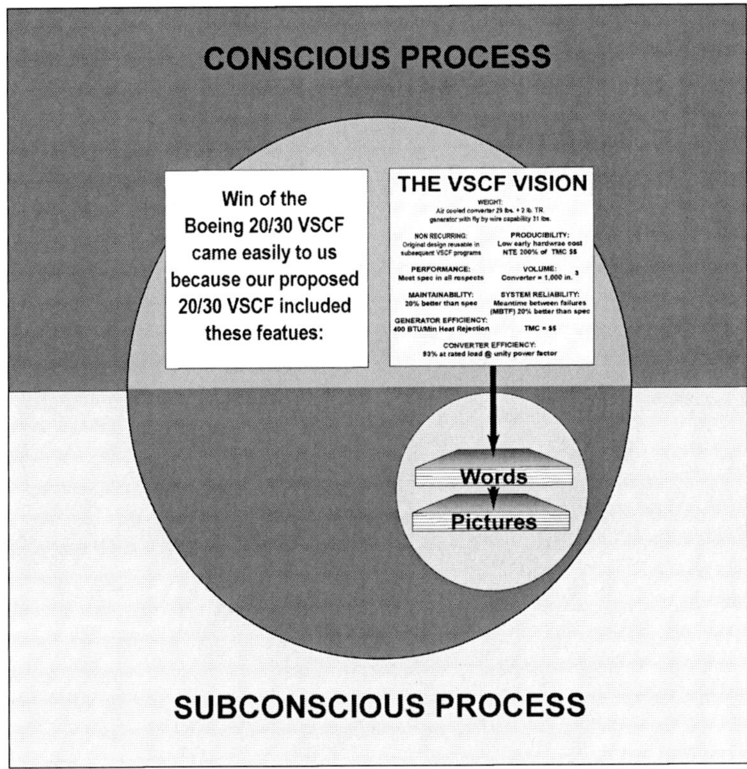


Fig. 18-7 VSCF Affirmation Visualization Process

However, simply delivering a series of thoughts that include words and pictures is not sufficient to initiate an incubation process that leads to the invention of a problem solution. As shown in Fig. 18-8, the mind must always consciously ask, How is it to be accomplished? HOW? HOW? HOW?

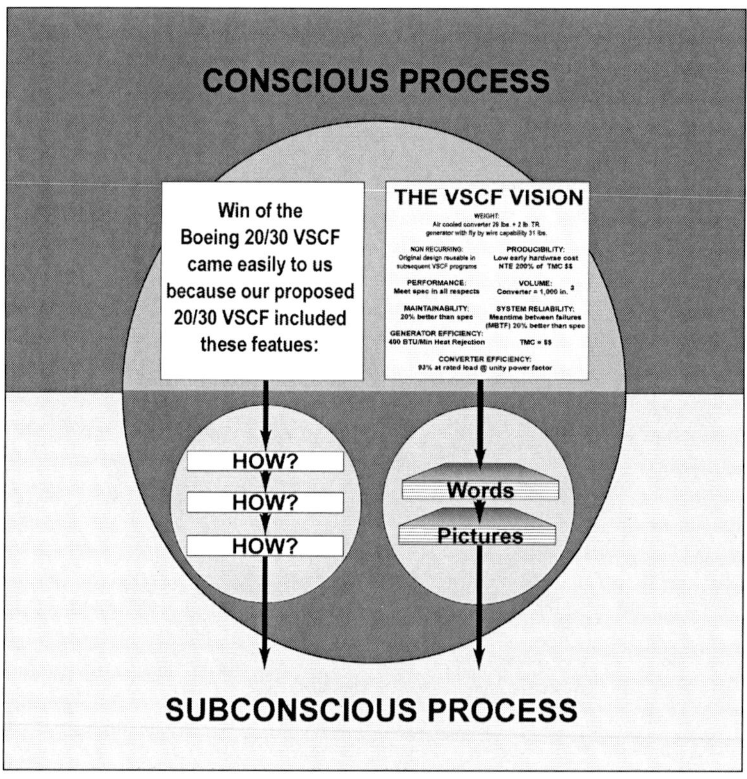


Fig 18-8 How?

The incubation of the problem solving loop in the subconscious is shown next, in Fig. 18-9.

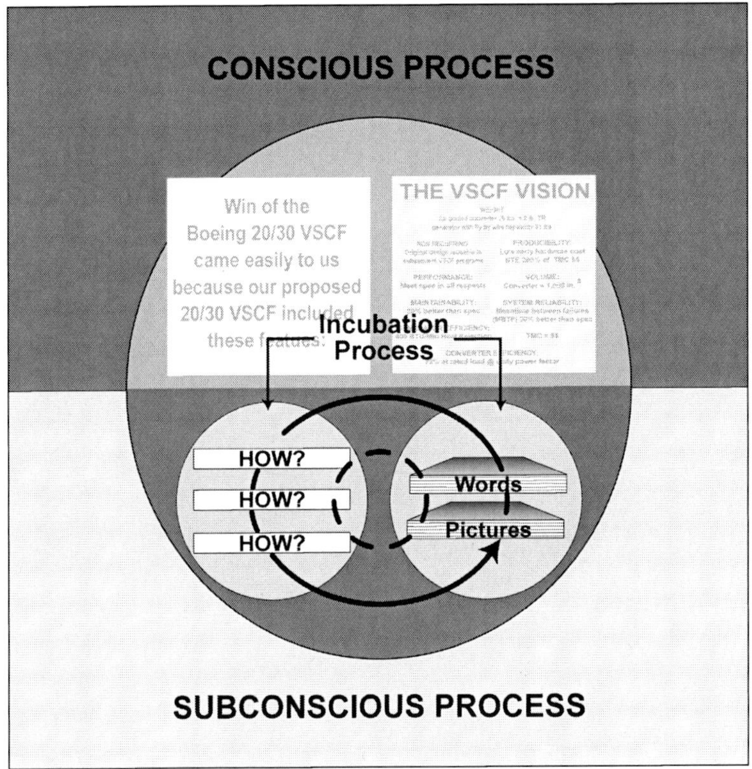


Fig. 18-9 Incubation

When the subconscious process generates a solution, it appears as a moment of illumination, symbolized by the light bulb, a revelation of the “how” as shown in Fig. 18-10.

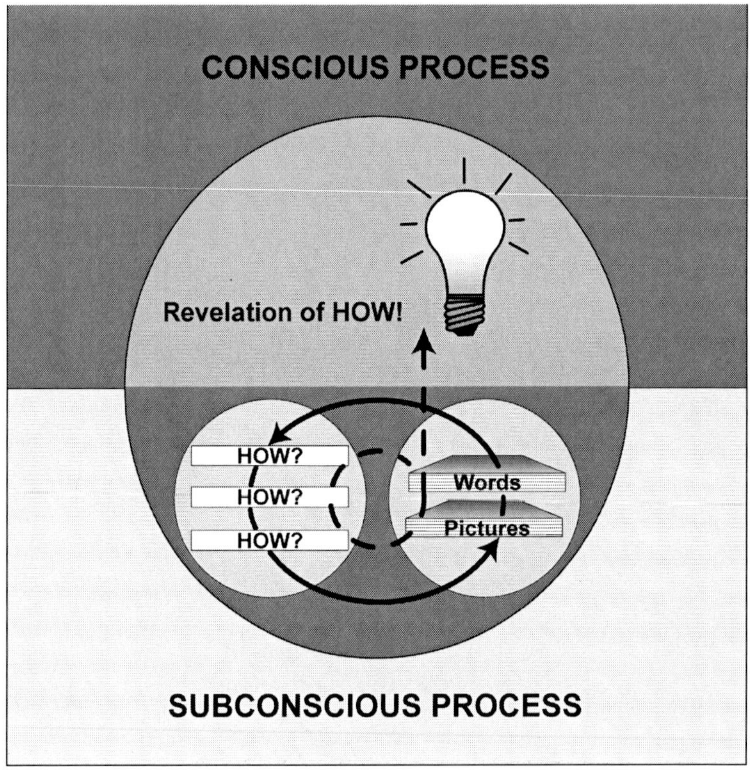


Fig. 18-10 Aha!

Recent research shows the "insight" phenomenon is located in the right hemisphere of the brain.

> This right anterior temporal area is associated with making connections across distantly related information during comprehension. Although all problem solving relies on a largely shared cortical network, the sudden flash of insight occurs when solvers engage distinct neural and cognitive processes that allow them to see connections that previously eluded them.[22]

It will come as no surprise that their proposal won. They were then faced with creating, in just a few short months, a prototype model that would provide evidence that the proposed device was technically feasible. The VSCF invented in just a few months worked and eventually became a standard component in the aircraft power generating industry.

The next time you have a problem to solve, try these steps. Solving problems in this way is so easy it seems almost magical.

1. Define the problem as simply as possible.
2. Create and begin to repeat an affirmation of how the world will look once the problem is solved. (When appropriate make the affirmation time specific. It can be a stretch, but not impossible.)
3. Ask your subconscious, *How do I solve (the problem)__?*
4. Repeatedly deliver the problem to the subconscious just before you fall asleep and just on waking.

# 19

## *Elements of a Life Well Lived*

> *Still more wonderful is the feeling that we do not have to be specially distinguished among our fellows in order to be useful and profoundly happy.*
>
> Bill Wilson

It has been said that happiness is a by-product of a life well lived. I take this to mean a life in line with our purpose, a life in which we actually live our values. It is in this context that we can become useful and profoundly happy. Sometimes people think when we talk about purpose and values, we have to get heavy and serious. Not so. One of my highest values is fun.

You read the story of my life in Chapter 1, and I return to it here to highlight an important shift that occurred inside of me gradually, culminating in the writing of this book to share my experiences with you. In late August of 1952 I found myself standing curbside, waiting for a Greyhound bus to take me to Madison, Wisconsin, to begin study in a dual degree program at the University of Wisconsin. I had decided to become an agricultural engineer, whatever that was. It made sense, I thought: born and raised on a farm, I loved science and hated math in high school. Math, chemistry and physics were extremely difficult for me, but I valued getting good grades in these classes more than in my easy courses.

What I found easy seemed to be worth less than subject matter I found difficult.

## *Something's Missing*

In my first week of college a dean from the Engineering School addressed the freshman class enrolled in the pre-engineering curriculum. He suggested that each of us look at the person seated on our left and then the person on our right. He then advised us that only one of the three of us would graduate as engineers. The dean's message made clear to me that I was about to face an academic challenge of a magnitude that would test my motivation, determination and mental fortitude.

Had someone asked me at that time what I wanted out of life, I think the truthful answer would be something like, "I want an education that will provide me with the academic credentials I need to get a good paying job that will afford me a lifestyle seen by others as living well." "Living well" for me meant "looking good." I wanted a solid marriage, healthy and accomplished children, a nice home, fine car and all the luxuries of the "good life" as seen on TV and depicted in the popular press.

Throughout engineering school I continued to be aware that I was not especially talented in the skills required to be an engineer. A closer look at the world of agriculture lead me to believe that small farms would be displaced by large, corporate enterprises. It also appeared that careers tied to the agricultural economy did not pay well. In the fall of my junior year, I met an alumnus of Wisconsin's College of Chemical Engineering who had gone on to law school and was now in his early thirties and a highly successful patent attorney. We enjoyed a conversation on a myriad of topics. Upon learning that I was studying mechanical engineering, he said to me "You know, Hal, with your gift for the use of words, you should really think about becoming a patent attorney." As we parted company, I noticed that he drove off in a brand new Lincoln Continental. Right then and there it became clear to me that I should go to law school when I graduated. My plan to become a patent attorney was born.

By the time I was 27, I had a beautiful home in the mountains of New Hampshire. I was married, had two delightful children, a devoted wife and a job as a patent attorney for a rapidly expanding electronic countermeasure defense company. I began to acquire vehicles, boats, a recreational vehicle (RV). However, these wonderful things were bought on credit, and the payment schedules for the credit cards and loans began to haunt me as I juggled finances to meet my monthly obligations.

I found the technological aspects of my work as a patent attorney exceptionally demanding. The advanced electronic systems the company was inventing exceeded the complexity of the technology in which I was trained. My days at work were filled with performance anxiety, from which I tried to escape at home by playing hard and living well. This was the era of the two-martini lunch and cocktails after work. The drinking seemed to make the work and financial stress more endurable.

Later, at age 37, I had moved on to another company, been promoted to a division patent counsel position and then to the executive offices where my walnut paneled corner office made it apparent I had made it to the top. I also had joined The Fellowship and was free from the bondage of alcohol. By this time I had four delightful children! I was not, however, free from wanting all the good things in life, which now included vacations in the Caribbean, ski trips in the winter, fancier cars, a bigger home with an in-ground swimming pool.

There were some ups and downs in my work. By the time I turned 50, my work life became increasingly less satisfying. I felt unfulfilled. I had no idea what was missing in my life. However, the service work I did in The Fellowship provided an increasing sense of spiritual satisfaction and an expanding sense of peace. Whenever I would begin to feel anxious, I could throw myself into working with newcomers to The Fellowship to move my thoughts away from myself and onto caring about the well-being of newly-arrived, struggling or recovering alcoholics.

My thoughts began to center on designing an exit strategy from the working world of intellectual property law. I embarked on a savings plan that would provide funds sufficient, by age 59, for me to buy a small yacht on which my wife and I would retire. I dreamed of being a sailor, setting sail to wander the world, free of any commitments. About this time, I was exposed to the work of Ned Herrmann as well as Lou Tice's curriculum, Investment in Excellence® and Willis Harman's book *Higher Creativity: Liberating the Unconscious for Breakthrough Insights.*[23] The impact of the work of these three men was to change the trajectory of my life and drive me to discover my purpose in life. With their help, I realized my dreams had changed. All the things I wanted and got didn't fulfill me. I wanted a meaningful life. A purpose.

> Peter Senge speaks eloquently about purpose and vision in his book, *The Fifth Discipline.*
>
> *Purpose for an individual is a sense of why they are alive.*
>
> *Real vision cannot be understood in isolation from the idea of purpose.*
>
> *A vision without an underlying sense of purpose is just a good idea and purpose without vision has no appropriate sense of scale.*

## *Purpose*

*It is not what the vision is.*
*It is what the vision does to you*[24]
Robert Fritz

Fritz's quote leads me to one of the key subjects of this book: Defining purpose for one's life. Focusing on purpose is important if you want to live a meaningful life full of moments of intense satisfaction and fulfillment. A vision is a specific destination, a mental image of a desired future. When Fritz wrote the above sentiment about vision, he was probably not thinking about the neurobiological consequences of visualization and the role cognitive dissonance plays in disturbing the human system and conditioning the RAS. Even without understanding the inner workings of the brain, Fritz recognized the profound significance of holding in mind a vision of what one wants to see manifested in the world.

The visions we have been talking about since Chapter 12 are much likelier to be realized if they line up with your purpose. Right now you may be unclear about what your own purpose is. In order to recognize it, you must know what purpose is and how to find it. Let me share my experience of defining my purpose.

My first foray into the subject of finding or defining purpose in one's life was to read Victor Frankl's book *Man's Search for Meaning*[25]. From it, I had written down and, in time, committed to memory the following:

> The more one forgets himself — by giving himself to a cause to serve or another person to love — the more human he is and the more he actualizes himself.

Frankl's quote explained to me why I found a deep satisfaction in working with others who were struggling with addiction and recovery. I was able to share the nature of the man I had been and the way I now lived. I began to feel that I was authentic, more of the person I was capable of being, rather than simply being an affluent patent attorney. The man these people met and came to know and trust was my best self.

In The Fellowship, it is commonly agreed that the members live a purposeful life by pledging themselves to being of service to God and their fellow men. Whenever I was involved in service work, I experienced a sense of personal fulfillment that did not seem to depend on my efforts having any particular outcome. It was enough to be willing and to show up. However, the generic purpose statement of being of service to God and my fellow man felt incomplete to me. When I was involved in Fellowship service work, I felt authentic and my efforts were meaningful. But I didn't do this service work all day, every day. In some way I felt my statement of purpose needed enhancement. The tension in my mind brought about by this motivated me to read everything I could find that involved defining purpose in one's life.

A small book, *The Power of Purpose*[26], by Richard J. Leider, was an easy read and a rich source of background material. I found this book most helpful in guiding my quest to define my purpose in life, a purpose tailored to the unique person I was and the person I was becoming. And, I was becoming convinced that living on purpose, or in alignment with my purpose, allowed me to live a meaningful life. It was becoming clear to me that purpose is something you live.

> *This is the true joy in life — the being used for a purpose recognized by yourself as a mighty one.*
>
> George Bernard Shaw

Finding and defining your personal purpose in life is a process of discovery that evolves over time. During the time I was beginning to think about purpose, I had a startling experience. I was thinking back to that time, at age sixteen, when I was sitting in church hearing the sermon on Excellence (see Chapter 1). Suddenly, at this moment years later, I could actually *hear* the pastor's words in his closing charge to the congregation (they were all stored in my neural circuits) and I realized I had been operating on only *half* of his message. The part I had ignored came at the beginning: "With God's help." "With God's help, there isn't anything you can't do or be if you want it badly enough and are willing to work hard enough for it." Remembering "With God's help" seemed important as I moved to uncover and articulate my purpose.

> We are born with our purpose in place in our spiritual DNA. All we have to do is uncover it.

As our life unfolds, we experience meaningful moments that provide affirming evidence of what we value in life, the virtues we live, and our gifts and talents. These provide clues to our purpose. Each is related and yet different from the others.

## *What We Value*

There is a distinction between what we value and the values we live as virtues. In one sense what we value in life is extrinsic, that is, outside of ourselves, and is directed to what the world has to offer us. Our values, lived out as virtues, have more to do with the intrinsic principles that guide our conduct.

How do you know what you value? Can you write a list of what you value in life? I submit that you can. Let me explain how to do it. But first, a little background.

I recall the moment when I came upon Kevin McCarthy's book, *The On-Purpose Person.*[27] I was waiting to catch the red-eye flight from San Diego to my home in Illinois. I was sitting at a counter in a Long's Drug Store having a milk shake, when I noticed a book and magazine display nearby. I wandered over to the display and for reasons I cannot explain my eyes were drawn to the top shelf. Providentially, my gaze fell upon and then focused on the smallest, thinnest book on the top shelf, barely visible between two much larger books. It was *The On-Purpose Person* book. I purchased it and carried it aboard my flight. Now, what I really wanted to do was get to sleep as quickly as possible, so that, upon arrival in the morning, I would be rested and ready to begin a full day's work. I flipped through the early pages of McCarthy's book and was immediately engaged in the narrative, which took the form of a parable. I decided to read the introduction and the first chapter and then get some much needed sleep. I finished reading the entire book on that flight. I sensed that the incubation period for defining my purpose in life was about to enter a final stage of labor before birthing a purpose statement that would embody the authentic soul that I am.

A month or so later I went to Orlando, Florida, where I attended one of McCarthy's workshops. There my purpose in life materialized clearly. After some guidelines from Kevin McCarthy it emerged in my mind, fully formed.

With McCarthy's permission I would like to share a number of elegantly simple exercises that helped me refine my understanding of what I valued in life and my values.

## *Exercise to Pinpoint What You Value*

In order to determine what you value, you need to examine what you want in life. Find below "category accounts" that McCarthy suggests:

- Physical/Health/Recreational
- Financial/Material
- Family
- Vocational/Career
- Social/Community
- Spiritual
- Mental/Intellectual
- Anything important in your life missing from this list

On the top of eight separate sheets of paper write a category account name. McCarthy then instructs,

> Quiet your thoughts and focus on your wants. Next write down, in the manner described below, every imaginable want in each category account. Let them flow freely; no matter how outrageous they may seem, write them all down.

In doing this, you are to alternate your wants, writing the first one at the top of the page, the second at the bottom, the third near the top, below the first, the fourth near the bottom, just above the second, etc. (See left side of fig. 19-1).

As your account fills up, over a span of days or weeks, your wants in each category will converge at the middle of the page. It is recommended that you let thoughts about what you want in life flow freely from your mind. You will be returning to your wants lists from time to time. Don't edit. List what you want, even if it's outrageous. Wanting to be a multimillionaire and/or President of the United States are appropriate if that is what you want at some level of your being. Remember that no one is ever going to see the lists but you.

Next, have a tournament among your "wants" in each category account. It is in this step that you experience an elegantly simple, but profound, insight into the relative value you place on each "want" in each account. Fig. 19-1 shows an example of a play-off sheet like those seen in the sports section of newspapers, only with an array of eight numbered "wants" from a single account. You may have more or fewer.

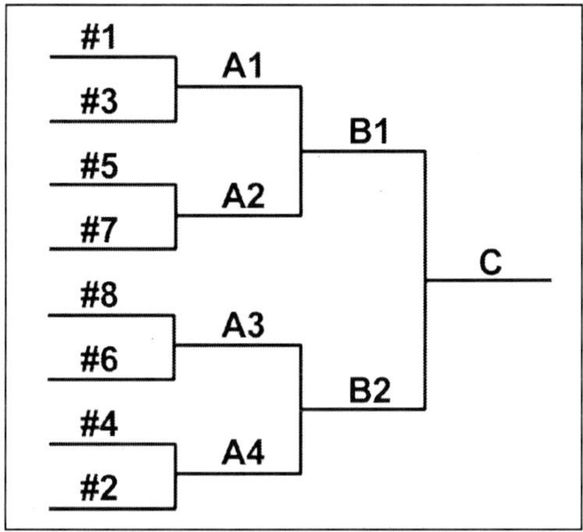


Fig. 19-1 Wants Tournament

Decide whether want #1 or want #3 is more important to you, and write the answer on line A1. Do the same for #5 and #7, etc. Repeat the process for each succeeding level. Your task is to consciously execute a serious competition among your "wants." Continue the playoff until you end up with a winner for each of the eight pages of category accounts. This may be difficult. Some people find it helpful to say the "wants" out loud, or to ask yourself a question out loud, such as, *Do I care more that my children are happy or successful? Do I want a new car more than a bigger savings account?*

The winners represent your "core wants." When you finally have your list of "core wants," you will be ready for a main draw tournament, a big time play-off of your "core wants."

We said before that defining one's purpose in life comes as the result of a process, a heartfelt examination. Even if you find the task of focusing on your "wants" very difficult, force yourself to do it.

Remember, it's not that you have to dream up these "wants." They're already there. Just bring them to the surface.

When you finish the main draw and a winner emerges, you will have a unique insight into what, at this moment in life, you value the most.

This exercise provides you with an answer. What meaning will you give it? This is but one of a number of illuminating steps that McCarthy takes his readers through on the way to uncovering their purpose. Time spent with your search for purpose guided by the text of *The On-Purpose Person* book will pay you huge dividends for the balance of your life. As McCarthy so beautifully puts it, "As you move boldly in the direction of your wants, your purpose will emerge in time." Understanding what you want will shed light on what you need to give to be of service to the world. Imbedded in your "wants" are the seeds of what you might give to some cause that is outside and greater than yourself.

The way you spend your time and money provides evidence of what you value. Of the two currencies, time and money, only time cannot be replaced. The time we have on the planet is finite. We have no way of knowing how much time we have left. All of us will eventually run out of it. Understanding your purpose will enable you to gain the greatest satisfaction from the time you have remaining.

If we are living our lives on purpose, does this mean the work we do to earn a living must line up with the purpose we have defined for our lives? What if our purpose in life has nothing to do with the nature of the work we do to earn a living? In an ideal world the work that we do would be in alignment with and provide an expression of our purpose in life. There are countless starving artists who do not consider their art to be work, for them it is a labor of love. Their efforts are their reward. For them joy and meaning come as a by-product of the very act of creation. It is often said that the day you find something you love to do you will never work another day in your life. This may be true, but it begs the question of how you pay your bills while doing what you love. Purposeful work is not the same as finding our purpose in life.

Several things can help you live well if there is not an alignment between your purpose and the way you make a living. You can change the way you think about your work, you can change the way you do the work or relate to the people you work with. You can request a transfer within your company that is more in line with your purpose, you can look for another job, you can go to school to prepare yourself for a different career (it's literally never too late), you can find a volunteer opportunity that fills your soul and think of your job as a necessary discipline.

## *Virtues – the Values that Animate our Lives*

Many people have found it helpful in the purpose discovery process to examine the values they hold both consciously and subconsciously. These are often different from *what* we value. Many values we hold are by-products of the culture in which we have been raised. Rather than talking about values in the abstract, I like to talk about values as they are lived. These are often called virtues. There appear to be virtues that are valued across many cultures.

> *A value in action is a virtue.*
> Loehr and Schwartz

Virtues are recognizable qualities and often involve moral thought and action. In other words a virtue may manifest its presence in behavior and be thought of as a character trait. When it was first suggested to me that I take a careful look at the virtues being manifested in my life, I simply came up blank. I had never given specific thought to the relative value I placed on the virtues that made their home in my mind and activities.

Assertiveness
Fidelity
Kindness
Spontaneity
Caring
Flexibility
Love
Steadfastness
Chastity
Focus
Loyalty
Tact
Cleanliness
Forgiveness
Moderation
Temperance
Commitment
Friendliness
Modesty
Thankfulness
Compassion
Frugality
Obedience
Tolerance
Confidence
Generosity
Openness
Toughness
Consideration
Gentleness
Orderliness
Trust
Cooperation
Gratitude
Patience
Trustworthiness
Courage
Helpfulness
Peacefulness
Truthfulness
Courtesy
Honesty
Perseverance
Tranquility
Creativity
Honor
Prudence
Understanding
Curiosity
Humility
Purposefulness
Unity
Detachment
Idealism
Reliability
Valor
Determination
Impartiality
Respect
Devotion
Industriousness
Responsibility
Diligence
Industry
Self-Discipline
Discretion
Integrity
Service
Enthusiasm
Joyfulness
Simplicity
Excellence
Justice
Sincerity

The most insightful work I have found on the subject of virtues is that of the Virtues Project (www.virtuesproject.com). Below is a chart that includes a list of virtues, many of which are featured in a set of 52 virtue cards offered by the Virtues Project.

### *Exercise to Identify Your Virtues*

Select 20 or more of the above virtues that seem to best characterize your behavior over your lifetime. Run a draw sheet tournament, just like you did with your "wants" lists.

What does the result tell you about yourself? When I completed my virtues tournament, it became apparent to me that the virtue that most fully embraced my conduct was that of perseverance in the face of obstacles.

## *Gifts and Talents*

What are your gifts — your natural, God-given talents? When answering this question, include behaviors and activities that don't seem like a big deal because they are nearly effortless for you. Sometimes we fail to notice our gifts because they are so much a part of us they don't stand out. Sometimes it takes comments from others or a tool like the HBDI™ to recognize our gifts.

The notion of thinking style preferences provides one answer to the question, "What comes naturally to you?" When you're operating within your thinking style preferences, things seem easy. Time passes quickly. You feel smart and energized.

Go back and look at the HBDI™ job profiles shown in Chapter 11. If you presently hold a job that you do not enjoy or are looking for work in the best possible world, I hope you have completed a HBDI™ survey and have your thinking style profile available to you. If not, Appendix A contains instructions on how to do so. If you are not able to have an HBDI™ profile, at least imagine what your thinking style profile might look like from the descriptions of the quadrants in this chapter.

My story is an example of the value of knowing your thinking style preference. In Chapter 11 there is a profile of the thinking styles required to execute the tasks of a patent attorney. Next to the patent attorney work profile is my thinking style preference profile. The basic nature of a patent attorney's work involves left brain mental activity, whereas my thinking style preference is clearly right-brained. Was I in the wrong kind of work, given what appeared to be a mismatch between my thinking style preferences and the thinking styles called for by my work? Did I find the work easy and purposeful or demanding and energy draining?

## *Thriving with a Thinking Style Mismatch*

I wanted to be a patent attorney. I wanted to provide well for my family. I wanted to look good. I wanted to do the job well. Yes, the work was demanding and difficult, probably because of the mismatch. But, it was also rewarding. In my first job out of engineering school, without realizing it, I found ways to engage my right brain and in the process helped some other people realize their greatness! I was working as a Patent Examiner in the U.S. Patent Office during the day, while attending law school at night. I found I possessed the unexplainable gift of being able to identify, within complex technology, the gist of an invention. This allowed me to focus my efforts and that of the inventors and attorneys on the broadest possible protection available for their ideas. Much later when I discovered my thinking style preference, which favored holistic thinking and visualization of complex structures and concepts, I understood my gift of perceiving the essence of invention. It was a by-product of my right brain thinking style preference. Later, in my corporate work as a patent attorney, I also found I had a talent for public speaking, for finding a natural way to teach my company's engineers and scientists how to identify and disclose invention in their work. During those years, the invention disclosure rate and patents issuing leaped twenty-fold (See Chapter 12).

It is appropriate to ask, "Did the classes I taught make the engineers and scientists more creative — that is, more inventive?" The answer is no. They were already creative; I helped them capitalize on it. Their job performance reviews were significantly improved when their invention disclosure activity that resulted in patents was noticed by the people in the Human Resources Department. Bear in mind that very few engineering school graduates will ever receive a patent in the course of their careers.

When head count reductions, downsizing, right sizing and other euphemisms for firing employees became more common, some of the engineers I'd worked with lost their jobs. I cannot count the number of laid-off engineers who found new work quickly and shared with me their belief that the patents listed in their resumes gave them a real edge over the competition in their job search. You can imagine how my spirits soared when I learned of my role in liberating their greatness in a form that would be with them for the rest of their lives.

As you learned in Chapter 1, I had first been told I had a gift for public speaking in high school. In 1974, I was invited to speak at Chautauqua Institution, a lovely summer learning community in New York state. I gave a talk in the evening. The crowd numbered more than 1000. The next morning I was jogging, and a number of cars slowed down after they passed me and each time a passenger got out and waved to me to stop. Each one said something like, "Thank you for your talk last night. You touched me." I figured it was the content of what I said that touched them.

Years later, in 1983, I'd been invited to give a talk at a half-way house for women who were recovering alcoholics. At the end of my talk, the woman in charge of the program approached me and thanked me for coming and said, "Hal, I heard you speak before." I responded, "I don't see how you could have....I've never been in this town before." She replied, "It wasn't here." She described having heard me speak at a regional gathering three years earlier. I remembered the time. After my talk that night, a small group had asked me to speak to a very sick woman in the audience. When I approached her it was apparent to me that she needed medical help. She'd been drinking non-stop for more than a week and she'd just called for help. She was disheveled, she was shaking, her eyes were rolling back into her head. I said, "I cannot help her. Get her to a hospital immediately." This scene flashed across my mind.

I then asked the half-way house director, "Do you know what ever happened to that woman?" She replied, "I was that woman." Then she added, "You know, Hal, I don't remember a single word that you said that night, but I knew, I knew at some level that I would never drink again." And it dawned on me that it was not the content of what I had said that reached her at some deep level. I think I have what is described in the Christian scriptures as the gift of "inspired speech." What I say may be helpful and insightful, but the deepest impact is when my God-given gift of inspired speech, offered in the spirit of service, communicates love. Love heals.

So, once again, what are your natural gifts and talents? Identifying them will help you uncover your purpose.

## *Making a Purpose Statement*

> *Purpose builds on our past, lives in our present and holds hope for our future...From a divine perspective, purpose is God's will for your life...Therefore purpose is the ultimate service concept.*
>
> Kevin McCarthy

He suggests that a good way to begin a purpose statement is with the words, "I exist to serve by ......."

Find below a sampling of purpose statements related in "On-Purpose Person" workshops.

I exist to serve by:
igniting and imparting joy
bringing light
liberating greatness
awakening dreams
cultivating growth

In contrast to a vision or mission statement, which may be long and complex, a purpose statement should be short and concise. All the books on finding purpose seem to agree on this. In fact, the shorter the better. A purpose statement is most valuable when you are able to remember it easily, so that if someone asked you, "What's your purpose in life?" you could answer effortlessly.

McCarthy's guidance in uncovering purpose has been very helpful to me. There does not appear to be any perfect form for a purpose statement. However it does seem best when purpose statements expand from a connection to oneself to include other people, or a bigger world in some way. It may suit you to include reference to God or a higher power. Purpose statements need to be broad enough to apply to all areas of life, personal and professional.

Of course, many people are living their lives on purpose without having written a purpose statement. That's partly because we don't create a purpose, we just uncover it. People arrive at it from many different paths.

You may recall my friend Jim, the anxiety-ridden job seeker from Chapter 17, who seemed at first to find affirmations ineffective in changing his life. More than a year after our first conversations, he came to visit. He was alive and enthusiastic. He was teaching as an adjunct professor at two local universities and loving it. It didn't matter that the pay did not equal his previous levels. He felt energized, appreciated, and useful. He had discovered his purpose. (A year later he was made a full-time instructor at one of the universities.)

Sharon and I had a funny experience with purpose during our courtship, which was mostly a long-distance correspondence. I wrote asking her to tell me what her purpose in life was. I was beginning to be very interested in her, and wanted to know that she lived a purpose-directed life, or lived "on-purpose," if this were going to get serious. She wrote back that the question "rankled" her. She had worked very consciously to live according to her values, to walk her talk, to be her best self. But she never asked herself this exact question, "What is your purpose in life?" and it seemed to imply that maybe she wasn't purpose directed. I explained to her that by living "on-purpose" I meant behaving day-to-day in concert with your purpose. After she got over being defensive, she thought seriously about the question and wrote back: "My purpose in life is to love well and help others do the same." That was good enough for me!

It has been my experience that those individuals who have been living their lives on-purpose easily state their purpose in simple declaration sentences. Find below, used with their permission, some examples of purpose statements.

*My purpose in life is to be of service to God and my fellow man.*
Bill Wilson

*My purpose in life is to help people find their voice and use it for the common good.* Gordon Mitchell

*My purpose in life is to make meaning of the things I see around me and create an environment where others can do the same.*
Jennifer Landau

*My purpose in life is to create safe environments for myself and others to be authentic and understand our gifts.* Susan Swearingen

When I joined The Fellowship in 1971, I adopted as my own purpose that of Bill Wilson (listed first above): *My purpose in life is to be of service to God and my fellow man.* This wonderful purpose statement has been instrumental in guiding countless other men and women in The Fellowship programs throughout the world.

Although the purpose statement's generic nature comforted me on the one hand at a spiritual level, it seemed ambiguous in terms of *how* the purpose would manifest itself in my life. I was in this frame of mind when I attended Kevin McCarthy's workshop, spending a day or so immersed in thought regarding my purpose in life. It was here that I was encouraged to consider writing a purpose statement with a preamble that begins with "I exist to serve by......... "

For me the word "by" was the key to thinking about the doing, the actions that could express my purpose in my daily life. The answer came instantly to me from my subconscious when I asked of my inner self how I was going to be of service to God and my fellow man? "By" what action? By doing what? It was at that moment I realized that I felt most fully alive when I was refining and delivering my program, "Pathways to Greatness," the primary purpose of which was to liberate the God-given gems of greatness embedded in the neural networks of every person's brain. As I noted earlier in this chapter, my purpose statement came to my conscious mind fully formed and it reads as follows:

> *My purpose in life is to be of service to God and my fellow man by liberating greatness in myself and others.*

That's my memory of discovering my purpose. When I wrote Kevin McCarthy asking his permission to quote his material, he called and asked if I would include the story as he remembers it. Here is what he wrote, with a follow-up in the chapter notes.

*Hallelujah! The Day Hal First Voiced His Purpose*

Working with individuals and organizations to articulate their purpose is a special privilege. One story I love telling is that of Hal

Williamson. He's an unforgettable and learned character with an infectious spirit who taught me a lesson about purpose statements and life.

It was in September 1994, when Hal and his wife, Trudy, attended a Train-the-Trainer program based on my first book, *The On-Purpose Person.* When the time came for Hal to write his personal purpose statement, this ever-the-engineer-and-lawyer had come with his homework done. He had completed the statement, "To the Glory of God, I, Hal Williamson, exist to serve by..." with great gusto. Proudly, he handed me a page and a half brief of single-spaced typed copy. "Here, please read this and give me your feedback," Hal invited.

I took one quick look and said, "No, Hal, I won't read it." A look mixed with confusion and disappointment crossed his face. I instructed him, "Shorten it to a paragraph."

"Impossible!" Hal replied. "I can't do that."

"Go do it, Hal. I'm sure you can," I unwaveringly encouraged.

Hal obeyed, and left to work some more. About twenty minutes later, he appeared with his now handwritten notes clutched in his hand. Shaking with excitement, he said, "Kevin, I did it! Now read my purpose statement."

"No. I won't." Once again Hal's bewildered expression said it all. I chuckled to myself and once more instructed, "Hal, go back and reduce your paragraph to a single sentence."

"Impossible!" he said. "It can't be done."

"Go do it, Hal."

Only minutes later Hal returned with a single sentence. It read, "My purpose in life is to be of service to God and my fellow man by liberating greatness in myself and others."

"Hal," I said, "Say it in two words." Right before my eyes, Hal lit up. "Liberating Greatness. That's it! In all of my 60 years of life, that's it!" His eyes twinkled with delight. I call this moment The Breath of Adam. It is like watching God breathe life into man. He glowed in the moment.

Later that day, Hal pulled me aside. "This way you do purpose

> statements makes a lot of sense, Kevin. As a patent attorney I always asked my staff lawyers and engineers to write their patent descriptions with the least number of words possible. It provided the broadest patent coverage and protection possible. The more words there were, the more loopholes existed for others to penetrate the patent. In much the same way, a simple two-word purpose statement provides the same." Hal was absolutely right. A purpose statement is a high internal personal standard that informs, directs, and protects us.[28]

Some people will find it useful to include a "doing" section to their purpose statements, as I did, but it is not required. Purpose is more about being than doing.

It is my belief that identifying your purpose in life provides a direction. It is a vector for the trajectory your life will take once you begin to live your life on purpose. It can also provide inspiration, guidance, and a sense of peace. When a new opportunity comes up, asking yourself, "Does this fit with my purpose in life?" can help you decide whether or not to take it.

However, actually taking the time and thought to uncover your purpose can be scary. In many "Pathways to Greatness" workshops people expressed enthusiasm about articulating their purpose. So I offered a guided workshop to help. No one came. I tried a few more times, with the same result. Conversations with people gradually helped me see the difficulty. If you clearly discover and articulate your purpose, you may have to change some things in your life. It can make you uncomfortable, give you cognitive dissonance. This is discomfort and cognitive dissonance you've already had on some level but, when it becomes conscious and written, it is hard to ignore. You can tell I feel strongly that uncovering your purpose is important, but proceed at your own risk!

Imagine, if you will, ten individuals who each have a purpose statement identical to my own. Do you think the purposeful lives they live day-to-day look just like mine? Of course not! You may not find a way to earn a living that fully engages your preferred thinking styles as well as your values, gifts and talents. Fortunately, there are opportunities in volunteer work or adjustments you can make in your emphasis and style in the workplace.

The powerful, hopeful message is that if you:

- get clear about what you value
- identify your virtues
- acknowledge and own your gifts and talents,

you will be on the path to uncovering your purpose in life. When your purpose is out in the open, clearly expressed, you know when it's right. It gives you a tingle it is so right, and it provides guidance much like a rudder, guiding you forward, toward your vision, your best self, your biggest contribution.

# 20

## *You Are In Charge of Your Life*

You now have the tools to change your life. They worked in my life. Thousands of individuals have successfully practiced the principles outlined in this book. Let them work for you too.

There are some in the world who see people in The Fellowship as flawed. Because of our addiction each of us is thought to be as weak as our weakest link, like a chain. I say this is a half-truth. I am as strong as my strongest link. And what is it fashioned of? My faith in those who travel the spiritual path, and in God and in myself. And with these spiritual links intertwined I journey through life, finding myself strengthened by the company of like-minded souls.

All the spiritual traditions seem to acknowledge that man must experience difficulties in the process of growing spiritually. Indeed, the writings of the Bahá'í Faith explain that it is often during the individual's determined and courageous struggle against physical, emotional and mental handicaps that the greatest spiritual growth occurs. The individual may come to view such handicaps as blessings in disguise that have, ultimately, helped him or her grow spiritually.[29]

I know that for people like me, success is a journey and not a destination. I live my life on purpose, a life of love and service, a life free from the bondage of alcohol. By every measure, by every test that counts in my life, I am a success. I now believe I am living the life my father envisioned when he admonished his sons, "Never forget that you are a Williamson."

*Photo by Lisa Mitchell*

Hal Williamson in 2006

Victor Frankl, who survived years in a concentration camp, pointed the way when he said:

> Everything can be taken from a man but one thing: the last of human freedoms – to choose one's attitude in any given set of circumstances, to choose one's own way.[30]

The purpose of this book has been to provide simple instructions that will allow you to cultivate and liberate your natural greatness. I've tried to give you insight into the biology of the process, and tools to live in a purposeful way the life you've always wanted.

If you are new to the concepts and principles of this book, accept this warm invitation: Come walk with us, come talk with us, come join us on the high road, on the road to a way of life that grows indescribably more wonderful with each passing day. The longest journey begins with a single step. You who have read this book have taken that step.

M. Scott Peck said, "Life is difficult." Oh, yes it is. He closes his book *The Road Less Traveled* with a passage from the poem by Robert Frost quoted in the Introduction to this book. "Two roads in a wood diverged and I took the one less traveled by and that has made all of the difference."

As you join me on that high road, consider the following lines that touched my heart when I read them.

If you would sense the past - touch a stone.
If you would capture the moment, touch a rose.
If you want to glimpse eternity, touch a life.

Anonymous

Touch a life. Begin with touching your own. And when you do, the effect of your presence in the world will cause a ripple that will wash up on the shores of eternity. Your life will have been a life well lived!

LIFE IS WONDERFUL!

# Chapter Notes

Introduction

1 Bahá'u'lláh, founder of the Bahá'i Faith

2 Frankl, Viktor E. *Man's Search for Meaning.* New York: Washington Square Press, 1985.

3 Frost, Robert. "The Road Not Taken." In *Selected Poems of Robert Frost.* New York, New York: Holt, Rinehart and Winston, Inc, 1963.

Chapter 2

4 Blakeslee, Sandra. "The Brain in the Gut." New York Times May 23, 1996.

5 Armour, Dr. Andrew J. *Neurocardiology – Anatomical and Functional Principles.* E-book. University of Montreal. Available at www.hearthmath.org.store. Armour discusses intriguing data documenting the complex neuronal processing and memory capabilities of the intrinsic cardiac nervous system, indicating that the heart brain can process information and make decisions about its control independent of the central nervous system. This monograph contributes to the newly emerging view of the heart as a complex, self-organized system that maintains a continuous two-way dialogue with the brain and the rest of the body.

Chapter 4

6 Damasio, Antonio R. *Descartes' Error: Emotion, Reason, and the Human Brain.* New York: Avon Books, 1994.

7 Pert, Candace B., Ph.D. *Molecules of Emotion.* New York: Simon & Schuster, 1999.

8 Howard, Pierce J., Ph.D. *The Owner's Manual for the Brain: Everyday Applications from Mind-Brain Research.* Austin, Texas: Bard Press, Second Edition, 2000.

Chapter 5

9 Goleman, Daniel. *Emotional Intelligence.* New York: Bantam Books, 1995.

Chapter 8

10 Barbara Curry has hidden four (4) four-leaf clovers in this picture.

Chapter 9

11 Leon Festinger (1919-1989) was, in the 1950s and 1960s, one of the most influential social psychologists in the world. He held teaching positions at Iowa, Rochester, MIT, Minnesota, Michigan and Stanford before joining the faculty of the New School for Social Research in New York City in 1968. He is best known for his Theory of Cognitive Dissonance. Festinger considered the human need to avoid dissonance as basic as the need for safety or the need to satisfy hunger. He theorized that cognitive dissonance creates a drive that motivates us to be consistent.

12 *Twelve Steps and Twelve Traditions.* New York, NY: The A.A. Grapevine, Inc., 1953.

Chapter 13

13 Senge, Peter M. , and Art Kleiner, Charlotte Roberts, Bryan Smith, and Richard Ross, *The Fifth Discipline Fieldbook: Strategies and Tools for Building a Learning Organization,* p. 195. New York: Doubleday, 1990.

Chapter 15

14 Investment in Excellence® is a program of the Pacific Institute. Founded in 1971 by Lou and Diane Tice, it provided my first taste of cognitive psychology and social learning theory. For more information, see www.pac-inst.com.

15 Richardson, Alan. *Mental Imagery.* Springer Publishing Co., Inc. 1969 (out of print).

16 Pascual-Leone, Alvaro, M.D., Ph.D. Director of the Center for Non-Invasive Brain Stimulation and Associate Professor of Neurology, Harvard Medical School.

17 Carson, Ben, M.D. Director of Pediatric Neurosurgery, Johns Hopkins Children's Center. Dr. Carson grew up in poverty in Detroit and Boston. He started out with terrible grades, anger and low self-esteem. But once he made a decision to change his life by harnessing the power of his mind, nothing could stand in his way.

Chapter 17

18 Peale, Norman Vincent. *The Power of Positive Thinking.* New York, Prentice-Hall, 1952.

19 Maltz, Maxwell., M.D., F.I.C.S. *Psycho-Cybernetic Principles for Creative Living.* New York: Pocket Books, 1974.

20 Rheinhold Niebuhr, apparent author of The Serenity Prayer. He recounted to interviewers on several occasions that he had written the prayer as a "tag line" to a sermon he had delivered on Practical Christianity. Yet even Dr. Niebuhr added at least a touch of doubt to his claim, when he told one interviewer, "Of course, it may have been spooking around for years, even centuries, but I don't think so. I honestly do believe that I wrote it myself."

Chapter 18

21 Toastmasters is a wonderful organization with branches in many communities, where you can learn how to give great speeches and practice in a non-threatening audience. Learn more at www.toastmasters.org

22 PLOS Biology Vol. 2, Issue 4, April, 2004, Chapter 16, p. 41.

Chapter 19

23 Harman, Willis, Ph.D. and Howard Rheingold. *Higher Creativity: Liberating the Unconscious for Breakthrough Insights.* Los Angeles: Jeremy P. Tarcher, Inc., 1984.

24 Fritz, Robert. *The Path of Least Resistance: Learning to Become the Creative Force in Your Own Life.* New York: Ballantine Books, 1984.

25 Frankl, Viktor E. *Man's Search for Meaning.* New York: Washington Square Press, 1985.

26 Leider, Richard, *The Power of Purpose.* New York: Ballantine Books, 1985.

27 McCarthy, Kevin W. *The On-Purpose Person, Making Your Life Make Sense.* Colorado Springs, Colorado: Piñon Press, 1992.

28 McCarthy, Kevin. Kevin's story continues, "Months passed and I was thinking of Hal. We hadn't connected since shortly after the training program so I picked up the phone to say hello to this wonderful man. A woman answered and I said, "Hi Trudy! This is Kevin McCarthy." There was an awkward silence. The woman's voice dropped. It was Hal's daughter. She said, "Kevin, you must not have heard about my parents."

"No."

"Mom and Dad were in Miami shortly after the workshop with you in Orlando and..." and she proceeded to tell me the story of the accident that took Trudy's life and put Hal in the hospital. She urged me, "Give Dad a call. He would love to hear from you." Stunned by the news I sat thinking and staring at Hal's hospital phone number on my notepad, *What do I say to a man who has lost his wife of thirty-plus years and lies in a hospital bed recovering from serious injuries?*

Pressing the numbers on the phone, I said a little prayer. Hal's distinctively chipper voice answered, "Hello!"

"Hi Hal, it's Kevin McCarthy. I'm so sorry to hear of your loss and your injuries."

"Kevin, I miss my Trudy with all my heart. I'll recover from my injuries. In the meantime, I'm Liberating Greatness in the hospital!"

Wow! I, who called to minister, was the one who gained comfort. After our brief conversation, I hung up the phone inspired by the model of Hal's life and renewed in the meaning of m work. So when you read my second book, *The On-Purpose Business,* you'll know why there's a wonderfully wise, kind, and spry character by the name of Hal Trudy. The memory of Hal and Trudy's love and marriage is honored. There's power in your purpose statement."

Chapter 20

29 *Fire and Gold, Benefiting from Life's Tests.* Compiled by Brian Kurzius. Oxford: George Ronald, 1997.

30 Frankl, Viktor E. *Man's Search for Meaning.* New York: Washington Square Press, 1985.

# *Appendix A*

## *Sample Affirmations*

(Especially useful for tape or CD use described in Chapter 17.)

- I am a good person.
- I am lovable and capable.
- I am smart enough, experienced enough and talented enough to get what I want.
- Everything good in me increases and multiplies.
- I am free to be the person I always wanted to be.
- My life is fun.
- I am worthy and deserving of wealth and success.
- I am constantly learning new and better ways to do things.
- I can do whatever I set my mind to.
- I always expect the best outcome.
- I take responsibility for every aspect of my life.
- Every day I become more the person I want to be.
- I have all that I need.
- My financial affairs are in order.
- I deserve to have my dreams come true.
- I take good care of my body.
- I have a slim, fit, beautiful body.
- I am relaxed, calm and healthy.
- I get enough physical exercise.
- I have a lifestyle that generates high energy.
- I spend my time in ways that fulfill me.

- My needs are as important as anyone else's needs.
- I surround myself with happy and successful people.
- I move confidently through life.
- I am flexible and creative.
- Abundance flows easily into my life.
- I am honest and unafraid.
- I find it natural to express myself more and more fully.
- I am open and receptive.
- I easily accept compliments.
- The more receptive I am, the more I receive.
- When I am my true self, I experience truth, peace, abundance and joy. My true self is my guide and teacher.
- I am aligned with my highest good.
- I let go of control.
- My life is perfectly balanced.
- Every problem is an opportunity for me to be creative.
- Every problem is an opportunity for me to grow and expand myself.
- I am enthusiastic and alive.
- My wisdom and my love are always expanding.
- I have many gifts and positive qualities.
- I trust my own intelligence.
- I have integrity.
- I accept the truth about myself and my life.
- It is not what happens but how I respond to what happens that determines the quality of my life.
- I am empowered to take action and I do so, now.
- I am honest with myself.
- I tell the truth with compassion.
- When I am one with my true self, I accept others exactly as they are.
- I release all present relationships based on fear.

- I choose to build a life of love and abundance.
- My being here makes a difference.
- I am strong.
- Life is good.
- I do what makes my heart sing.
- I take on challenges easily.
- I trust myself.
- I have an inner wisdom that provides perfect guidance.
- I start each new day with wonder and joy.
- I am financially successful.
- I always add value wherever I am.
- I am living life fully.
- I am patient.
- My intellect supports my intuition.
- I am aware of my life's purpose and know why I am here.
- I act in alignment with my mission.
- The universe rewards my actions.
- I am self-disciplined.
- I do whatever I need to do to succeed.
- I experience great satisfaction in completing things.
- I take necessary risks easily and joyfully.
- I give myself permission to make mistakes.
- I constantly stretch myself into new comfort zones.
- I keep all my agreements.
- I say no to things that take me off purpose.
- I get things done.
- People can depend on me to get results because I take action. I expect only the best.
- I deserve only the best.
- I enjoy the support of many people.
- I am open to feedback.

- My life is a celebration of love and abundance.
- I acknowledge all those who assist me.
- I am grateful for all that I have.
- I see opportunity every where.
- I am doing everything I can to make my world a better place.
- My life is in balance.

Affirmations Specific to Recovery

Samples can be downloaded from www.halwill.com.

Many thanks to the *Pathways to Greatness* participants from whom these have been received over the years.

# *Appendix B*

## Order copies of *Liberating Greatness*

You can order copies of *Liberating Greatness, The Whole Brain Guide to an Extraordinary Life* in a number of ways:

On the Web:

- www.halwill.com
- www.wordassociation.com
- www.amazon.com

E-mail hal@hopellc.com

Call 1-888-907-HOPE (4673) or (412) 741-1709

## Order Your HBDI™ Thinking Style Preference Profile

Discover your own thinking style preference by ordering the HBDI™ for your self. You can do this from our website, www.hopellc.com, or e-mail us at hope@hopellc.com.

There is a fee for processing and debriefing the HBDI™. Call us for pricing.

1-888-907-HOPE (4673) or (412) 741-1709

For information on HBDI™ Certification, call or e-mail us.

## Understand More about Whole Brain Thinking

To learn more about Whole Brain Thinking and to get a sense of your thinking style preference without actually taking the HBDI™, read Ned Herrmann's *Whole Brain Business Book*, which includes many ways of looking at yourself and your thinking style preferences. This book can be found in most libraries and bookstores, or ordered from online bookstores.

## Services of Hope Unlimited, LLC

Hal Williamson, Sharon Eakes and Hope Unlimited, LLC offer a variety of services, including:

- Keynote speeches
- "Pathways to Greatness" seminar series
- Liberating Greatness workshops
- Couples Workshops
- Teambuilding
- Personal and Executive Coaching

Contact us.

**Hope Unlimited, LLC**
Phone: 1-888-907-HOPE (4673)
(412) 741-1709
www.hopellc.com
www.halwill.com
E-mail: hal@hopellc.com
sharon@hopellc.com

# *BIBLIOGRAPHY*

Adler, Mortimer J. *Six Great Ideas.* New York: McMillan Publishing, 1984.

Albrecht, Karl. *Brain Power: Learn To Improve Your Thinking Skills.* New York: Prentice Hall Press, 1980.

Alkon, Daniel L., M.D. *Memory's Voice: Deciphering The Mind-Brain Code.* New York: HarperCollins, Inc., 1992.

Allman, William F. *Apprentices of Wonder: Inside the Neural Network Revolution.* New York: Bantam Books, 1989.

Armour, J. Andrew, M.D., Ph.D. *Neurocardiology—Anatomical and Functional Principles.* University of Montreal, 1991.

Baars, Bernard J. *A Cognitive Theory of Consciousness.* Cambridge: Cambridge University Press, 1988.

Benson, Herbert, M.D. *The Relaxation Response.* New York: William Morrow and Company, 1975.

Benson, Herbert, M.D. *Your Maximum Mind.* New York: Random House, 1987.

Benziger, I. Katherine, and Anne Sohn. *The Art of Using Your Whole Brain.* Rockwall, Texas: The Benziger Publishing Company, 1989.

Bloodworth, Venice J., Dr. *Key To Yourself.* Marina del Rey, California: DeVross & Company, 1952.

Boden, Margaret A. *The Creative Mind: Myths & Mechanisms.* New York: BasicBooks, 1992.

Briggs, John and F. David Peat. *Turbulent Mirror.* New York Harper & Row, 1989.

Burke, James and Robert Ornstein. *The Axemaker's Gift.* New York: G.P. Putnam's Sons, 1995.

Buzan, Tony and Barry Buzan. *The Mind Map Book.* New York: Dutton, 1994.

Buzan, Tony. *Use Both Sides of Your Brain.* New York: Dutton, 1974.

Buzan, Tony. *Use Your Perfect Memory.* New York: Plume, 1991.

Cade, C Maxwell and Nona Coxhead. *The Awakened Mind.* Great Britain: Element Books, 1989.

Calvin, William H. *How Brains Think.* New York: BasicBooks 1996.

Capra, Fritjof. *The Tao Of Physics.* Boston: Shambhala, 1991.

Chopra, Deepak, M.D. *Ageless Body, Timeless Mind.* New York: Harmony Books, 1993.

Chuck "C". *A New Pair of Glasses.* Irvine, California: New-Look Publishing, 1984.

Churchland, Patricia S. and Terrence J. Sejnowski. *The Computational Brain.* Cambridge: The MIT Press, 1992.

Churchland, Patricia Smith. *Neurophilosophy: Toward a Unified Science of the Mind-Brain.* Cambridge: The MIT Press, 1992.

Cohen, David. *The Secret Language of the Mind: A Visual Inquiry into the Mysteries of Consciousness.* San Francisco: Chronicle Books, 1996.

Corballis, Michael C. *The Lopsided Ape: Evolution of the Generative Mind.* New York: Oxford University Press, 1991.

Covey, Stephen R, A. Roger Merrill and Rebecca R. Merrill. *First Things First: To Live, to Love, to Learn, to Leave a Legacy.* New York: Simon & Schuster, 1995.

Covey, Stephen R. *The Seven Habits of Highly Effective People: Restoring the Character Ethic.* New York: Simon & Shuster, 1990.

Covey, Stephen R. *The Seven Habits of Highly Effective People: Powerful Lessons in Personal Change.* New York: HarperCollins, 1992.

Csikszentmihalyi, Mihaly. *Flow: The Psychology of Optimal Experience.* New York: Harper & Roe, 1990.

Czerner, Thomas B., M.D. *What Makes You Tick?: The Brain in Plain English.* New York: John Wiley & Sons, 2001.

Damasio, Antonio R. *Descartes' Error: Emotion, Reason, and the Human Brain.* New York: Avon Books, 1994.

de Bono, Edward. *The Mechanism of Mind.* New York: Penguin Books, 1990.

de Bono, Edward. *Practical Thinking: 4 ways to be right. 5 ways to be wrong. 5 ways to Understand.* New York: Penguin Books, 1991.

de Bono, Edward. *Lateral Thinking: A Textbook of Creativity.* New York: Penguin Books, 1990.

de Bono, Edward. *The Happiness Purpose.* New York: Penguin Books, 1990.

de Bono, Edward. *The Use of Lateral Thinking.* New York: Penguin Books, 1990.

de Bono, Edward. *Six Thinking Hats: The Power of Focused Thinking: 6 Proven Ways To Effectively Focus Your Creative Thinking.* Boston: Little, Brown and Company, 1985.

de Bono, Edward. *Teaching Thinking.* New York: Penguin Books, 1991.

de Bono, Edward. *I Am Right – You Are Wrong: From This To The New Renaissance: From Rock Logic To Water Logic.* New York: Penguin Books, 1991.

de Bono, Edward. Sur/Petition: *Creating Value Monopolies When Everyone Else Is Merely Competing.* New York: Penguin Books, 1991.

Dennett, Daniel C. *Kinds of Minds: Toward an Understanding of Consciousness.* New York: Basic Books, 1996.

Dewey, John. *How We Think.* Buffalo, New York: Prometheus Books, 1991.

Dyer, Dr. Wayne W. *Real Magic: Creating Miracles In Everyday Life.* New York: HarperCollins, 1992.

Einstein, Albert. *The Theory of Relativity (and Other Essays).* New York: First Carol Publishing Group, 1996.

Esslemont, J.E. *Bahá'u'lláh and The New Era.* US: Allen & Unwin, 1976.

Fezler, William, Ph.D. *Creative Imagery: How to Visualize in All Five Senses.* New York: Simon & Schuster, 1989.

Frankl, Viktor E. *Man's Search For Meaning.* New York: Washington Square Press, 1985.

Frankl, Viktor E. *The Unheard Cry for Meaning: Psychotherapy & Humanism.* New York, NY: Simon & Schuster, 1978.

Fritz, Robert. *The Path of Least Resistance: Learning to Become the Creative Force in Your Own Life.* New York: Ballantine Books, 1984.

Fritz, Robert. *Creating.* New York: Ballantine Books, 1991.

Fromm, Erich. *The Revolution of Hope: Toward A Humanized Technology.* New York: Harper & Row, 1968.

Gallwey, Timothy W. *The Inner Game of Tennis. Revised Edition.* New York: Random House 1998.

Gallwey, Timothy W. *The Inner Game of Golf. Revised Edition.* New York: Random House 1997.

Gallwey, Timothy W. *The Inner Game of Work: Focus, Learning, Pleasure, and Mobility in the Workplace.* New York: Random House 2000.

Gardner, Howard. *The Disciplined Mind: What All Students Should Understand.* New York: Simon & Schuster, 1999.

Gardner, Howard and Emma Laskin. *Leading Minds: An Anatomy of Leadership.* New York: BasicBooks, 1995.

Gelb, Michael J. *How to Think Like Leonardo da Vinci: Seven Steps To Genius Every Day.* New York: Delacorte Press, 1998.

Gleick, James. *Chaos: Making a New Science.* New York: Viking Penguin, 1987.

Gleick, James. *Genius: the Life and Science of Richard Feynman.* New York: Vintage Books, 1992.

Goleman, Daniel. *Emotional Intelligence.* New York.: Bantam Books, 1995.

Gordon, Barry, M.D., Ph.D. and Lisa Berger. *Intelligent Memory: Improve the Memory That Makes You Smarter.* New York: Viking Penguin, 2003.

Greenfield, Susan A. *Journey to the Centers of the Mind: Toward a Science of Consciousness.* New York: W.H. Freeman, 1995.

Greenspan, Stanley I., M.D. with Beryl Lieff Benderly. *The Growth of the Mind and the Endangered Origins of Intelligence.* New York: Addison-Wesley Publishing, 1997.

Gross, Stanislav, M.D. with Hal Zina Bennett, Ph.D. *The Holotropic Mind: The Three Levels of Human Consciousness and How They Shape Our Lives.* San Francisco: HarperSanFrancisco, 1993.

Hampden-Turner, Charles. *Maps of the Mind.* New York: Macmillan Publishing, 1982.

Harary, Keith, Ph.D. and Pamela Weintraub. *Right-Brain Learning in 30 Days: The Whole Mind Program.* New York: St. Martin's Press, 1991.

Harman, Willis, Ph.D. *Global Mind Change: The New Age Revolution In The Way We Think.* New York: Warner Books, 1988.

Harman, Willis, Ph.D. and Howard Rheingold. *Higher Creativity: Liberating the Unconscious for Breakthrough Insights.* Los Angeles: Jeremy P. Tarcher, Inc., 1984.

Harrison, Allen F. and Robert M. Bramson, Ph.D. *The Art Of Thinking: Strategies for Asking Questions, Making Decisions, and Solving Problems.* New York: Berkley Books, 1982.

Hatcher, William S. and J. Douglas Martin. *The Bahá'í Faith, The Emerging Global Religion.* Wilmette, Illinois: Bahá'í Publishing Trust. 1998.

Healy, Jane M. Ph.D. *Endangered Minds: Why Our Children Don't Think.* New York: Simon & Schuster, 1990.

Herrmann, Ned. *The Creative Brain.* North Carolina: Brain Books. 1989.

Herrmann, Ned. *The Whole Brain Business Book.* New York: McGraw-Hill, 1996.

Hobson, J. Allan. *The Dreaming Brain.* New York: BasicBooks, 1988.

Hooper, Judith and Dick Teresi. *The Three-Pound Universe.* New York: Jeremy P. Tarcher, 1992.

Howard, Pierce J., Ph.D. *The Owner's Manual For The Brain: Everyday Applications From Mind-Brain Research.* Austin, Texas: Leornian Press, 1994.

Hubel, David H. *Eye, Brain, And Vision.* New York: Scientific American Library, 1987.

Jaynes, Julian. *The Origin of Consciousness in the Breakdown of the*

*Bicameral Mind.* Boston: Houghton Mifflin, 1976.

Joseph, R., Dr. *The Right Brain and the Unconscious: Discovering the Stranger Within.* New York: Plenum Press, 1992.

Kahaner, Larry. *Competitive Intelligence: From Black Ops To Boardrooms-How Businesses Gather, Analyze, And Use Information To Succeed In The Global Marketplace.* New York: Simon & Schuster, 1996.

Kauffman, Stuart. *At Home In The Universe: The Search for Laws of Self-Organization and Complexity.* New York: Oxford University Press, 1995.

Kosko, Bart. *Fuzzy Thinking: The New Science of Fuzzy Logic.* New York: Hyperion, 1993.

Kotulak, Ronald. *Inside The Brain: Revolutionary Discoveries of How the Mind Works.* Kansas City, Missouri: Andrews McMeel Publishing, 1996.

Krauss, Lawrence M. *Fear Of Physics: A Guide for the Perplexed.* New York: BasicBooks, 1993.

Leider, Richard J. *The Power of Purpose.* New York: Ballantine Books, 1985.

Leider, Richard J. and David A. Shapiro. *Repacking Your Bags: Lighten Your Load for the Rest of Your Life.* San Francisco: Berrett-Koehler Publishers, 1995.

LeShan, Lawrence. *How to Meditate.* New York: Bantam Books, 1975.

McCarthy, Kevin W. *The On-Purpose Business: Doing More of What You Do Best More Profitably.* Colorado Springs, Colorado: Piñon Press, 1998.

McCarthy, Kevin W. *The On-Purpose Person, Making Your Life Make Sense.* Colorado Springs, Colorado: Piñon Press, 1992.

Maltz, Maxwell., M.D., F.I.C.S. *Psycho-Cybernetic Principles for Creative Living.* New York: Pocket Books, 1974.

Maltz, Maxwell, M.D., F.I.C.S. *Psycho-Cybernetics: A New Way to Get More Living Out of Life.* New York: Simon & Schuster, 1989.

Mandino, Olg. *University Of Success.* New York: Bantam Books, 1982

Mapes, James J. *Quantum Leap Thinking: An Owner's Guide to the Mind.* Beverly Hills, CA: Dove Books, 1996

Mark, Vernon, M.D., F.A.C.S. with Jeffrey Pl Mark, M. Sc. *Brain Power: A*

*Neurosurgeon's Complete Program to Maintain and Enhance Brain Fitness Throughout Your Life.* Boston: Houghton Mifflin, 1989.

Marshall, Ian. and Danah Zohar. *Who's Afraid Of Schrödinger's Cat? New Science Ideas You Need To Keep Up With The New Thinking.* New York: Morrow and Company, 1997.

Michaud, Ellen, Russell Wild and the Editors of Prevention Magazine. *Boost Your Brain Power.* New York: MJF Books, 1991.

Miller, William C. *The Creative Edge: Fostering Innovation Where You Work.* Reading, MA: Addison-Wesley Publishing Company, 1986.

Moir, Anne and David Jessel. *Brain Sex: The Real Difference Between Men and Women.* New York: Dell Publishing, 1989.

Moyers, Bill. *Healing and The Mind.* New York: Doubleday, 1993.

Murphy, Joseph, D.R.S., D.D., Ph.D., LL.D. *The Power of Your Subconscious Mind.* Englewood Cliffs, NJ: Prentice-Hall, 1963.

Naylor, Thomas H., William H. Willimon, Magdalena R. Naylor. *The Search for Meaning.* Nashville, TN: Abingdon Press, 1994.

Neville. *Feeling Is The Secret.* New York: Goddard Publications, 1994.

O'Connor, Joseph and John Seymour. *Introducing Neuro-Linguistic Programming: Psychological Skills For Understanding and Influencing People.* San Francisco, CA: HarperCollins, 1990.

O'Hanlon, William Hudson and Michele Weiner-Davis. *In Search of Solutions: A New Direction In Psychotherapy.* New York: W.W. Norton, 1989.

Ornstein, Robert and Richard F. Thompson. *The Amazing Brain.* Boston, MA: Houghton Mifflin, 1984.

Ornstein, Robert. *The Evolution Of Consciousness: Of Darwin, Freud, and Cranial Fire: The Origins of the Way We Think.* New York: Prentice Hall Press, 1991.

Ornstein, Robert. *Multimind.* New York: Doubleday, 1986.

Ornstein, Robert and Paul Ehrlich. *New World New Mind: Moving Toward Conscious Evolution.* New York: Simon and Schuster, 1989.

Ornstein, Robert. *The Psychology of Consciousness.* New York: Penguin, 1973.

Page, George. *Inside the Animal Mind.* New York: Broadway Books, 1999.

Parker, Marjorie. *Creating Shared Vision: The Story Of A Pioneering Approach To Organizational Revitalization.* New York: Essandess Special Editions, 1960

Peale, Norman Vincent. *You Can If You Think You Can.* New York: Simon & Schuster, 1974.

Peale, Norman Vincent. *The Power of Positive Thinking.* New York: Prentice-Hall, 1952.

Peat, F. David. *Synchronicity: The Bridge Between Matter And Mind.* New York: Bantam Books, 1987.

Peck, M. Scott, M.D. *The Road Less Traveled: A New Psychology Of Love, Traditional Values And Spiritual Growth.* New York: Simon & Schuster, 1978.

Pert, Candace B., Ph.D. *Molecules Of Emotion.* New York: Simon & Schuster, 1999.

Pinker, Steven. *The Blank Slate: Modern Denial of Human Nature.* New York: Penguin Books, 2002.

Pinker, Steven. *How the Mind Works.* New York: W.W. Norton & Company, 1997.

Pinker, Steven. *Words and Rules: The Ingredients of Language.* New York: HarperCollins, 1999.

Pinker, Steven. *The Language Instinct: How the Mind Creates Language.* New York: William Morrow and Company, 1994.

Powers, William T. *Behavior: The Control of Perception.* New York: Aldine De Gruyter, 1973.

Prentiss, Robert Swayne. *Omnicom: Success through Brain Power.* Pittsburgh, PA: Hoechstetter, 1977.

Prigogine, Llya and Isabelle Stengers. *Order Out Of Chaos: Man's New Dialogue With Nature.* New York: Bantam Books, 1984.

Quen, Jacques M., M.D. *Split Minds/Split Brains: Historical and Current Perspectives.* New York: New York University Press, 1986.

Ramachandran, V.S., M.D., Ph.D. and Sandra Blakeslee. *Phantoms in the Brain.* New York: William Morrow and Company, 1998.

Restak, Richard M., M.D. *The Modular Brain: How New Discoveries in Neuroscience Are Answering Age-Old Questions about Memory, Free Will, Consciousness, and Personal Identity.* New York: Charles Scribner's Sons, 1994.

Restak, Richard, M.D. *The Brain Has a Mind of Its Own: Insights from a Practicing Neurologist.* New York: Harmony Books, 1991.

Restak, Richard, M.D. *Mozart's Brain and the Fighter Pilot: Unleashing Your Brain's Potential.* New York: Harmony Books, 2001.

Restak, Richard M., M.D. *Receptors.* New York: Bantam Books, 1994.

Revel, Jean-Francois and Matthieu Ricard. *The Monk And The Philosopher: A Father and Son Discuss the Meaning of Life.* New York: Schoken Books, 1998.

Ribarich, Cindy, D.V.M. and Delzio, Suzanne. *Felinestein, Pampering the Genius in Your Cat.* New York: HarperCollins, 1999.

Rodriguez, Richard. *Hunger of Memory.* New York: Bantam Books, 1982.

Russell, Peter. *The Brain Book.* New York: E.P. Dutton, 1979.

Sacks, Oliver. *The Man Who Mistook His Wife for a Hat and Other Clinical Tales.* New York: Harper Perennial, 1990.

Senge, Peter M., et. al., *The Fifth Discipline: The Art And Practice Of The Learning Organization.* New York: Doubleday, 1990.

Senge, Peter M. *The Fifth Discipline Fieldbook: Strategies and Tools for Building a Learning Organization.* New York: Doubleday, 1994.

Silva, Jose and Philip Miele. *The Silva Mind Control Method.* New York: Pocket Books, 1977.

Spielberg, Nathan and Bryon D. Anderson. *Seven Ideas that Shook the Universe.* New York: John Wiley & Sons, 1987.

Springer, Sally P. and Deutsch, Georg. *Left Brain, Right Brain.* New York:

W.H. Freeman, 1981.

Sternberg, Robert J. *Successful Intelligence: How Practical and Creative Intelligence Determine Success in life.* New York: Simon & Schuster, 1996.

Stewart, Ian. *Does God Play Dice? The Mathematics of Chaos.* Cambridge, MA: Blackwell, 1989.

Tolle, Eckhart. *The Power of Now: A Guide to Spiritual Enlightenment.* Novato, CA: New World Library, 1999.

Tracy, Brian. *Maximum Achievement: The Proven System of Strategies and Skills That Will Unlock Your Hidden Powers to Succeed.* New York: Simon & Schuster, 1993.

Volk, Tyler. M*etapatterns: Across Space, Time, and Mind.* New York: Columbia University Press.

Von Bertalanffy, Ludwig. *General System Theory: Foundations, Development, Applications.* New York: George Braziller, 1968.

Vos Savant, Marilyn. *The Power of Logical Thinking: Easy Lessons in the Art of Reasoning...and Hard Facts About Its Absence in Our Lives.* New York: St. Martin's Press, 1996.

Waitley, Denis. *Empires of the Mind: Lessons to Lead and Succeed in a Knowledge-Based World.* New York, William Morrow, 1995.

Watson, Richard. *Cogito, Ergo Sum: The Life of René Descartes.* Boston, MA, David R. Godine, 2002.

Weiner, David L. *Brain Tricks: Coping with Your Defective Brain.* Amherst, NY: Prometheus books, 1995.

West, Thomas G. *In The Mind's Eye: Visual Thinkers, Gifted People with Learning Difficulties, Computer Images, and the Ironies of Creativity. Buffalo,* NY: Prometheus Books, 1991.

Wheatley, Margaret J. *Leadership and the New Science: Learning about Organization from an Orderly Universe.* San Francisco, CA: Berrett-Koehler, 1992.

Winnicott, D.W. *The Maturational Processes and the Facilitating*

*Environment: Studies in the Theory of Emotional Development.* New York: International Universities Press, 1965.

White, William L. *Slaying the Dragon: The History of Addiction Treatment and Recovery in America.* Bloomington, IL: Chestnut Health Systems, 1998.

Wiener, Norbert. *Cybernetics or Control and Communication in the Animal and the Machine.* Cambridge, MA: the M.I.T. Press, 1994.

Wills, Christopher. *The Runaway Brain: The Evolution of Human Uniqueness.* New York: BasicBooks, 1993.

Wonder, Jacquelyn and Priscilla Donovan. *Whole-Brain Thinking: Working From Both Sides of the Brain To Achieve Peak Job Performance.* New York: Ballantine Books, 1984.

Wynn, Charles M. and Arthur Wiggins. *The Five Biggest Ideas in Science.* New York: John Wiley & Sons, 1997.

Zohar, Danah. *Quantum Self.* New York: William Morrow & Company, Inc. 1990

Zohar, Danah. *Rewiring The Corporate Brain: Using the New Science to Rethink How We Structure and Lead Organizations.* San Francisco, CA: Berrett-Koehler, 1997.

_________. *Alcoholics Anonymous – Big Book.* New York: Alcoholics Anonymous World Services, 1976.

_________. *Twelve Steps and Twelve Traditions.* New York, NY: The A.A. Grapevine, Inc., 1953.

_________. Blakeslee, Sandra. "The Brain in the Gut." New York Times May 23, 1996.

_________. *The Science Times Book of the Brain.* Edited by Nicholas Wade. New York Times, 1998.

_________. "Mind and Brain." In *Readings From Scientific American Magazine.* New York: W.H. Freeman, 1993.

_________. "The Biology of the Brain from Neurons to Networks." In *Readings from Scientific American Magazine.* Edited by Rodolfo R. Llinas. New York: W.H. Freeman, 1977.

__________. *New Metaphysical Foundations of Modern Science.* Edited by Willis Harman and Jane Clark. Sausalito, CA: Institute of Noetic Sciences, 1994.

__________. *Memory: History, Culture and the Mind.* Edited by Thomas Butler. New York: Basil Blackwell Ltd., 1989.

__________. "The Road Not Taken." In *Selected Poems of Robert Frost.* New York, New York: Holt, Rinehart and Winston, Inc., 1963.

__________. *Evidence of Purpose: Scientists Discover the Creator.* Edited by John Marks Templeton. New York: The Continuum Publishing Co, 1994.

__________. *Brain Development and Cognition, a Reader.* Edited by Mark H. Johnson. Cambridge, MA: Blackwell Publishers, 1993.

__________. *Companion to The Mind.* Edited by Richard L. Gregory. New York: Oxford University Press, 1987.

__________. *Transforming Work. A Collection of Organizational Transformation Readings.* Edited by John D. Adams, Ph.D. Alexandria, VA: Miles River Press, 1984.

__________. "Traumatic Brain Injury Survival Guide." Dr. Glen Johnson, www.tbiguide.cm/howbrainworks.html, 1998.

# *ACKNOWLEDGEMENTS*

Writing *Liberating Greatness* has been a long, amazing journey. It simply would not have happened without the help of many, many people. Generous collaborators showed up at every step of the way to provide encouragement, support and hours and hours of hard work.

I want to extend heartfelt thanks to all who have contributed, beginning with Hal and Joanne Zenisek, who founded Couples in Recovery in Rockford, Illinois, in 1985. Without them, there would have been no Couples in Recovery Conference, where I heard Dr. Robert Henry, who introduced me to the HBDI™ and Investment in Excellence® and suggested that the integration of these two models would be powerful. Dale Daniel was a great thought partner at Sundstrand, and introduced Investment in Excellence® there. My daughter, Sue Williamson Dixon, created the original graphics for the "Pathways to Greatness" seminars and was instrumental in making many synthesized ideas visible. She has supported me in every way imaginable through the years. I cannot thank her enough. I'm grateful to Harry Stonecipher for making it possible for me to take the "Pathways to Greatness" program to all the people of Sundstrand and many of their families.

Thanks also to Gene Stroyan, who believed in this material and organized opportunities for me to deliver the "Pathways" program to groups of every kind. Ann Brown helped move the material forward and designed the corporate logo for Hope Unlimited. I treasure Sue Hutcheson for the way she helped, transcribing hours of tape and my handwritten manuscript, and then reporting she had read the material as she typed and found it useful. My brother Garfield Williamson has been a supporter, a sounding board, and a constructive critic of mine throughout this project (and many others).

I will be eternally grateful to Faranak and Farid Samandari, whom I met because they came to one of my public "Pathways to Greatness" series. They introduced me to the Bahá'í Faith, which has enriched my life enormously, including bringing me into contact with many people who have collaborated on this book. Thanks to Faranak and Farid and also Astrid Kersten, who have provided validation, encouragement and numerous opportunities to share this material.

We are grateful to Stephanie Parrott who seemed to know when we needed new energy. She brought soup, humor, Healing Touch, and her calming presence. Dave and Dona Luedde fed and cared for us, listened to us, and encouraged us throughout the project. Jackie and Tim Hoag have been steadfast and supportive friends at every step. Siobhan Murphy provided support, prodding, and wisdom all along the way.

Thanks to Ralph Yearick for urging me to change the name of the book and send the manuscript to many people for their reactions and suggestions. Heartfelt thanks to Sharon Lippincott, Marlene McCann, Susan Crossley, Hugh Leonard, George Theotocatos, Karim Jaude, Kirk Snyder, Dona Luedde, Michael Penn, Robin Heid, and Sallie Davis. who spent hours reading and giving us valuable feedback. Sharon Lippincott and Marlene McCann have been workhorses. Or call them angels. They have dedicated literally hundreds of hours to reading, collaborating and editing. They came with enormous skills and generous hearts and have given so much time and energy and love to this book that their names should be on the cover. One day Sharon Lippincott said, "Let's use some of the techniques in the book to manifest a great graphic artist." So we did: Barbara Curry, creative, patient and tireless. An inspiring artist, she is both a friend and a joy to work with. Lisa Mitchell, a talented photographer, is Sharon's daughter. We asked her to take Hal's picture because her photos always carry peoples' spirit.